LAND TRANSFERS
A Case Study

LAND TRANSFERS
A Case Study

Kripa Shankar

GIAN PUBLISHING HOUSE
NEW DELHI—110002

GIAN PUBLISHING HOUSE
4-C Ansari Road, Daryaganj
New Delhi—110002

ISBN 81—212—0325—2

PRINTED IN INDIA

Published by Mrs. Gayatri Garg for Gian Publishing House, New Delhi 110002. Printed at Godwall Printers, Delhi.

Preface

Land alienation in an agrarian economy characterised by highly skewed distribution of land, adverse land man ratio and vast landlessness has important bearing on the dynamics of rural transformation. Various forces—institutional and technological – determine its contours and a delineation of such forces is necessary for a correct understanding of the dynamics of land market. The present study has not gone into the analysis of all such forces but has confined to the delineation of magnitude of the land alienation, its direction and the reasons for land alienation and the manner in which various classes/castes have been affected. Again land transfers which are duly registered have been taken into account and land transfers by way of lease or mortgage have not been studied as, among other things, they are not final transfers.

At first the idea was to study the phenomenon as a case study of selected villages but it was Prof. Nasim Ansari of this Institute (GBPSSI) who suggested that the study might be extended to cover the whole of U.P. so that some generalisations could be made about the dynamics of the land market in the state. I am thankful to Prof. Nasim Ansari for his valuable suggestion which was followed.

I am thankful to ICSSR for funding this project and to Prof. A.D. Pant, Director, GBPSSI who took keen interest in the progress of the study and provided all the facilities for its successful completion.

The field data was collected by Sarvashri V.N. Lal, Kishori Lal, S.N. Singh, R.K. Tewari, N.K. Agarwal, R.P. Singh and Arun Kumar. The tabulation work was done mainly by Dr. V.N. Lal who has done it in a very meticulous manner. Shri Kishori Lal was also involved in tabulation work. I express my gratefulness to all of them. Sarvashri P.K. Agarwal and Ratan Lal were associated with the typing work and the final draft was neatly typed by Shri P.K. Agarwal to whom I am thankful.

Allahbad

Kripa Shankar

Contents

List of Tables

1

Introduction

In agrarian economies the land, by and large, is the only means of sustenance in rural areas where the bulk of the population is concentrated. In a situation where the landless is on the increase, the desire to acquire land on the part of those who have no or little and the desire to retain as well as to extend if possible on the part of those who have it will be equally intense. In the absence of a growing non-farm sector within the rural economy as well as outside, land will assume still greater importance, more so if land productivity rises.

During the colonial period agriculture was in stagnation, as the Zamindars were interested only in rack renting of the peasantry. They were unconcerned about investments and the colonial state also was not favourably disposed towards agricultural development as Zamindari system on which they relied, was itself the greatest drag on agriculture.

In the post-Independence period Zamindari system was abolished but it was not accompanied by any redistribution of land although its distribution was highly skewed. But the fact that the vast majority of peasants were granted proprietary rights was itself a great landmark. The state also had taken up the responsibility of providing the infrastructure. Investment on irrigation and power occupied a prominent place in the plan investments and development of tube-well irrigation which was hitherto untapped was emphasised. Besides, canal irrigation was also extended. Use of fertilizers was popularised through extension agencies.

Soon after the abolition of Zamindari consolidation of holdings was taken up. It largely helped the peasants and induced them to make investments more so in private tube-wells which increased phenomenally. A feeble attempt to impose ceilings on land holdings was also made in early sixties.

It was during the mid-sixties that high yielding varieties of wheat, rice, maize *etc.* were introduced in a big way commanly known as the green revolution. The new agricultural technology was based on high yielding varieties of seeds, chemical fertilizers and adequate supply of water. The farmers were also assisted by cooperative societies and Land Development Banks for investing in private irrigation sources, agricultural machinery and also for other modern inputs. All this resulted in an increase of agricultural production. The large farmers were the main beneficiaries but medium and small farmers also took to the new technology in so far as it was possible within their means.

Agriculture which hitherto was not a paying proposition now became profitable. Agricultural prices also rose, particularly after the PL-48 wheat supplies were brought to an end. Large farmers began to produce for the market and the Government also pursued a policy of price support to help the surplus farmers. The terms of trade moved in favour of agriculture and although the gains were positively related with the size of the holdings yet the medium and to some extent small farmers and even marginal farmers also gained. The only class which had little to gainfrom the new agricultural technology was the landless, for they had no land, the productivity of which was sought to be raised through various devices. Yet there was some diversification in the wake of increased purchasing power of a section of the peasantry and although there was rapid increase in the number of landless their condition does not seem to have deteriorated in absolute terms.

Thus under the impetus of land reforms and the new agricultural technology, a class of surplus rich farmers has emerged on the rural scene which has gained from public investments and public policies. By virtue of their control over land and the rising income they have come to dominate the village life and control all the local organs of power and other institutions.

It was hoped that the gains of new technology will trickle down to the poorer sections of the rural population but that did not materialise as the surplus owners were strong enough to resist any percolation to the agricultural labourers. Besides, as no diversification of any significance could occur in the economy, the rising population was forced to fall back on agriculture with the result that the number of agricultural labourers grew fast[1] which could not but have a depressing effect on agricultural wages. The introduction of labour saving agricultural machinery particularly tractors[2] and the liberal manner of financing it also aggravated the problem of surplus labour. It can well be argued that tractors have multi-purpose uses and many tractor owners manage to keep it by undertaking haulage and transportation but it seems that tractors have eliminated the dependence of employers on agricultural labourers for tilling the field. All this has resulted in the weakening of the bargaining power of the agricultural labourers.

If the large farmers were to utilize their surplus in improving and diversifying the production base in the rural areas there could still be justification for their private accumulation. But there is little evidence to show that the rural rich are utilizing their surplus in a productive manner.[3] In a status ridden society conspicuous consumption gets the upper hand. It is the latter that determines one's status in such societies. Besides, the rural rich by the very logic of their existence are not likely to play an entrepreneurial role as argued by Djurfeldt and Lindberg.[4]

There is vast scope of investment on intensification of agriculture itself, on soil and water conservation schemes, afforestation[5] on all vacant and culturable waste land, on land reclamation and construction activity of various types but investment on such schemes cannot be made by individuals in most of the cases as firstly, it is beyond the resources of individuals and more importantly it requires some sort of collectivism as Hayami[6] has argued which at present is completely lacking again because of highly iniquitous land holdings in the first instance.

The net result is that although there are savings and capital funds in the economy[7] to gainfully employ the rural poor within the rural sector itself the same is not coming forth in the desired channels and in desired magnitude.

The emerging rural scenario is thus characterised by sharp cleavage between two opposing classes. On the one hand there is a class of big landowners who control a large part of the land and other resources and who have gained all round through state policies. They are acquiring surpluses which are not being used in raising the productive base of the rural economy. On the other, there is a vast class of agricultural labourers, marginal and small farmers who find that work on land is not sufficient to provide them subsistence but in the absence of non-farm employment they stick to it howsoever unremunerative it may be.

And land continues to be the centre of attraction in rural economy. For it is the control over it that determines the power structure and the manner in which gains of development will be shared. And the tendency to retain and, if possible, to enlarge the land on the part of the rich and the scramble of poor to get land continues to govern the overall contours of the land market.

NOTES AND REFERENCES

1. Agricultural labourers constituted 11.3 per cent of the workforce in 1961, the same rose to 19.4 per cent in 1971.
2. The number of tractors in U.P. increased from 7139 in 1961 to 10,139 in 1966 and further to 1,40,821 in 1982.
3. All India Debt and Investment Survey 1971-72 found that capital

formation per household in farm business among cultivators was Rs. 52 only. Further, of the total capital formation of rural households one-fourth went to residential housing. Capital formation accounted for only 0.2 per cent of the tangible assets of rural households in U.P.

4. Djurfeldt and Lindberg (1975) : *Behind Poverty* : *The Social Formation in Tamil Village*, London.
5. The latest satellite data show that the forest cover has dwindled to just 11 per cent of the land surface altough officially it was given that the forest cover is round 18 per cent.
6. Yujiro Haymant (1981) : *Understanding Village Community and the Direction of Agrarian Change in Asia.* H.P. Corporation, New Delhi, p. 29.
7. It has been one of the riddles of economic growth in India that despite high savings in the economy it is not moving fast. Probably the answer is that savings under private sector are not available to the state authorities which could make a productive utilization of the same.

2

Objectives, Methodology and Coverage

Objectives

The objective of the study has been to delineate the working of the land market in the state of U.P. and its different regions. The working of the land market has been analysed in the context of the forces that are at work in shaping the agrarian relations. The impact of the various land reform measures after independence on the land market and the consequences that followed after the introduction of new agricultural technology and its bearing on the land market have all been delineated. The behaviour of land market and the manner in which it has affected various strata of rural population in terms of their asset holding, income etc. has also been analysed. The forces governing the supply as well as demand and the direction of land market and its implications for agrarian transformation and growth have also been delineated.

Methodology and Coverage

Land can be transferred through outright sale but it can also be transferred on a temporary basis, when land is leased out or is given on mortgage. The latter two phenomena are common in the countryside. Land can also be gifted or donated.

Leasing is fairly prevalent in U.P. though it is legally banned in this state. In many cases when one gets a regular job in an urban area and there is no one else to look after the agricultural operations the whole or a part of the holding is leased out. Similarly when one is hard pressed for money the only alternative, short of land sale, may be to mortgage the land. Nowhere these transactions are recorded in black and white.

As land transfers through leasing or mortgage is not a permanent transfer, and also because the lessors will like to hide the fact that they have leased out, and similarly those who have given land on mortgage will not like that such a fact should be recorded it was decided to leave out these types of transfer for the purpose of this study. Transfers of land on a permanent basis which were made through Registration Office alone were taken into consideration. Land transfer in the form of gift or donation is almost non-existent in U.P. and, therefore, excluded. We did not also come across any such case in our study.

U.P. has more than one lakh villages and 8791 Nyaya Panchayats. As the study was to cover the whole of the state it was considered desirable to cover about 20 Nyaya Panchayats so that the sample may cover about 0.2 per cent of the Nyaya Panchayats. The latter consists an average of 10 villages. The villages would also in that case number about 200 approximately.

There are five regions in the state and consequently the Nyaya Panchayats were to be selected from each region. The Panchayats were to be selected roughly on the basis of population from all region. Thus 7 Panchayats were selected from eastern and western region each, 3 from central region and one each from Bundelkhand and Hill Region. The study thus covered 19 Nyaya Panchayats in 19 districts out of a total of the then 57 districts in the state.

The selection of Nyaya Panchayats was done on a random basis. Seven districts each in eastern and western regions were selected randomly. One Block, again, was randomly selected in each district and one Nyaya Panchayat in each selected Block was again randomly selected. All the villages in the jurisdiction of the selected Nyaya Panchayats were studied for the purpose of land transfers. All households in the selected villages that had sold or purchased any land after Zamindari abolition (1952) constituted the universe of the sample. As Zamindari abolition was a major event it was taken as a cut-off point. The reference period was 1952-53 to 1982-83 or, a period of 30 years. As the new agricultural technology was introduced in mid-sixties it was hoped that the study would be able to throw light on the behaviour of the land market in both the pre-green as well as post-green revolution period as they will be nearly equally divided in the 30 year span.

The difficulty in getting the data about land transfers for the earlier period was obvious. In many cases family partitions had taken place and the households would just not own the earlier transactions. There was pariticular difficulty where the transactions were made by forefathers, and the heirs had little know ledge about the same. This is why the magnitude of land transfers for earlier period is quite small and should not be taken on its face value because of highly underreporting due to the above factors.

No less difficult was the case of those who had migrated to cities or elsewhere after selling their entire holding. The only source of information about such persons were the purchasers of their land who generally knew about their landholding and caste. They were also relied upon while providing an idea of their income and assets. But little information could be supplied by them as to what forced them to sell their entire holding and to leave the village. This aspect was very important for investigation but it was physically not possible to contact such persons (and their number was also quite large) given the constraint of time and resources. Consequently a very important gap persists in the knowledge about the functioning of the land market and this study throws no light on the reasons which force people to sell their entire holding and migrate elsewhere.

While the sellers of land had no hesitation in providing the required information, a reticence was observed in the case of a few purchasers in the higher categories who were somewhat apprehensive about the nature of the survey. The difficulty was very apparent where land was purchased by relatively bigger farmers.

The land transactions are registered and recorded in the Registration Office and the records give exact area of the land that changes hands. But the focus of the study was to know something about the characteristics of those who sell and buy land, their landholding, caste, the reasons why they sell the land, the source of finance for land purchase etc. The Registration Office records do not contain any information on these counts. All they contain is the name of the seller and the purchaser and the area of the land involved. There is no information as to how much land the purchaser or seller had or any other relevant information.

Under the circumstances it was thought desirable to administer the questionnaire on all the sellers and buyers of land who alone could reply to all the queries. The only advantage that could be had from culling the information from Registration Office could relate to the exactness of the area. But the sellers and buyers, could also give reliable information about the area under transactions. And the margin of error would, if at all, be only nominal. Consequently recourse was not taken to cull the records of the Registration Office which in any case were not easy to handle for as many as 19 Tehsils. There was particular difficulty in getting the records of earlier years. Besides, the land transactions are recorded on Tehsil basis and to cull village-wise data for so many villages for a period of 30 years would have been a highly time consuming process whose utility may not be much in terms of focus of this study.

The list of selected Nyaya Panchayats in different districts of U.P. in whose jurisdiction all the buyers and sellers of land were interviewed is as follows :

Region		*District*	*Nyaya Panchayat*
Eastern U.P.	1	Ghazipur	Chaukia
	2	Ballia	Kharsara
	3	Jaunpur	Balrampur
	4	Deoria	Siswa Bhokraha
	5	Sultanpur	Bhawalpur
	6	Bahraich	Hasulia
	7	Mirzapur	Gangahara Kalan
Central U.P.	8	Fatehpur	Alipur Bhadar
	9	Sitapur	Paraspur
	10	Farrukhabad	Jahanganj
	11	Barabanki	Aunalia
	12	Unnao	Mirzapur Samhari
Western U.P.	13	Agra	Dharera
	14	Saharanpur	Ghunna
	15	Etah	Patna
	16	Bulandshahar	Hridaipur
	17	Bijnor	Mohammadpur Deomal
Bundelkhand	18	Jalaun	Majeeth
Hill Region	19	Pitthoragarh	Kimtoli

3

Land Reforms and Agrarian Structure in U.P.

All evidences lead to the fact that prior to the advent of British the rural economy was quite balanced. About half of the rural population was dependent on agriculture. Crafts supported the rest. Almost all the households depending on agriculture had some land as the same was in plenty. There did not exist a class of landless agricultural labourers as such although high caste landowners employed agricultural labourers but in most of the cases they had some land.

The advent of British rule changed the situation very drastically. It was the policy of the foreign rulers to deliberately destroy the flourishing handloom industry to make way for British made cotton goods. How the British destroyed this industry in a brutal manner is a story well known. A British Governor was constrained to report to the Imperial Government that the bones of cotton weavers were bleaching the plains of Ganges.

The sudden destruction of hand spinning, weaving and many allied activities connected with the production of cloth put lakhs of persons without any source of livelihood. They had no alternative but to fall back on agrieulture as the only source of sustenance.

The British also introduced a western type of feudalism which was unknow in India. The revenue collectors of late Moghal period turned into Zamindars to create a class of persons who would be loyal to the British and also keep the rural ryot under their domination and control. These Zamindars were declared the owners of land, which they were not and the working peasantry was deprived of all security as the Zamindars could evict them at their sweet will.

The foreign rulers wanted cheap foodgrains and other agricultural products and raw materials which they imported from India to feed the population and also the industries. The agricultural prices were deliberately kept very low with the result that agriculture was no longer a paying proposition but it had to be carried out as a way of life. The rental demand by the Zamindars were frequently raised and in view of very low agricultural prices peasants found it difficult to meet the same. Ejectment on account of failure to pay the land revenue became the order of the day. The U.P. Zamindari Abolition Committee (ZAC) found that during the 1930s, on an average, peasants were evicted annually from an area of 2.05 lakh acres of land. In early thirties during the depression period when agriculture prices fell steeply it increased to nearly 2.5 lakh acres per annum.[1]

The U.P. Tenancy Act, 1939 put an end to arbitrary ejectments but the Act suffered from certain loopholes. Taking advantage of these loopholes the landlords continued to get a larger number of tenants evicted every year. The ZAC had noted that during 1940-41 to 1943-1944 the tenants were evicted from 1.1 lakh acres of land or annually from about 27,000 acres and under Secs. 163-165 of the same Act, on an average, from an area of 36,000 acres annually. Again under Secs. 175-179 they were evicted from 31,000 acres annually on an average and under Sec. 180 they were evicted from 38,000 acres annually.[2] Baljit Singh and Shridhar Misra have noted that during mid-forties evictions took place on 0.7 per cent of the cultivated area annually. They note that "During the ten years preceding

Zamindari abolition tenants were ejected from more than a million acres of land. This represents 2.37 per cent of the total area under holdings."[3] In their sample study it was found that tenants were ejected from an area of 1.5 per cent of the total cultivated area during 1951-52 to 1959-60.[4]

Land revenue had always been a big burden for small peasants throughout the colonial period and even in early years of Independence. It was only when agricultural prices began to rise in late fifties and after the advent of new agricultural technology a decade later, that the burden was lessened. An idea of the coercive process that was used to realise all dues which were realisable as arrears of land revenue can be had from the fact that more than fifty thousand warrants of arrest were issued annually in mid-fifties to realise the dues as arrears of land revenue.[5] It also speaks of the distress of the peasantry even after Zamindari was abolished.

The utter ruin of peasantry under the British rule brought it in the vortex of the national movement for independence and it was this basic factor which transformed it into a powerful mass movement for independence. The peasantry was mobilised on the slogan of "land to the tiller" and abolition of Zamindari systems. Consequently after independence on the recommendations of Zamindari Abolition Committee, U.P. Zamindari Abolition and Land Reforms Act, 1950, was passed in January 1951, but as the Zamindars challenged the Act in the High Court and the Supreme Court, the Act could be enforced only after July 1952. This gave the Zamindars ample time and opportunity to evict tenants and to corner the *Gram Samaj* land. The Zamindari Abolition Committee had recommended that all *Sir* and *Khudkast* land be retained by the erstwhile landlords. Such land formed about 18 per cent of the cultivated land of the state. Significantly the tenants were to be made *Bhumidhars* by paying 10 times the land revenue and the ex-Zamindars were made *Bhumidhars* of such land without paying any multiple of the land revenue. The total *Sir* and *Khudkast* land was of the order of 74 lakh acres out of a total of 413 lakh acres of agricultural land on the eve of abolition of Zamindari. Out of 42.5 lakh acres of *Sir* land as much as 9.3 lakh acres was let out and out of 31.3 lakh acres of *Khudkast* land 2 lakh acres was let out.[6] Obviously a large number of such sub-tenants were evicted by the Zamindars. There were occupiers of land on 14.5 lakh acres who were occupying land without the consent of the person entitled to admit as tenants.[7] They must have been the first to be evicted by the Zamindars.

Baljit Singh and Shridhár Misra have noted that the area under *Sir* and *Khudkast* increased immediately preceding Zamindari abolition and "it was for the purpose of resumption of cultivation or for establishment of farm by the Zamindars to retain as much land as possible".[8]

At the time of passing of the Act in 1950 a restriction on future acquisition of holdings up to 30 acres was made. This limit was reduced to 12.5 acres by an amendment in 1958. But it had been made clear that land cannot be transferred to any person (other than an institution established for a charitable purpose), where he would come to possess in all *i.e.* his own holding as well as the new land, more than 12.5 acres. Similarly if lessee gets land which together with his own land exceeds 12.5 acres he would be ejected from the surplus land.

It was also stipulated (Sec. 157A of Zamindari Abolition and Land Reforms Act, 1950) that a member of the Scheduled Caste or Scheduled Tribe cannot transfer any land by way of sale, gift, mortgage or lease to a person who is not a member of Scheduled Caste or Scheduled Tribe without the prior permission of the Collector. This was incorporated in 1969 by way of an amendment so that higher castes may not force them to transfer land.[9]

Through the U.P. Zamindari Abolition and Land Reforms Act, 1950 all agricultural land whether cultivated or not was vested in the state. Thus all the rights of intermediaries were terminated. The only right that was not taken over was in case of mines. Groves and buildings were also left untouched and more importantly the *Sir* and *Khudkast* land was converted into *Bhumidhari* of the erstwhile intermediaries. In place of a bewildering variety of about forty types of tenures only three types of tenures, *viz.*, *bhumidhar*, *sirdar* and *asami* were introduced. A temporary right known as *adhivasi* was also introduced for the transitional phase.

Bhumidhari rights were conferred on all the *Sir* and *Khudkast* land as well as groves and plantations of Zamindars. Others could acquire *Bhumidhari* right by paying an amount equal to ten times the land revenue if paid in lump sum or twelve times if paid in instalments. *Bhumidhars* have permanent, heritable and transferable rights over their land. They cannot be ejected and can use their land as they like.

The majority of cultivators consisting of tenants, sub-tenants and occupiers of land without consent were declared *sirdars*. *Sirdars* have permanent and heritable rights but they cannot transfer their land. A *sirdar* on the other hand could acquire *Bhumidhari* rights by paying 10 times the land revenue and thereby acquires the right to transfer the land. A *sirdar* may use his land for agricultural, animal husbandry and for horticultural purposes, but is liable to be ejected in case he violates it.

An inferior mode of tenure was also created in the form of *asamis*. Former tenants of grove land, those who held pasture land or land under water etc., were conferred *asami* rights. The *asami* rights are heritable but they are neither permanent nor can they transfer the land. They are also liable to be ejected under certain circumstances.

The large body of cultivators of land, sub-tenants and occupants of land other than grove land who did not enjoy any security of land was conferred the right of *adhivasies*. They were given security of tenure and could become *Bhumidhars* after 5 years or within this period with the consent of landlord on payment of sum equal to fifteen times the rent computed at hereditary rates.

But in a sudden move in 1954 by an amendment all *adhivasies* were made *sirdars* and thus got permanent and heritable right on the land that they were cultivating but in fact were at the mercy of the landlords and were liable to be ejected. It is also axiomatic that no landlord would have given his consent to such cultivators to acquire *Bhumidhari* rights within the stipulated period of five years. This naturally was hailed as a radical measure.

By an amendment in the Zamindari Abolition and Land Reforms Act in 1977 all *Sirdars* were made *Bhumidhars*. But they were given non-transferable rights while the erstwhile *Bhumidhars* had been recognised as *Bhumidhars* with transferable rights.[10] Thus the measure was of little consequence in actual practice.

The Act also provides that no *Bhumidhari* rights can be acquired on pasture land, land covered by water or in beds of rivers, on grove land of *gram samaj* or on land held for public purposes. Such land can be let out by the Land Management Committee of the *Gaon Sabha* as *asami* if the same is vacant and is vested in the Land Management Committee. The Land Management Committee can admit persons as *Bhumidhars* on other lands vested in it but such persons cannot transfer the land.

It is also stipulated that the land allotted to any person by the Land Management Committee should not exceed 3.125 acres or 1.26 hectares including any land held by him.

The Act also provides that any holding that does not exceed 3.125 acres cannot be partitioned. The Act provides that "no person shall transfer whether by sale, gift or exchange any fragment situated in a consolidated area except where the transfer is in favour of tenure holder who has a plot contiguous to the fragment or where the transfer is not in favour of any such tenure holder, the whole of the plot to which the fragment pertains is thereby transferred".

Although the Act had prohibited sub-letting yet it has provided for a kind of "arrangement whereby a person is entitled to a right merely to share in the produce grown on the land in consideration of such person assisting or participating with a tenure holder in the actual performance of agricultural operation...." Thus it may be stated that indirectly the system of share cropping has been permitted under the garb of partnerships.[11]

One distinguishing feature of land reforms in U.P. was that despite the categorical recommendation of the First Year Plan that landlords should be allowed to resume land upto three times the family holding, the U.P. Act did not provide for resumption of land for personal cultivation by the landlords. In other states where such a measure was incorporated in the Act there was large scale resumption of land from tenants. Despite this havoc the Second Five Year Plan reiterated that landlords should be given the right to resume land for personal cultivation. In U.P. not only this right was not given but as mentioned earlier in 1954 all tenants of home-farm land of Zamindars who paid a land revenue of Rs. 250 or less in a year and sub-tenants called Shikmies were conferred permanent and hereditary rights on the land that they cultivated.[12] Such right was already given to tenants of bigger Zamindars in 1952 itself. Had the right of resumption of land for personal cultivation been granted 38 lakh *shikmies* who later on were called *adhivasies* would have been evicted and it would have created a disastrous situation for the poorest peasantry.

Another noticeable feature of the Zamindari Abolition Act was that it abolished sub-letting except in certain special cases such as persons in the defence services, widows, disabled persons, minors *etc.* Had sub-letting been allowed, it would have meant reemergence of feudal relations and landlordism by the back door. If the principle of land to the tiller were to be implemented sub-letting could not be allowed. Those who sub-let land have either excess land which they cannot till and/or have regular jobs mostly in the cities and therefore cannot till the land. In a situation of extreme land hunger it is logical that the land should belong to those who reside in the villages and personally perform agricultural operations.

Zamindari abolition in the state has been a noteworthy event next only to the achievement of independence. As far as the vast multitude of oppressed peasantry was concerned it was a more important event even as Zamindari abolition not only provided security of tenure but it also freed the peasants from the feudal bondage. As is well known the Zamindars used to take *begar* on their land and the agricultural labourers, particularly members of the Scheduled Castes had to work on their fields without wages for certain agricultural operations. The other small peasants were also made to pay various kinds of exactions from time to time and were subjected to humiliation. Inability to pay land revenue not only brought public humiliation and physical punishment but it also led to eventual ejectment. Scheduled Caste population was virtually considered their chattel as they were supposed to have their homestead on Zamindar's land. They were subjected to all sorts of indignities. So was the lot of other poor farmers. Zamindari abolition was for this vast section a social as well as economic liberation despite the fact that this measure of land reform was neither accompanied by any land redistribution nor any change in the power equation.

Another important piece of land reforms was the enactment of the Uttar Pradesh Imposition of Ceiling on Land Holdings Act, 1960 which came into force the following year. It imposed a ceiling of 40 acres on "fair quality land" for a family of five persons. Additional members in the family were provided 8 acres each subject to a maximum of 24 extra acres. For second grade land the ceiling limit was fixed at 60 acres plus 12 acres for each additional member subject to a maximum of 36 extra acres. For the third grade land the ceiling limit was 80 acres plus extra 16 acres for additional members subject to a limit of 48 extra acres. So if there were 8 or more persons in a family, the ceiling limit would be 64 acres for good quality land, 96 and 128 acres respectively for second and third grade land. The Act provided for may exemptions. The grove and plantation land was exempted and so was the case with land under cooperative societies *etc.* The ceiling limit was itself placed so high that little land could be declared surplus. Besides, taking advantages of the time lag[13] large landowners partitioned the land often through *benami* transfers to escape the ceiling laws. Another easier course was to plant trees on surplus land so as to show it as grove land. Bogus cooperatives were formed with the purpose of circumventing the ceiling laws.

The ceiling limit was reduced to 7.3 hectares or 18 acres of irrigated land for a family of five members in 1973. If the family size exceeded five, 2 extra hectares of land per additional member was allowed subject to a maximum of six extra hectares. In that case a family could retain 13.3 hectares of irrigated land. In case of unirrigated land the ceiling limit was 1.5 times the ceiling of irrigated land and in case of groves or *usar* land it was fixed at two and half times the ceiling limit fixed for irrigated land.

Various exemptions granted in the original Act were withdrawn and the same was limited to land held by Government, local authority, Government undertakings, educational institutions, banks *etc.* A significant alteration was made in the definition of family also. While in the original Act family was defined to constitute husband, wife dependent mother and father, sons and grandsons, daughters-in-law, unmarried daughter and grand-daughters, the amending act limited it to husband, wife, minor sons and minor daughters (other than married daughters). The original Act also stipulated that the excess land can be temporarily allotted to the original land owner but the same was repealed by an amendment in 1969.

On account of *benami* transfers and other fraudulent means the estimated surplus land could not materialise. In 1960 it was estimated that the surplus land would be around 14 lakh acres.[14] By 1972 only 2.32 lakh acres could be declared as surplus out of which 2.01 lakh acres was acquired and 1.10 lakh acres distributed. Not much land also could be acquired after lowering the ceiling limit in 1973. Upto 1980 only 2.8 lakh acres was declared surplus out of which 2.54 lakh acre was acquired and 2.23 lakh acres could be distributed among 1.81 lakh persons.[15]

The ceiling laws have failed to bring about changes in the distribution pattern[16] for which they were primarily aimed but they have brought about a situation where bigger landowners now somewhat desist from purchasing more land. They are now concerned with retaining their existing land through all types of fraudulent transfers and partitions. As the ceiling limit was reduced almost a decade after the first enactment, the bigger landowners have a lurking fear that in days to come the ceiling may still be lowered and then it would be difficult to retain even the existing holding. Hence, they as a class, have almost ceased to act in terms of extending their direct ownership although as surplus farmers they can purchase and do purchase the land of others most easily. Not that land has ceased to be attractive to them. In reality the rise in productivity has made it attractive but all the same the large landowners feel that in future large holdings may come under greater pressure and if nothing else may invite larger taxation. So the tendency to parcel their land to evade future lowering of the ceiling is more in evidence than further acquisition of land although the later is by no means absent.

Obviously this change has been brought about by ceiling laws. Thus although the impact of ceiling laws in terms of surplus land acquired is not at all impressive[17] yet it cannot be denied that this legislation has restrained the tendency of the large landowners to acquire freely more land as in its absence they would have used their surplus in acquiring more of it.

The near passivity of the large land owners in the land market has obviously given opportunities for the middle farmers to become active in the land market as purchasers of land as corroborated by this study. If the land distribution pattern has not further worsened despite unusual gains to richer sections, it is probably because of the impact of these laws which have forced them not to think in terms of acquiring more land. There is also a likelihood that the surplus of the rich which otherwise would have gone in purchasing the land of others might be utilized in some other productive ventures for which there are some indications although it cannot be denied that conspicuous consumption and consumerism have also their sway.

Agrarian Structure

The Zamindari Abolition Committee had found that "a bare 1.49 per cent of the bigger landlords own nearly 57.77 per cent of the land while the overwhelming majority of 98.51 per cent of small landlords owns only 42.43 per cent of the land."[18] It observed that 804 landlords out of a total of more than 20 lakhs own anything between one-fifth and one-fourth of the province".[19] It had also found that their *sir* and *khudkast* land was more than one-fourth of the agricultural land and that about nine thousand top landlords had more than 100 acres each of such land on an average.[20]

Despite this heavy concentration of land in few hands and even admitting the case of land distribution in such a situation[21] the Committee observed".... we do not think that the results achieved by the redistribution of land would be commensurate with the discontent and hardship resulting from it. We, therefore, recommend that no limit be placed on the maximum area held in cultivation either by landlord or tenant.[22] It felt that it would "increase the difficulty of Zamindars in adjusting them to changed condition."[23] and feared "that an immediate cutting down of large farms might reduce the quantity of grain available for the market."[24] And further "the dismemberment of large holdings would have the result of displacing a large number of agricultural labourer.[25]

As Zamindari Abolition and Land Reforms Act did not envisage any land redistribution and there were eviction in many cases the pattern of land ownership remained as skewed after Zamindari abolition as was the case previously. The ceiling laws that were enacted did not result in any reduction of concentration in land holdings either. The first Agricultural Census of 1970-71 and the subsequent censuses of 1976-77 and 1980-81 have exhibited continued concentration of land holdings in the state as is shown in Table 3.1.

It will be observed that in 1970-71, 66.8 per cent of the holdings were below one hectare and by 1980-81 the percentage increased to 70.6. Holdings above 5 hectares constituting 3.5 per cent of the holdings in 1970-71 accounted for 15.7 per cent of the area and in 1980-81 the same accounted for 2.5 per cent of the holdings and 20.1 per cent of the area. The area held by top 3.5 per cent of the households in 1970-71 was more than the area held by bottom 70 per cent of the households. In fact the Area held by top 0.7 per cent of the household was more than what was held by bottom 50 per cent of the households. Concentration ratio which was 0.59 in 1970-71 remained almost stationary at 0.58 in 1976-77. In 1980-81 top 0.4 per cent of the households held more than half of the area held by bottom 50 per cent of the households. Concentration ratio again remained almost stationary at 0.57. It is well known that the large landowners have partitioned their holdings in a fraudulent manner. The concentration may thus be actually more than what is depicted by official records. In any case the failure of theland reform measures to bring about a change in the agrarian structure is obvious.[26]

TABLE 3.1

Percentage Distribution of Holdings and Area in Different Size Categories in U.P.

Size Category (in hectare)	Percentage Distribution of Holdings			Percentage Distribution of Area		
	1970-71	1976-77	1980-81	1970-71	1976-77	1980-81
1	2	3	4	5	6	7
Below 0.5	46.74	49.74	50.52	8.67	10.43	11.29
0.5—1.0	20.09	19.63	20.04	12.42	13.45	14.39
1.0—2.0	17.19	16.39	16.27	20.79	21.58	22.61
2.0—3.0	7.11	6.46	6.16	14.79	14.74	14.72
3.0—4.0	3.46	3.12	2.90	10.20	10.11	9.84
4.0—5.0	1.94	1.78	1.59	7.40	7.45	7.04
5.0—10.0	2.75	2.37	2.11	15.79	14.84	13.92
10 and above	0.72	0.51	0.41	9.94	7.40	6.19
Total	100.00	100.00	100.00	100.00	100.00	100.00

Source : "Agricultural Census in Uttar Pradesh 1980-81", Board of Revenue Lucknow, 1985.

NOTES AND REFERENCES

1. Calculated from Table on p. 349 of ZAC Report, Vol. I, Allahabad, 1948.
2. Calculated from Table on pp. 351-352, *Ibid.*
3. Baljit Singh and Shridhar Misra, *A Study of Land Reforms in U.P.* East-West Centre Press, Honolulu, p. 163.
4. *Ibid.*, p. 163.
5. Charan Singh, *Agrarian Revolution in Uttar Pradesh*, Government of the U.P. Lucknow, p. 23.
6. Report of U.P. Zamindari Abolition Committee Vol. I, Allahabad, 1948, p. 174.
7. *Ibid.*, p. 174.
8. Baljit Singh and Shridhar Misra, *Ibid.*, p. 36.
9. It has been found that in many cases particularly in the Tarai area the land was permitted to be sold to higher castes particularly to Sikhs by the Collectors when the tribals approached them with the plea that someone in the house was seriously ill and land sale was the only way to meet the medical expenses. The Collectors even if they knew the reality had no choince but to permit such sales. Vide P.D. Shrimali : Agrarian Change, Agrarian Tension, Peasant Movement and Organisation in U.P. Mimeo 1981, Lucknow.
10. Secs. 129, 130-131.
11. Baljit Singh and Shridhar Misra, *Ibid*, p. 72.
12. Charan Singh, Agrarian Revolution in Uttar Pradesh, Government U.P. Lucknow, p. 42.
13. Ladejinsky mentions about the "wide time gap between the enactment and the initiation of implementation" Vide, *Agrarian Reforms as Unfinished Business*. New York, 1977, p. 390.
14. P.D. Shrimali, *Ibid.*
15. Rajasva Vibhag ka Karya Vivaran U.P. Government, Lucknow, 1980, p. 7.
16. The Report of the Task Force on Agrarian Relation (Planning Commission March 1973) lists several reasons for poor performance of land reform like "lack of political will". For an exhaustive survey on the work of evaluation of land reforms see Joshi P.C. *Land Reforms in India : Trends & Perspectives*. Allied, Bombay 1975. Referring to political will Joshi says, "The concept of 'political will' is however too vague to be of practical use in planning for effective implementation of land reform", p. 87.
17. The surplus land does not account for even 1 per cent of the cultivated land and consists of most inferior land ,a part of which is unfit for cultivation as admitted officially.
18. Report of United Provinces Zamindari Abolition Committee, Vol. I, Allahabad, 1948, p. 343.
19. *Ibid*, p. 343.
20. *Ibid.*, p. 389.
21. *Ibid.*, p. 385.
22. *Ibid.*, p. 389.
23. *Ibid.*, p. 389.
24. *Ibid.*, p. 389.
25. *Ibid.*, p. 389.
26. Ladejinsky observes in this context "The built-in land lord opposition, abetted by public servants can be dealt with successfully if the political leadership is bent on carrying its goal. This is especially important because the peasantry has not developed a popular political movement of its own capable of effectively representing and advocating its own cause". *op. cit.* p. 362.

4

Magnitude of Land Transfers in U.P.

Land transfers in the sample villages according to size category of owned land of sellers have been shown in Table 4.1. It will be seen that 5.6 per cent of the total land in eastern U.P. had been transferred during the reference period spanning for about 30 years. It ranged from 1.35 per cent in Deoria to 11.08 per cent in Mirzapur. It is significant to note that in the size category of less than 2.5 acres (marginal farmers), nearly ten per cent of the total land had been transferred in the sample villages of eastern U.P. Mirzapur registered the highest percentage of land transfer to total land *i.e.* 32.2 per cent whereas in Ballia, it was only 1.1 per cent. In the size category of 2.5—5 acres of owned land (small farmers), 3 per cent of the land was sold by the households in the region. It ranged from 0.7 per cent in Deoria to 9.6 per cent in Jaunpur. Households in the size category of 5 to 10 acres (semi-medium farmers), transferred nearly 4 per cent of the land in eastern U.P. It ranged from 0.43 per cent in Deoria to 11.23 per cent in Sultanpur. The medium and large farmers having more than 10 acres of land transferred nearly 4 per cent of their land. It ranged from 0.53 per cent in Deoria to 6.12 per cent in Bahraich.

TABLE 4.1

Land Transfers in U.P. According to Size Category of owned Holdings During 1952-53 to 1982-83

Eastern U.P.

(Area in Acres)

	Less than 2.5 acres		2.5 to 5 acres		5 to 10 acres		10 & above		Total	
District	Total land-holding	Sold Land	Total land-holding	Land Sold	T.L.H.	L.S.	T.L.H.	L.S	T.L.H.	L.S.
1	2	3	4	5	6	7	8	9	10	11
Jaunpur	794.97	43.89 (5.53)	318.58	30.86 (9.67)	409.86	25.01 (6.10)	456.59	20.45 (4.48)	1980	120.15 (6.07)
Sultanpar	1077.35	73.44 (6.82)	523.16	38.70 (7.40)	672.77	75.54 (11.23)	798.72	27.89 (3.49)	3072	215.57 (7.07)
Ghazipur	653 .50	22.74 (3.48)	557.14	29.34 (5.27)	627.90	28.07 (4.47)	576.46	19.92 (3.46)	2415	100.03) (4.14)
Ballia	969.55	10.63 (1.10)	831.83	17.28 (2.08)	778.46	31.86 (4.09)	863.16	18.91 (2.19)	3443	78.68 (2.29)
Deoria	1400.91	42.23 (3.01)	960.48	6.84 (0.71)	878.67	3.75 (0.43)	1111.94	5.88 (0.53)	4352	58.70 (1.35)
Bahraich	942.03	89.84 (9.54)	844.37	25.30 (3.00)	772.22	18.20 (2.36)	797.38	48.79 (6.12)	3356	182.12 (5.43)
Mirzapur	1366.30	439.98 (32.20)	954.83	12.72 (1.33)	1313.75	44.55 (3.39)	1620.12	84.80 (5.23)	5255	582.05 (11.08)
Eastern U.P.	7204.61	722.75 (10.03)	4990.39	161.04 (3.23)	5453.63	226.98 (4.16)	6224.37	226.63 (3.64)	23873	1337.40) (5.60)

Table 4.1 *Contd.*

1	2	3	4	5	6	7	8	9	10	11
				CENTRAL U.P.						
Sitapur	1465.21	58.10 (3.97)	1309.58	17.00 (1.30)	1041.00	21.30 (2.05)	1389.21	47.4 (3.41)	5205	143.80 (2.76)
Unnao	1864.79	95.28 (5.11)	1618.71	35.94 (2.22)	1370.77	33.19 (2.42)	1328.73	14.73 (1.11)	6183	179.14 (2.90)
Fatehpur	795.88	37.78 (4.75)	849.36	26.28 (3.09)	1270.04	15.80 (1.24)	1295.72	33.40 (2.50)	4211	113.26 (2.69)
Barabanki	1475.19	16.00 (1.08)	843.65	37.22 (4.41)	1003.53	73.66 (7.34)	664.63	— —	3987	126.88 (3.18)
Farrukha-bad	1431.80	70.23 (4.91)	1029 .28	37.15 (3.61)	1194.70	26.91 (2.55)	939.22	1.39 (0.15)	4595	135.68 (2.95
Central U.P.	7032.87	277.29 (3.94)	5650.58	153.59 (2.72)	5880.04	170.86 (2.91)	5617.51	96.92 (1.73)	24181	698.76 (2.89)
				WESTERN U.P.						
Buland-shahar	405.07	8.79 (2.17)	559.02	22.66 (4.05)	776.34	4.27 (0.55)	673.27	— (0.0)	2414.00	35.72 (1.48)
Bijnor	693.50	123.82 (17.85)	1285.90	16.66 (1.30)	2481.73	22.43 (1.51)	1446.87	36.89 (2.55)	4908.00	199.80 (4.07)
Agra	518.06	73.32 (14.15)	959.27	29.75 (3.10)	1064.11	42.12 (3.96)	873.56	34.51 (3.95)	3415.00	179.70 (5.26)

1	2	3	4	5	6	7	8	9	10	11
Etah	885.38	2.07 (0.23)	815.00	4.55 (0.56)	997.99	16.51 (1.65)	820.63	10.75 (1.31)	3519.00	33.88 (0.96)
Saharan-pur	596.99	120.16 (20.13)	1143.80	30.30 (2.65)	1398.03	67.73 (4.84)	1077.18	67.74 (6.29)	4216.00	285.93 (6.78)
Western U.P.	3099.00	328.16 (10.59)	4763.29	103.92 (2.18)	5718.20	153.06 (2.68)	4891.51	149.89 (3.06)	18472.00	735.03 (3.98)
Bundel-khand	269.96	36.68 (13.40)	670.51	23.74 (3.54)	750.46	32.33 (4.31)	974.07	29.51 (3.03)	2665.00	132.39 (4.97)
Hill Region	1230.36	2.40 (0.20)	501.40	1.00 (0.20)	376.05	3.35 (0.89)	426.19	— (0.0)	2507.00	6.75 (0.27)
U.P.	18809.80	1367.51 (7.27)	16576.17	453.29 (2.73)	18178.38	586.58 (3.23)	18133.65	502.95 (2.77)	71698.00	2910.33 (4.06)

N.B. : Total Land-holding connotes the land in the given size category of all the households in that category in the sample villages. Land sold is for a total period of 30 years (1952-53 to 1982-83). Figures in parentheses are percentages of land sold to the total land in the given category by the respondents.

T.L.H. = Total Land-holding
L.S. = Land Sold

It will be thus seen that land transfers were of a very moderatenature. Hardly 0.2 per cent of the cultivated land changed hand annually, on an average, in eastern U.P. The distressing situation in eastern U.P. is the fact that the marginal farmers sold the largest percentage of their owned land (10%) which was nearly twice the average for all cultivators (5.6%).

In central U.P. nearly 3 per cent of the land owned had been transferred during the reference period. It ranged from 2.69 per cent in Fatehpur to 3.18 per cent in Barabanki. The households which had less than 2.5 acres of owned land, transferred nearly 4 per cent of their land. It ranged from 1.08 per cent in Barabanki to 5.11 per cent in Unnao. Nearly 3 per cent of land owned had been transferred by those households which had owned land in the size category of 2.5 to 5.0 acres. It ranged from 1.3 per cent in Sitapur to 4.41 per cent in Barabanki. Households having land holding of 5 to 10 acres transferred nearly 3 per cent of the land which ranged from 1.24 per cent in Fatehpur to 7.34 per cent in Barabanki. It is remarkable to note that the lowest percentage of land owned (1.73 per cent) had been transferred by medium and large farmers having more than 10 acres of owned land. It ranged from nil in Barabanki to 3.41 per cent in Sitapur.

In central U.P. also it would be seen that the marginal farmers had transferred a higher percentage of their land (3.94 per cent) as was the case in eastern U.P. although the magnitude of land transfers was significantly low in all the categories as compared to eastern U.P. Land transfers as percentage to total land had generally an inverse relationship with the size category in central U.P. also.

In western U.P. nearly 4 per cent of the owned land had been transferred during the reference period. It ranged from 0.96 per cent in Etah to 6.78 per cent in Saharanpur. It is significant to note that households which had less than 2.5 acres of land have sold nearly 11 per cent of their land. It ranged from 0.23 per cent in Etah to as high as 20.13 per cent in Saharanpur. Slightly more than 2 per cent of owned land had been alienated by those households which had owned holdings of 2.5 to 5.0 acres. It ranged from 0.56 per cent in

Etah to 4.05 per cent in Bulandshahar. Households in the size category of 5 to 10 acres had sold 2.68 per cent of their land. The same ranged from 0.55 per cent in Bulandshahar to 4.84 per cent in Saharanpur. Three per cent of land had been transferred by households having more than 10 acres of owned land. It ranged from nil in Bulandshahar to 6.29 per cent in Saharanpur.

It is significant to find that in western U.P. also the marginal farmers having less than 2.5 acres of owned land sold highest percentage of the land (10 per cent) as has been the case in eastern U.P. as well as central U.P. In other categories the land sold ranged from 2 to 3 per cent only.

In Bundelkhand nearly 5 per cent of owned land had been transferred during the reference period. In this region also the marginal farmers sold the highest percentage (13 per cent) of their land as was the case in other regions. In other categories the land sold ranged between 3 to 4 per cent of owned land. Hill region witnessed the least alienation of land (0.27 per cent) during the reference period.

Taking the State as a whole it would be seen that during the reference period 4 per cent of the land was alienated, or in other words, the annual transfer of land was not more than 0.13 per cent of the total land. Marginal farmers witnessed the largest degree of alienation as 7 per cent of their land was alienated followed by households in the size category of 5-10 acres (3.23 per cent). Households in the size category of 10 acres and above witnessed land alienation to the extent of 2.77 per cent of their land followed by households in the category of 2.5—5 acres in whose case 2.73 per cent of the land was alienated.

Thus it can be concluded that while the magnitude of land alienation was not much the fact stands out clearly that the poorest section of the peasantry was hardest hit by the process as they had to part with a larger percentage of their land.

Latest Trend in Land Transfers

It was also thought desirable to analyse the land transfers during the closing 5 years of the reference period to discern the latest trends in the land market and to discern if it materially differed from the general trend. Size category-wise land transfers during last 5 years *viz.* 1978-79 to 1982-83 can be seen from Table 4.2. It will be seen that only 1.21 per cent of the owned land in eastern U.P. had been transferred which ranged from 0.11 per cent in Ballia to 2.51 per cent in Ghazipur. Those households which had owned less than 2.5 acres sold nearly 2 per cent of their land. It ranged from 0.12 per cent in Ballia to 3.35 per cent in Mirzapur. It will be further noted that 1.33 per cent of the owned land had been alienated in the landholding category of 2.5—5.0 acres. In this category land transfers ranged from 0.1 per cent in Ballia to 4.15 per cent in Ghazipur. Land transfers in the size category of 5 — 10 acres accounted for 1.13 per cent of the owned land. The same ranged from 0.18 per cent in Deoria to 2.85 per cent in Sultanpur. The largest category of farmers in the size category of 10 acres and above sold 0.61 per cent of the land which ranged from nil in Ballia to 1.71 per cent in Ghazipur.

It would be seen that there is an inverse relationship between the size of holding and the percentage area sold in eastern U.P. although this does not hold true for all the districts surveyed. The inverse ratio can possibly be explained by the fact that as land cannot be sold in extremely tiny parcels as in that case it will not meet the requirements of the sellers the smaller farmers have to sell a higher percentage of land. Large landowners having more land and higher incomes will sell a smaller portion of their land which will meet their monetary requirements.

It is also significant to note that the highest sale among marginal farmers was in Mirzapur followed by those in Bahraich both of which are agriculturally poor districts while the percentage was lower in agriculturally progressive districts. It lends support to the hypothesis that when agricultural productivity rises marginal farmers find it more worthwhile to cling to the land.

In central U.P. 0.8 per cent of the owned land was transferred through sales during the five year period *viz.*, 1978-79 to 1982-83. In only Unnao more than 1 per cent of the land was transferred whereas in other sample districts it was less than 1 per cent. While marginal farmers sold 0.88 per cent

TABLE 4.2

Land Transfers in U.P. According to Size Category of owned Holdings During 1978-79 to 1982-83.

EASTERN U.P.

(Area in Acres)

District	Lass than 2.5		2.5 to 5.0		5.0 to 10.0		13 & above		Total	
	Total Land-holding	Land Sold	Total Land-holding	Land Sold	Total Land-holding	Land Sold	Total Land-holding	Land Sold	Total Land-holding	Land Sold
1	2	3	4	5	6	7	8	9	10	11
Jaunpur	794.97	8.43 (1.06)	318.58	6.56 (2.06)	409.86	6.59 (1.61)	456.59	17.8 (0.39)	1980.00	22.36 (1.18)
Sultanpur	1077.35	16.66 (1.55)	523.16	16.95 (3.24)	672.77	19.19 (2.85)	798.72	9.68 (1.21)	3072.00	62.48 (2.03)
Ghazipur	653.50	11.92 (1.82)	557.14	23.12 (4.15)	627.90	15.61 (2.49)	576.46	9.86 (1.71)	2415.00	60.50 (2.51)
Ballia	969.55	1.20 (0.12)	831.83	0.87 (0.10)	778.46	1.79 (0.23)	863.16	—	3443.00	3.86 (0.11)
Deoria	1400.91	13.70 (0.98)	960.48	2.08 (0.22)	878.67	1.59 (0.18)	1111.94	0.88 (0.08)	4352.00	18.25 (0.42)
Bahraich	942.03	25.64 (2.72)	844.37	12.10 (1.43)	772.22	4.90 (0.63)	797.88	9.68 (1.21)	3356.00	52.32 (1.56)

(*Table 4.2 Contd.*)

1	2	3	4	5	6	7	8	9	10	11
Mirzapur	1366.30	45.78 (3.35)	954.83	4.86 (0.51)	1313.75	11.71 (0.89)	1620.12	6.06 (0.37)	5255.00	68.41 (1.30)
Eastern U.P.	7204.61	123.32 (1.72)	4990.39	66.54 (1.33)	5433.63	61.38 (1.13)	6224.37	37.94 (0.61)	23873.00	289.18 (1.21)
CENTRAL U.P.										
Sitapur	1465.21	12.30 (0.84)	1309.58	8.60 (0.66)	1041.00	4.80 (0.46)	1389.21	9.30 (0.67)	5205.00	35.00 (0.67)
Unnao	1864.79	19.45 (1.04)	1618.71	30.30 (1.87)	1370.77	16.28 (1.19)	1328.73	2.73 (0.21)	6183.00	68.77 (1.11)
Fatehpur	795.88	8.42 (1.06)	849.36	1.15 (0.84)	1270.04	6.46 (0.51)	1295.72	6.40 (0.49)	4211.00	28.41 (0.67)
Barabanki	1475.19	2.30 (0.16)	843.65	11.35 (1.35)	1003.53	16.03 (1.60)	664.63	—	3987.00	29.68 (0.74)
Farrukhabad	1431.80	19.70 (1.38)	1029.20	8.37 (0.81)	1194.70	3.23 (0.27)	939.22	—	4595.00	31.32 (0.68)
Central U.P.	7032.87	92.20 (0.88)	5650.58	65.75 (1.16)	5880.04	46.80 (0.80)	5617.51	18.43 (0.33)	24181.00	193.18 (0.80)

WESTERN U.P.

1	2	3	4	5	6	7	8	9	10	11
Bulandshahr	405.07	6.19 (1.53)	559.32	9.69 (1.73)	776.34	2.50 (0.32)	673.27	—	2414.00	18.38 (0.76)
Bijhor	693.52	98.40 (14.19)	1285.90	1.44 (0.11)	1481.73	13.77 (0.93)	1446.87	14.51 (1.00)	4908.00	128.12 (2.61)
Agra	518.06	25.08 (4.84)	959.27	14.46 (1.51)	1064.11	20.93 (2.81)	873.56	21.86 (2.50)	3415.00	91.33 (2.67)
Etah	885.38	1.84 (0.21)	815.00	2.14 (0.26)	997.99	6.51 (0.65)	820.63	4.93 (0.60)	3519.00	15.42 (0.44)
Saharanpur	596.99	44.47 (7.45)	1143.80	17.10 (1.50)	1398.03	43.94 (3.14)	1077.18	19.34 (1.80)	4216.00	124.85 (2.96)
Western U.P.	3099.00	175.98 (5.68)	4763.29	44.83 (0.94)	5718.20	96.65 (1,69)	4891.51	60.64 (1.24)	18472.00	378.10 (2.05)
Bundel-khand	269.96	16.68 (6.18)	670.51	25.75 (3.84)	750.46	20.42 (2 72)	974.07	22.71 (2.33)	2665.00	85.56 (3.21)
Hill Region	1203.36	—	501.40	1.0 (0.20)	376.05	2.0 (0.53)	426,19	—	2507.00	3.00 (0.12)
U.P.	18809.80	378.18 (2.01)	16576.17	203.87 (1.23)	18178.38	227.25 (1.25)	18133.65	139.72 (0.77)	71698.00	949.02) (1.32)

N.B. : Total landholding connotes the land in the given size category of all the households in that category in the sample villages. Figures in parentheses are percentages of land sold to total land in the given category.

of their land during this period, the small farmers sold 1.16 per cent of their land, the percentage share declined to 0.8 per cent in case of semi-medium farmers and further to 0.33 per cent in case of medium and large farmers. Small farmers had sold a larger percentage of their land as compared to other categories. But surprisingly in Farrukhabad, agriculturally the most progressive district of this region, the marginal farmers had sold the highest percentage (13.8 per cent) of their land and the percentage declined as the size of landholdings increased. A similar trend was discernible in Sitapur also barring the category which again has a higher agricultural productivity.

In Western U.P. 2.05 per cent of the land changed hands during this period and the same ranged from 0.44 per cent in Etah to 2.96 per cent in Saharanpur. The latter is well developed and significantly registered the highest percentage of land sale followed by Agra (2.67 per cent) and Bijnor (2.61 ler cent). Here also an inverse relationship was more or less found between the percentage area sold and size of land holding. Significantly 5.68 per cent of the land of marginal farmers was alienated which declined to 0.94 per cent in case of small farmers but rose to 1.69 per cent in case of semi-medium farmers and declined again to 1.24 per cent in case of medium and large farmers having holdings of 10 acres and above.

It is somewhat intriguing to find that while only 1.7 per cent of the land of marginal farmers in eastern U.P. was alienated the ratio was higher at 5.7 per cent in Western U.P. Saharanpur, one of the most developed districts, in the whole the state, witnessed an alienation of 7 per cent of the land of marginal farmers during this period. It may be that faster growth of agriculture and diversification of the ccconomy might have induced marginal farmers to move out of agriculture.

In Bundlekhand region 3.21 per cent of the land was transferred during this period. Here also there was on inverse relationship with the size of holding. The marginal farmers transferred 6.18 per cent of their land which declined to 3.84 per cent in case of small farmers, 2.72 per cent in case of semi-medium farmers and 2.33 per cent in case of medium and large farmers.

In the Hill region only 0.12 per cent of the land was transferred. It was confined to small and semi-medium farmers only as marginal, medium and large farmers did not undertake any land sale during the period.

Taking the state as a whole it will be seen that 1.32 per cent of the land was transferred during 1978-83. The marginal farmers sold 2.01 per cent of their land while the percentage was 1.23 in case of small farmers, 1.25 in case of semi-medium farmers and 0.77 in case of medium and large farmers. The inverse relationship between the percentage area sold and the size of landholdings was generally true for the state also.

Land transfers have not become significant in U.P. as annually only about 0.26 per cent of the land changed hands through land sale in the recent past. Although this rate is double of what was in the 30 year period yet again not much should be read into it as the data for the earlier part of the reference period is highly underreported. Land alienated as percentage to total land continued to have an inverse relationship with the size of holding during this period also. Thus there does not seem to be any change in the closing quinquennium of the reference period and the general trends observed earlier regarding land alienation in the state prevailed in later period also.

5

Land Transfer Matrix

Size-wise land transfer matrix in eastern U.P. (Table 5.1) shows that landless accounted for 42 per cent of all the land that was alienated. Sellers in the category of less than 2.5 acres accounted for 12 per cent of the alienated land while those in the category of 2.5—5 acres also accounted for the same proportion (12 per cent). The two higher categories of 5—10 acres and 10 acres and above accounted for 17 per cent each of the alienated land.

Thus it will be seen that the lower categories were the main sellers of land and the alarming aspect is that more than 40 per cent of the land was sold by those who became landless as they sold their entire land-holding. Such persons sold 70 per cent of their land to those who had over 5 acres of land. The marginal farmers sold 56 per cent of their land to marginal and small farmers. Small farmers sold 70 per cent of their land to small and semi-medium farmers. The latter sold only about one-fourth of their land to categories that stood above them while the medium and large farmers sold 46 per cent of their land to the same category.

It will further be seen that of the total land that was

TABLE 5.1

Land Transfer Matrix in eastern U.P. According to size Category of Owned Holdings

(Size and Area in acres)

SELLERS	BUYERS Less than 2.5	2.5—5	5.0—10	10 & above	Total
1	2	3	4	5	6
Landless	64.10 (11.43) (31.15)	97.76 (17.43) (30.71)	224.17 (39.97) (50.87)	174.80 (31.17) (46.91)	560.83 (100.00) (41.93)
Less than 2.5	45.55 (28.13) (22.14)	45.86 (28.33) (14.41)	45.65 (28.19) (10.36)	24.86 (15.35) (6.67)	161 92 (100.00) (12.11)
2.5—5	31.38 (19.49) (15.25)	59.26 (36.80) (18.62)	55.77 (34.63) (12.65)	14.63 (9.08) (3.93)	161.04 (100.00) (12.04)
5—10	39.59 (17.44) (19.24)	72.60 (31.99) (22.81)	60.67 (26.73) (13.77)	54.12 (23.84) (14.52)	226.98 (100.00) (16.97)
10 & above	25.15 (11.10) (12.22)	42.81 (18.89) (13.45)	54.42 (24.01) (12.35)	104.52 (46.00) (27.97)	226.63 (100.00) (16.95)
Total	205.77 (15.39) (100.00)	318.29 (23.80) (100.00)	440.68 (32.95) (100.00)	372.66 (27.86) (100.00)	1337.40 (100.00) (100.00)

N.B—Figures in first parenthesis are percentages of land sold to different categories while the second parentheses are percentage of land purchased by different categories.

alienated the lowest category among the purchasers accounted for 15 per cent of the land followed by 24 per cent and 33 per cent by the two next higher categories of 2.5—5 acres and 5—10 acres respectively. The highest category of 10 acres and above accounted for 28 per cent of the land that was purchased. It is significant that marginal farmers (less than 2.5 acre category) accounted for almost one-sixth of the land that was purchased. The small farmers' (2.5—5 acre category) share at 24 per cent was also quite significant. The semi-medium farmers (5—10 acre category) accounted for one-third of the land purchased. This shows that although purchasers were from all categories of farmers yet the semi-medium farmers constituted the biggest chunk followed by medium and large farmers (28 per cent). The share of marginal and small farmers taken together at nearly 40 per cent is quite impressive and shows that purchasers of land are not confined to large farmers. A category-wise distribution of area sold and purchased is summarised in Table 5.2.

It is interesting to find that all the land owning categories gained as they purchased more land than was sold at the cost of those who became landless. The latter accounted for 42 per cent of the alienated land as noted earlier. Marginal farmers with less than 2.5 acres of owned land purchased 206 acres but sold 162 acres during the reference period thereby gaining 44 acres. Land purchased by such farmers was 127 per cent of the land sold by them. Similarly the small and semi-medium farmers purchased land was almost twice that of the land sold by these categories. Land purchased by medium and large farmers was 164 per cent of the land sold by them. Thus although all the land owning categories gained yet the largest gain was to small and semi-medium farmers although the gain of medium and large farmers was also substantial.

Land transfer matrix according to size of owned holding in central U.P. is shown in Table 5.3. It will be seen that landless accounted for 21 per cent of all the land sold and another 19 per cent of the land was sold by less than 2.5 acre category. Roughly 22 per cent of the land was sold by 2.5—5 acre category and 24 per cent of the land was sold by 5—10 acre category while the category of 10 acres and above accounted

TABLE 5.2

Size Category-wise Land Sold and Purchased in eastern U.P.

(Area in acres)

Size category of owned land	Land Sold	Land Purchased	Land Purchased as % of Land Sold	Net gain or loss	(+) As per- (—) centage
1	2	3	4	5	6
Landless	560.83 (41.93)	—	—	(—) 560.83	(—) 100.00
Less than 2.5	161.92 (12.12)	205.77 (15.39)	127.08	(+) 43.85	(+) 7.82
2.5—5	161.04 (12.04)	318.29 (23.80)	197.65	(+) 157.25	(+) 28.04
5--10	226.98 (16.97)	440.68 (32.95)	194.15	(+) 213.70	(+) 38.10
10 & above	226.63 (16.94)	372.66 (27.86)	164.44	(+) 146.03	(+) 260.47
Total	1337.40 (100.00)	1337.40 (100.00)	100.00	—	—

N.B.—Figures in parentheses are percentages.

TABLE 5.3

Land Transfer Matrix in central U.P. According to size Category of Owned Holdings

(Size and Area in acres)

SELLERS	BUYERS				
	Less than 2.5	2.5—5	5—10	10 & above	Total
1	2	3	4	5	6
Landless	12.06 (8.27) (21.56)	29.02 (19.89) (12.55)	59.41 (40.72) (21.41)	45.39 (31.12) (33.83)	145.88 (100.00) (20.88)
Less than 2.5	24.69 (18.78) (44.41)	63.63 (48.38) (27.25)	30.39 (23.11) (10.95)	12.80 (9.73) (9.54)	131.51 (100.00) (18.82)
2.5—5	12.17 (7.92) (21.76)	66.10 (43.04) (28.58)	51.34 (33.43) (18.51)	23.98 (15.61) (17.88)	153.59 (100.00) (21.98)
5—10	4.07 (2.38) (7.28)	58.52 (34.52) (25.31)	91.07 (53.30) (32.83)	17.20 (10.07) (12.82)	170.86 (100.00) (24.45)
10.0 & above	2.94 (3.03) (5.26)	13.97 (14.41) (6.04)	45.22 (46.66) (16.30)	34.79 (35.90) (25.93)	96.92 (100.00) (13.87)
Total	55.93 (8.01) (100.00)	231.24 (33.09) (100.00)	277.43 (39.70) (100.00)	134.16 (19.20) (100.00)	698.76 (100.00) (100.00)

N.B.—Figures in first parenthesis are percentages of land sold to different categories while the figures in second parenthesis are percentages of land purchased by different categories.

for 14 per cent of the all sold land. Thus roughly 40 per cent of the land was sold by those who had less than 2.5 acre of holding including the landless. It will further be seen that the landless, by and large, preferred higher categories while those in the size category of less than 2.5 acres preferred the 2.5—5 acres category as about half of their land was sold to this category. Sellers in the size category of 2.5—5 acre seem to prefer their own category as highest share (43 per cent) was accounted for by that category. This was all the more true about 5—10 acre category among the sellers who sold 53 per cent of the land to the same category. The highest category did not exhibit this tendency as 36 per cent of their land was sold to the same category while 47 per cent of the land was sold to 5—10 acre category.

As regards the buyers, those in the size category of less than 2.5 acres accounted for 8 per cent of the land purchased. Roughly 44 per cent of the land was bought from the same category of sellers. The next higher category of 2.5—5 acres accounted for one-third of all the land purchased and their own category among the sellers accounted for 29 per cent of the land sold. The 5—10 acre category accounted for the highest share (40 per cent) of the total land purchased and significantly one-third of their land was purchased from the same land ownership category. The highest category which accounted for less than 20 per cent of all land purchased had made largest purchases from the landless (34 per cent) followed by its own category (26 per cent). The net position of different categories is summarised in Table 5.4.

It will be seen that apart from landless the marginal farmers were also net losers. The latter accounted for 19 per cent of the land alienated but purchased only 8 per cent of the land. Their purchased land was only 42 per cent of the land that they sold. All the other categories were gainers. The gain of small, semi-medium and medium and large farmers was 50 per cent, 62 per cent and 38 per cent respectively.

Size-wise land transfer matrix in western U.P. is shown in Table 5.5. It will be seen that landless accounted for more than one-third (35 per cent) of the total land that was sold. Another 10 per cent of the land was sold by less

TABLE 5.4

Size Category-wise Land Sold and Purchased in central U.P.

(Area in acres)

Size category of owned land	Land Sold	Land Purchased	Land Purchased as% of Land Sold	Net gain (+) or loss (—)	As percentages
1	2	3	4	5	6
Landless	145.88 (20.88)	—	—	(—) 145.88	(—) 65.87
Less than 2.5	131.51 (18.82)	55.93 (8.01)	42.53	(—) 75.58	(—) 34.13
2.5—5	153.59 (21.98)	231.24 (33.09)	150.26	(+) 77.65	(+) 35.06
5—10	170.86 (24.45)	277.43 (39.70)	162.37	(+) 106.57	(+) 48.12
10 & above	96.92 (13.87)	134.16 (19.20)	138.42	(+) 37.24	(+)16.82
Total	698.76 (100.00)	698.76 (100.00)	100.00	—	—

N.B.—Figures in parentheses are percentages.

TABLE 5.5

Land Transfer Matrix in western U.P. According to size of Owned Holdings

(Size and area in acres)

SELLERS	BUYERS				
	Less than 2.5	2.5–5	5—10	10 & above	Total
1	2	3	4	5	6
Landless	10.83 (4.25) (17.58)	37.25 (14.58) (26.01)	53.04 (20.76) (26.18)	154.32 (60.41) (47.10)	255.44 (100.00) (34.75)
Less than 2.5	16.62 (22.85) (26.98)	22.46 (30.89) (15.69)	21.88 (30.09) (10.80)	11.76 (16.17) (3.59)	72.72 (100.00) (9.90)
2.5—5.0	15.36 (14.78) (24.93)	48.72 (46.88) (34.02)	23.99 (23.09) (11.84)	14.85 (15.25) (4.84)	103.92 (100.00) (14.14)
5.0—10.0	6.09 (3.98) (9.88)	22.84 (14.92) (15.95)	73.54 (48.05) (36.29)	50.59 (33.05) (15.44)	153.06 (100.00) (20.82)
10.0 & above	12.71 (8.48) (20.63)	11.93 (7.96) (8.33)	30.16 (20.12) (14.89)	95.09 (63.44) (29.03)	149.89 (100.00) (20.39)
Total	61.61 (8.38) (100.00)	143.20 (19.48) (100.00)	202.61 (27.57) (100.00)	327.61 (44.57) (100.00)	735.03 (100.00) (100.00)

N.B.—Figures in first parenthesis are percentages of land sold to different categories while figures in the second parenthesis are percentage of land purchases by defferent categories.

than 2.5 acre category while the 2.5- 5 acre category accounted for 14 per cent of the land sold. Roughly 21 per cent of the land was sold by 5—10 acre category and another 20 per cent by 10 and above category. Thus 44 per cent of the land was sold by those who had less than 2.5 acres of land.

As regards the buyers it will be seen that those in the category of less than 2.5 acres accounted for 8 per cent of the land purchased. The next two higher categories accounted for 19 and 28 per cent respectively while the highest category accountted for as high as 45 per cent of the land purchased. Thus the landless category was largely alienated from land and the higher categories mainly purchased the land. A size-category-wise area of land sold and purchased is summarised in Table 5.6.

Landless accounted for 96 per cent of the net loss but what is more disconcerting is the fact that the highest category of 10 acres and above accounted for two-thirds of the net gain in land transactions unlike in eastern or central U.P. where small and semi-medium farmers were the largest gainers. Green revolution seems to have strengthened the position of bigger land owners relative to that of semi-medium and small ones.

Size-wise land transfer matrix in Bundelkhand is shown in Table 5.7. It will be seen that the landless accounted for 15 per cent of the total land sold. The less than 2.5 acre category accounted for another 13 per cent of the sold land. The highest share (26 per cent) was accounted for by 2.5—5 acre category while another 24 per cent and 22 per cent was accounted for by the next two higher categories respectively.

The lowest category among the purchasers accounted for 4 per cent of the land purchased while 2.5—5 acre category accounted for 14 per cent and the 5-10 acre category accounted for 20 per cent of the land purchased. Significantly 62 per cent of the land was purchased by 10 and above category.

A category-wise distribution of land sold and purchased is summarised in Table 5.8. It is significant to note that the only category to gain was the highest category of 10 acres and above whose gain was as high as 177 per cent and all the other categories sold more land than they purchased. Agricultural productivity being very low in Bundelkhand it appears tha

TABLE 5.6

Size Category-wise Land Sold and Purchased in western U.P.

(Area in acres)

Size category of owned land	Land Sold	Land Purchased	Land Purchased as% of Land Sold	Net gain (+) or loss (—)	As percentage
1	2	3	4	5	6
Landless	255.44 (34.75)	—	—	(—) 255.44	(—) 95.83
Less than 2.5	72.72 (9.90)	61.61 (8.38)	84.72	(—) 11.11	(—) 4.17
2.5—5	103.92 (14.14)	143.20 (19.48)	137.80	(+) 39.28	(+) 14.74
5—10	153.06 (20.82)	202.61 (27.57)	132.37	(+) 49.55	(+) 18.59
10 & above	149.89 (20.39)	327.61 (44.57)	218.57	(+) 177.72	(+) 66.67
Total	735.03 (100.00)	735.03 (100.00)	100.00	—	—

N.B.—Figures in parentheses are percentages.

TABLE 5.7

Land Transfer Matrix in Bundelkhand according to size Category of owned Holdings

(Size and Area in acres)

SELLERS	BUYERS				
	Less than 2.5	2.5—5	5—10	10 & above	Total
1	2	3	4	5	6
Landless	0.98 (4.95) (19.48)	5.12 (25.83) (26.60)	9.75 (49.19) (37.14)	3.97 (20.03) (4.85)	19.82 (100.00) (14.97)
Less than 2.5	—	4.13 (24.31) (21.46)	3.20 (18.83) (12.19)	9.96 (56.86) (11.80)	16.99 (100.00) (12.83)
2.5—5.0	1,95 (5.78) (38.77)	3.60 (10.67) (18.70)	9.90 (29.34) (37.72)	18.29 (54.21) (22.34)	33.74 (100.00) (25.49)
5 0—10.0	1.20 (3.71) (23.86)	3.10 (9.59) (16.10)	0.90 (2.78) (3.43)	27.13 (83.92) (33.14)	32.33 (100.00) (24.42)
10 & above	0.90 (3.05) (17.89)	3.30 (11.18) (17.14)	2.50 (8.47) (9.52)	22.81 (77.30) (27.87)	29.51 (100.00) (22.29)
Total	5.03 (3.80) (100.00)	19.25 (14.54) (100 00)	26.25 (19.83) (100.00)	81.86 (61.83) (100.00)	132.39 (100.00) (100 00)

N.B.—Figures in first parenthesis are percentages of land sold to different categories while figures in the second perenthesis are percentage of land purchased by different categories.

TABLE 5.8

Size Category-wise Land sold and Purchased in Bundelkhand

(Area in acres)

Size category of owned land	Land Sold	Land Purchased	Land Purchased as% of land sold	Net gain (+) or loss (—)	As percentage
1	2	3	4	5	6
Landless	19.82 (14.97)	—	—	(—) 19.82	(—) 37.86
Less than 2.5	16.99 (12.83)	5.03 (3.80)	29.61	(—) 11.96	(—) 22.85
2.5—5	33.74 (25.49)	19.25 (14.50)	57.05	(—) 14.49	(—) 27.68
5—10	32.33 (24.42)	26.25 (19.83)	81.19	(—) 6.08	(—) 11.61
10 & above	29,51 (22.29)	81.86 (61.83)	277.40	(+) 52.35	(+) 100.00
Total	132.39 (100.00)	132.39 (100.00)	100.00	—	—

N.B.—Figures in parentheses are percentages.

only large farmers are doing well. They are in a position to acquire land while other categories are losing land. A process of concentration of land in upper most group and landlessness at the bottom seems to be at work in this region also.

In Hill Region (Table 5.9) half the land was sold by 5 — 10 acre category and the same category purchased 36 per cent of the land. The 2.5—5 acre category accounted for 15 per cent of the land sold but it accounted for half of the land that was purchased. The 2.5—5 acre category was the sole gainer at the cost of less than 2.5 acre and 5—10 acre categories. In this region there was no case of selling the entire holding.

Land transfer matrix in U.P. according to size category of holdings is shown in Table 5.10. It will be seen that landless accounted for 34 per cent of the total land sold. The share of less than 2.5 acre category was 13 per cent and that of 2.5—5 acre category was 16 per cent. Households in the size category of 5 –10 acres accounted for 20 per cent of the total land sold whereas the highest category accounted for 17 per cent of the land.

The landless had sold the bulk of their land to highest two categories but the less than 2.5 acre category had preference for lower categories as 58 per cent of their land was sold to those who had less than 5 acres. Households in the size category of 2.5—5 acre category had largest transactions with the same size group as 39 per cent of the land was sold to that group. This was also true for 5—10 acre category as well as for the highest category. In case of the latter more than half of the land was sold to households in the same size category whereas :9 per cent of the land of 5—10 acre category was sold to the same category. It appears that the households belonging to the same hierarchy in terms of land-holding had greater social affinity which probably led them to have greater mutual preference in land dealings.

As regards purchase of land the lowest category of less than 2.5 acres accounted for 11 per cent of the total land purchased. The next higher category of 2.5 – 5 acres accounted for one-fourth of the land and the 5—10 acres category accounted for another one-third of the land while the highest

TABLE 5.9

Size Category-wise Land Sold and Purchased in Hill Region

(Area in acres)

Size Category of owned land	Land Sold	Land Purchased	Land Purchased as % of Land Sold	Net gain (+) or loss (—)	As Percentages
1	2	3	4	5	6
Landless	—	—	—	—	
Less than 2.5	2.40 (35.55)	1.00 (14.82)	41.67	(—) 1.40	(—) 59.57
2.5—5	1.00 (14.82)	3.55 (49.63)	335.00	(+) 2.35	(+) 100.00
5—10	3.35 (49.63)	2.40 (35.55)	71.64	(—) 0.95	(—) 40.43
10 & above	—	—	—	—	
Total	6.75 (100.00)	6.95 (100.00)	100.00	—	—

N.B.— Figures in parentheses are percentages.

TABLE 5.10

Land Transfer Matrix in U.P. According to size Category of owned Holdings

(Size and Area in acres)

SELLERS	BUYERS				
	Less than 2.5	2.5—5	5—10	10 & above	Total
1	2	3	4	5	6
Landless	87.97 (8.96) (26.72)	169.15 (17.23) (23.65)	346.38 (35.27) (36.49)	378.48 (38.54) (41.31)	981.98 (100.00) (33.74)
Less than 2.5	86.86 (22.53) (26.37)	136.08 (35.30) (19.02)	103.52 (16.85) (10.90)	59.08 (15.31) (6.45)	385.54 (100.00 (13.25)
2.5—5	61.86 (13.65) (18.78)	177.68 (39.20) (24.84)	140.99 (31.10) (14.85)	72.75 (16.05) (7.93)	453.28 (100.00) (15.57)
5—10	50.95 (8.69) (15.47)	160.41 27.35 (22.43)	226.18 (38.56) (23.82)	149.04 (25.40) (16.27)	586.58 (100.00) (20.16)
10 & above	41.70 (8.29) (12.66)	72.01 (14.32) (10.07)	132.30 (26.30) (13.94)	256.94 (51.09) (28.04)	502.95 (100.00) (17.28)
Total	339.34 (11.32) (100.00)	715.33 (24.58) (100.00)	949.37 (32.62) (100.00)	916.29 (31.48) (100.00)	2910.33 (100.00) (100.00)

N.B.— Figures in first parentheses are percentages to the total land sold to different categories while figures in second parentheses are percentages to total land penchased by different categories.

TABLE 5.11

Size-Category-wise Land Sold and Purchased in U.P.

(Area in acres)

Size category of owned holdings	Land Sold	Land Purchased	Land purchased as % of Land Sold	Net gain (+) or loss (—)	As Percentages
1	2	3	4	5	6
Landless	981.98 (33.74)	—	—	(—) 981.98	(—) 94.59
Less than 2.5	385.54 (13.25)	329.34 (11.32)	85.42	(—) 56.20	(—) 5.41
2.5—5	453.28 (15.57)	715.33 (24.58)	157.81	(+) 262.05	(—) 25.24
5—10	586.58 (30.16)	949.37 (32.62)	161.85	(+) 362.79	(+) 34.95
10 & above	502.95 (17.28)	916.29 (31.48)	182.18	(+) 413.34	(+) 39.81
Total	2910.33 (100.00)	2910.33 (100.00)	100.00	—	—

N.B.—Figures in parentheses are percentages

category of 10 acres and above accounted for 31 per cent of the total purchased land. Thus the two highest categories accounted for almost two-thirds of the land purchased. A size-wise classification of land sold and purchased according to size category of owned holdings is summarised in Table 5.11. The table highlights the fact that at the bottom landlessness is increasing as they accounted for 95 per cent of the net loss in land transactions. Households with less than 2.5 acres also show a negative balance *i.e.* as a category they had sold more land than what was purchased although the margin was not very large. The other categories had a positive balance indicating that they purchased more land than what was sold. Land purchased as a percentage of land sold was 158 per cent in case of 2.5—5 acre category, 162 per cent in the category of 5—10 acres and 182 per cent in the size category of 10 acres and above. Thus the gain was positively associated with the size of holding *i.e.* percentage gain increased with an increase in the size category of owned holding.

It can be surmised that the land market in U.P. is witnessing a process of polarisation. Landlessness at the bottom and concentration at the top seems to be increasing through its working. The growth process appears to be favouring the rural landed elements mostly at the top and is bypassing the lowest peasantry.

6

Land Market in Pre-Green Revolution and Post-Green Revolution Periods

The introduction of high yielding varieties in mid-sixties can be said to be a watershed in Indian agriculture. The new technology being size neutral was adopted by all categories of cultivators although the bigger cultivators were the first to adopt it. There was a significant increase in production and yield with its introduction. An attempt was made to analyse the behaviour of land market in the pre-green revolution period which in this particular study refers to the period 1952-53 to 1967-68 and in the post-green revolution period which refers to the period 1968-69 to 1982-83 to discern if there was any marked change in the behaviour of the land market between the two periods in the State as a whole and in each of the five regions of the State.

It will be seen that in pre-green revolution period 38.81 per cent of the owned land of sellers was transferred in eastern U.P. (Table 6.1). It came down to 21.15 per cent in the post-green revolution period. It would be further seen that 38.41 per cent of owned land had been alienated by those households who had land-holding of less than 2.5 acres. The land

TABLE 6.1

Land sold as Percentage of total Landholding according to size Category of owned Holdings in eastern U.P.

Pre-Green Revolution Period (1952-53 to 1967-68)

(Area in acres)

Size Category	No. of land sales	As percentage	Total land holding	Total land sold	Sold land as percentage of total land
1	2	3	4	5	6
Landless	47	27.33	340.87	340.87	100.00
Less than 2.5	29	16.86	64.05	24.60	38.41
2.5 to 5.0	32	18.60	88.64	19.56	22.07
5.0 to 10.0	27	15.70	220.58	37.77	17.12
10.0 & above	37	21.51	599.90	87.21	14.54
Total	172	(100.00)	1314.04	510.01	38.81
Post-Green Revolution Period (1968-69 to 1982-83)					
Landless	65	9.75	219.96	219.96	100.00
Less than 2.5	175	26.28	369.11	137.32	37.20
2.5 to 5.0	166	24.93	656.63	141.48	21.55
5.0 to 10.0	173	25.98	1251.67	189.21	15.12
10.0 & above	87	13.06	1414.06	139.42	9.86
Total	66	100.00	3911.43	827.39	21.15

holding categories of 2.5 to 5.0 acres and 5—10 acres sold 22.07 per cent and 17.12 per cent of their owned land respectively in pre-green revolution period. The mediem and large farmers who had more than 10 acres of owned land transferred nearly 15 per cent of their land in this period. It would be seen that the land transferred as percentage of total owned land had an inverse relationship with the size of land-holding during pre-green revolution period in eastern U.P. It is significant to note that more than one-fourth (27 per cent) of the total sellers had sold their entire landholding and had thus, become landless. The next largest group of sellers came from those who had holdings of over 10 acres (22 per cent) followed by those in the size category of 2.5—5 acres (19 per cent).

During the post-green revolution period land transferred as a percentage of total land owned declined to 21 per cent as compared to 39 per cent in the pre-green revolution period. But the total area involved increased considerably. But this may not be true as during the pre-green revolution period, as already noted, not all the land transfers could be recollected because of time lag and also because of the fact that in many a case a new generation had come up which had no idea of the land transferred during the earlier period. In several cases family partitions had taken place and the new family unit would not own the earlier transfers. On account of these factors not much should be read into the finding that the area involved in land transfers was much larger in the post-green revolution than in the pre-Green one. In fact it may have been otherwise.

In this period also land transferred as a percentage of land owned had an inverse relationship with the size of land holding. In the size category of less than 2.5 acres the land transferred constituted 37 per cent of the land owned by this category, the same declined to 15 per cent in the size category of 5—10 acres and still further to 10 per cent in the highest size category of 10 acres and above.

It is significant to note that in the post-green revolution period only 10 per cent of the sellers sold their entire landholding as compared to 27 per cent in the pre-green revolution period. As agriculture became profitable the tendency to give up agriculture altogether was weakened in the second period. Households in the size category of 2.5 to 10 acres formed half the sellers of land during the second period while those owning more than 10 acres formed 13 per cent of all sellers. Average land sold per seller in the pre-green revolution period was 2.96 acres while in the second period it came down to 1.24 acres. Land alienated as per cent of total land was inversely related to the size of land holding in the second period as well.

In central U.P. (Table 6.2) during the pre-green revolution period nearly 29 per cent of the land of sellers was transferred. Households with less than 2.5 acres of land had transferred 35 per cent of their land while households in the size category of 2.5—5 acres had transferred 45 per cent of their total land. In the next higher category it declined to 19 per cent and was 11 per cent in the highest category of 10 acres and above. Roughly 18 per cent of the sellers had sold their entire land-holding. They generally belonged to the lower category as average land sold per household was less than 3 acres. Marginal farmers constituted 28 per cent of all sellers and small farmers constituted another 20 per cent. If we include 18 per cent of the households who had become landless after selling their entire land it can be said that two-thirds of all sellers were marginal and small farmers and together they had sold 57 per cent of their land during a span of 15 years.

During the post-green revolution period, land alienation as percentage of that land had come down to 23 per cent. It also showed an inverse relationship with size of land-holding. The alienated land of the marginal farmers accounted for nearly 38 per cent ef their land ; the same declined to 24 per cent in the case of small farmers and further to 18 per cent in case of semi-medium farmers. It was 11 per cent in case of medium and large farmers having holdings of 10 acres and above. Eleven per cent of all those who had sold their land had become landless. Twenty nine per cent of the sellers of land belonged to the marginal farmers' category while 28 per cent were small farmers having 2.5 to 5 acres of land.

By and large, land sold as per cent of total land owned declined with the size of holding both in the first as well as

TABLE 6.2

Land sold as Percentage of total Landholdings According to Size Category of owned Holdings in central U.P.

(Area in acres)

Size Category	No. of land sales	As Percentage	Total land-holding	Total land sold	Sold land as percentage to total land
1	2	3	4	5	6
		Pre-Green Revolution Period			
Landless	16	17.77	45.69	45.69	100.00
Less than 2.5	25	27.77	50.42	17.67	35.05
2.5 to 5.0	18	20.00	65.66	29.42	44.83
5.0 to 10.0	21	23.34	167.06	31.93	19.12
10.0 & above	10	11.12	172.79	18.79	10.88
Total	90	100.00	501.62	143.51	28.61
		Post-Green Revolution Period			
Landless	48	11.22	109.19	100.19	100.00
Less than 2.5	124	28.96	290.60	109.91	37.82
2.5 to 5.0	118	27.57	541.72	128.09	23.65
5 0 to 10.0	100	23.37	780.91	133.93	17.79
10.0 & above	38	8.88	717.77	78.13	10.89
Total	428	100.00	2431.19	555.25	22.84

the second period as was the case in eastern U.P. also. The average sold area also declined from 1.59 acre during the first period to 1.29 acres during the second period.

In western U.P. (Table 6.3) 19 per cent of total land of sellers had been transferred during pre-green revolution period as against 28 per cent during post-green revolution period. Nearly half of owned land (46 per cent) was alienated of those farmers who had less than 2.5 acres of land in the pre-green revolution period whereas land holding category of 2.5—5.0 acres sold only 18 per cent of their land. It is interesting to note that there were no land transfers in the land holding category to 5—10 acres of land. Among the sellers 27 per cent had sold their entire landholdings and had become landless. Eighteen per cent of the sellers were marginal farmers and another 36 per cent were small farmers. Adding those who had sold their entire landholding, it can be said that 82 per cent of the sellers were marginal and small farmers and together they had sold 42 per cent of their land during a span of 15 years.

In the post the green revolution period 41 per cent of owned land was transferred by farmers having less than 2.5 acres of land whereas one-fourth of the owned land had been sold by those in the size category of 2.5 to 5.0 acres. The next higher category had sold 28 per cent of their land whereas the extent of alienation was only 14 per cent among farmers in the highest category. Here again, by and large, there was an inverse relationship between land sold as a percentage of total land and size of landholding as was the case in other regions.

Among those who had sold any land 17 per cent had sold their entire holdings. Marginal farmers and small farmers constituted 23 per cent and 25 per cent respectively of the sellers. Adding those who had sold their entire land it can be said that 65 per cent of the sellers belonged to the marginal and small farmers category and together they had sold more than half of their land during a span of nearly 15 years in the post-green revolution period. The average area of land sold declined to 2.62 acres in the second period as compared to 3.25 acres during the first period.

In Bundelkhand region (Table 6.4) 37 per cent of the land of sellers was alienated during the pre-green revolution period

TABLE 6.3

Land sold as Percentage of total Landholding according to size Category of owned Holdings in Western U.P.

(Area in acres)

Size Category	No. of land sales	As percentage	Total !and holding sold	Total land	Sold land as percentage of total land
1	2	3	3	5	6
Pre-Green Revolution Period					
Landless	3	27.28	10.16	10.16	100.00
Less than 2.5	2	18.18	5.72	2.63	45.98
2.5 to 5.0	4	36.36	24.41	4.42	18.11
5.0 to 10.0	—	—	—	—	—
10.0 & above	2	18.18	180.68	18.59	10.29
Total	11	100.00	220.97	35.80	16.20
Post-Green Revolution Period					
Landless	46	17.23	245.28	245.28	100.00
Less than 2.5	62	23.22	169.68	70.09	41.31
2.5 to 5.0	66	24.72	391.03	99.50	25.45
5.0 to 10.0	65	24.34	736.56	153.06	27.78
10.0 & above	28	10.49	965.56	131.30	13.60
Total	267	100.00	2508.11	699.23	27.88

TABLE 6.4

Land sold as Percentage of Total Landholding According to Size Category of owned Holdings in Bundelkhand

Pre-Green Revolution Period

(area in acres)

Size Category	No. of land sales	As percentage	Total land holding	Total land sold	Land sold as percentage of total land
1	2	3	4	5	6
Landless	4	33.33	6.85	6.85	100.00
Less than 2.5	4	33.33	11.21	6.82	60.84
2.5 to 5.0	2	16.68	7.66	1.40	18.28
5.0 to 10.0	1	8.33	8.00	2.00	25.00
10.0 & above	1	8.33	15.00	1.00	6.68
Total	12	100.00	48.72	18.07	37.09
Post-Green Revolution Period					
Landless	7	8.75	12.97	12.97	100.00
Less than 2.5	14	17.50	33.23	10.17	30.61
2.5 to 5.0	31	38.75	144.54	32.34	22.38
5.0 to 10.0	15	18.75	147.98	30.33	20.50
10.0 & above	13	16.25	211.11	28.51	13.51
Total	83	100.00	549.83	114.32	20.79

as against 21 per cent in the post-green revolution period. In the pre-green revolution period one-third of the sellers had sold their entire landholding. Surprisingly the marginal farmers had sold 61 per cent of their total land while the small farmers had sold 18 per cent of their land. Semi-medium farmers had sold 25 per cent of the land and medium and large farmers with 10 acres or more of owned land had sold 7 per cent of their land.

In the post-green revolution period only 9 per cent of the sellers had sold their entire holdings. Marginal and small farmers had sold 31 per cent and 22 per cent respectively of their land. Semi-medium farmers having holdings of 5—10 acres had sold 21 per cent of their land and the medium and large farmers had sold 14 per cent of their land. Marginal and small farmers together with those who had sold their total holdings constituted 65 per cent of the total sellers and together they had sold 29 per cent of their land. Land sold as percentage of land owned generally declined with an increase in the size category of owned land in both the periods as was generally the case in other regions as well.

In the Hill region (Table 6.5) the only size category which witnessed any land sale during pre-green revolution period was the 5—10 acres category in which 15 per cent of the owned land was alienated. But during the post-green revolution period the marginal farmers who sold any land had transferred as high as 71 per cent of their land and the share of small and semi-medium farmers was 25 per cent and 28 per cent respectively. The medium and large farmers did not transfer any land during this period nor had any household sold its entire land. The marginal and small farmers constituted two-thirds of all sellers of land and together they had sold 46 per cent of their land during a span of nearly 15 years. The average area of land sold in the first period were 1.35 acres but it rose slightly to 1.80 acres during the second period.

For the State as a whole (Table 6.6) during the pre-green revolution period the sellers had sold more than one-third of their land as against 23 per cent of their land in the post-green revolution period. In the pre-green revolution period almost one-fourth of the sellers had sold their entire holding but the

TABLE 6.5

Land Sold as Percentage of Total Landholding according to Size Category of owned Land holding in Hill Region

Pre-Green Revolution Period

(Area in acres)

Size Category	No. of land sales	As Percentage	Total land holding	Total land sold	Land sold as percentage of total land
1	2	3	4	5	6
Landless	—	—	—	—	—
Less than 2.5	—	—	—	—	—
2.5 to 5,0	—	—	—	—	—
5.0 to 10.0	1	100.00	9.25	1.35	14.60
10.0 & above		—	—	—	—
Total	1	100.00	9.25	1.35	14.60
		Post-Green Revolution Period			
Landless	—	—	—	—	—
Less than 2.5	1	33.33	3.40	2,40	70.59
2.5 to 5.0	1	33.33	4.00	1.00	25.00
5.0 to 10.0	1	33.33	7.00	2.00	28.57
10.0 & above	—	—	—	—	—
Total	3	100.00	14 40	5.40	37.50

TABLE 6.6

Land Sold as Percentage of Total Landholding according to Size Category of owned landholding in U.P.

Pre-Green Revolution Period 1952-53 to 1967-68

(Area in acres)

Size Category	No. of land sales	As percentage	Total land holding	Total land sold	Land sold as percentage of total land
1	2	3	4	5	6
Landless	70	24.48	403.57	403.57	100.00
Less than 2.5	60	20.98	131.40	55.65	42.35
2.5 to 5.0	56	19.58	186.37	50.88	27.30
5.0 to 10.0	50	17.48	404.89	73.05	18.04
10.0 & above	50	17.48	968.37	125.59	12.69
Total	286	100.00	2094.60	708.74	33.83
Post-Green Revolution Period 1968-69 to 1982-83					
Landless	166	11.49	578.40	578.40	100.00
Less than 2.5	376	26.03	866.02	329.89	38.09
2.5 to 5.0	382	26.45	1737.92	402.41	23.15
5.0 to 10.0	354	24.51	2924.14	513.53	17.56
10.0 & above	166	11.49	3308.50	377.36	11.40
Total	1444	100.00	9414.96	2201.59	23.38

same came down to 11 per cent during the post-green revolution period. Marginal farmers had sold 42 per cent of their land in the pre-green revolution period but their share declined to 38 per cent during post-green revolution period. The share of small farmers was 27 per cent and 23 per cent respectively in the two periods. There was nominal change in the share of land alienated by semi-medium and medium and large farmers who had alienated 18 and 13 per cent of their land respectively in the pre-green revolution period and which marginally declined to 17.56 per cent and 11.4 per cent respectively during the post-green revolution period.

Both in the pre-green revolution as well as the post-green revolution period land transferred as a percentage of total land holdings had an inverse relationship with the size of landholding. Marginal and small farmers together with those who had sold their entire holding constituted 65 per cent ot the total sellers of land in the pre-green revolution period and 64 per cent of the sellers during the post-green revolution period. Average land sold per seller declined from 2.48 acres in the first period to 1.52 acres during the second period. The soaring price of land in the post-green revolution period as well as rising productivity appear to be the reason behind this decline.

We also tried to analyse the behaviour of the land market in pre-green revolution period (1952-53 to 1967-68) and post-green revolution period (1968-69 to 1982-83) in terms of land transfer among the various categories of sellers and buyers of land and to discern if there has been any change in it.

As has already been mentioned on account of various reasons the magnitude of land transfers in pre-green revolution period was highly underreported. Any comparison in absolute terms therefore will be of little use. But changes in percentage share of different categories in total land transactions might give a more meaningful idea of the working of the land market.

An analysis of Table 6.7 relating to eastern U.P. clearly brings to home that land purchased by highest category (10 acres and above) sharply declined. Whereas this category accounted for almost half (48 per cent) of all the land purchased during the pre-green revolution period in eastern U.P. its share declined to only 16 per cent in the post-green revolution

TABLE 6.7

Land Transfer Matrix in eastern U.P. according to size Category of owned Holdings

Pre-Green Revolution Period

(Size and Area in acres)

SELLERS	BUYERS Less than 2.5	2.5—5	5—10	10 & above	Total
1	2	3	4	5	6
Landless	45.32 (13.30)	25.42 (7.45)	120.50 (35.35)	149.63 (43.90)	340.87 (100.00)
Less than 2.5	4.10 (16.66)	8.36 (33.98)	8.12 (33.01)	4.02 (16.35)	24.60 (100.00)
2.5—5 0	5.05 (25.82)	3.77 (19.28)	10.29 (25.60)	0.45 (2.30)	19.56 (100.00)
5.0—10.0	2.85 (7.55)	7.34 (19.44)	12.91 (34.18)	14.67 (38.84)	37 77 (100.00)
10.0 & above	2.86 (3.28)	2.47 (2.84)	6.87 (7.88)	75.01 (86.00)	87.21 (100 00)
Total	60.18 (11.80)	47.36 (9.28)	158.69 (31.12)	243.78 (47.80)	510.01 (100.00)

(*Table 6.7 Contd.*)

	Post-Green Revolution Period				
Landless	18.78	72.34	103.67	25.17	219.96
	(8.54)	(32.88)	(47.14)	(11.44)	(100.00)
Less than 2.5	41.45	37.50	37.53	20.84	137 32
	(30.18)	(27.31)	(27.33)	(15.18)	(100.00)
2.5—5.0	26.33	55.49	45.48	14.18	141.48
	(18.61)	(39.22)	(32.15)	(10.03)	(100.00)
5.0—10.0	36.74	65.26	47.76	39.45	189 21
	(19.42)	(34.48)	(25.25)	(20.85)	(100.00)
10.0 & above	22.29	40.34	47.55	29.24	139.42
	(15.98)	(28.94)	(34.10)	(20.98)	(100.00)
Total	145.59	270.93	181.99	281.88	827.39
	(17.60)	(32.74)	(34.08)	(15.58)	(100.00)

N.B.—Figures in parentheses are percentages.

period. Clearly the ceiling laws had its effect in so far as they were dissuaded from investing money in purchase of more land. There appears to be little change in the behaviour of land owners in the category of 5—10 acres for in both the periods they accounted for nearly one-third of the total land purchased. But there was marked change as regards the category of 2.5—5 acres. Whereas this category accounted for only less than 10 per cent of the land purchased during the first period, in the latter period its share rose to one-third. There was also an improvement in the share of lowest category of less than 2.5 acres whose share in the total purchased land increased from 12 to 18 per cent. Thus in the post-green revolution period the lower categories have emerged as significant buyers of land.

It is also worth mentioning that in the earlier period those who became landless after disposing off their entire agricultural land accounted for as high as 67 per cent of the total land sold during that period, but the same percentage came down to 26 in the latter period (Table 6.8). The profitability of land has induced people to retain land in the post-green revolution period. The highest category which accounted for 17 per cent of the sales in the former period maintained the same ratio in the post-green revolution period. But there was an increase in the share of middle categories. Category of less than 2.5 acres accounted for only 4.8 per cent of the total land sales during the first period but its share increased to 16 per cent in the latter period. Households in the category of 5—10 acres accounted 7 per cent of the total sold in the first period but their share increased to 23 per cent in the latter period. The two highest categories accounted for one-fourth of the land sold during the first period but their share also increased to nearly 40 per cent in the second period.

Interestingly whereas 75 per cent of the total land purchased by the lowest category of less than 2.5 acres was from those who had become landless in the first period, the share came down to 13 per cent in the second period. The highest category accounted for only 5 per cent of the land purchases by the lowest category in the first period but in the second period the former accounted for 15 per cent of the land

TABLE 6.8

Size Category-wise Land Transfer as Percentages to total in Eastern U.P.

(Pre-Green Revolution Period

(Size and Area in acres)

SELLERS	BUYERS				
	Less than 2.5	2.5—5	5—10	10 & above	Total
1	2	3	4	5	6
Landless	75.31	53.68	75.93	61.38	66.83
Less than 2.5	6.81	17.65	5.12	1.65	4.83
2.5—5.0	8.40	7.95	6.48	0.18	3.84
5.0—10.0	4.73	15.50	8.14	6.02	7.40
10.0 & above	4.75	5.22	4.33	30.77	17.10
Total	100.00	100.00	100.00	100.00	100.00
Post-Green Revolution Period					
Landless	12.90	26.70	36.77	19.53	26.58
Less than 2.3	28.34	13.85	13.31	16 17	16.60
2.5—5.0	18.09	20.48	16.13	11.01	17.10
5.0—10.0	25.25	24.08	16.93	30.61	22.87
10.0 & above	15.32	14.89	16.86	22.68	16.85
Total	100.00	100.00	100.00	100.00	100.00

purchased the lowest category. A more or less similar trend was discernible in case of other categories as well excepting the largest one.

In central U.P. also (Table 6.9) the total land alienated in the post-green revolution period was larger than what it was in the previous period but as already mentioned the reporting in land sales in the pre-green revolution period was highly underreported for various reasons enumerated earlier. In the pre-geen revolution period about 70 per cent of the alienated land was purchased by household in the highest two categories but the percentage declined to 56 per cent in the second period. In fact the highest category of 10 acres and above which accounted for 37 per cent of the total land purchased in the first period declined to 15 per cent in the second period. The share of the lowest three categories increased in the second period. The lowest category of less than 2.5 acres accounted for only 2 per cent of the total land purchased in the first period but its share incrcased to nearly 10 per cent in second period. Likewise the share of the 2.5—5 acre category increased from 28 per cent in the first period to 34 per cent in the second period and that of 5—10 acre category increased from 33 per cent in the first period to 41 per cent in the second period. Thus in the post-green revolution period the relative share of lower categories in the total land purchased increased and the highest category alone witnesed a relative decline.

In the first period nearly one third of the land was sold by such households as became landless *i.e.* they sold their entire land holding but in the second period the percentage of such households declined to 18 (Table 6.10). There was a marginal increase in the percentage share of land sold by other categories in the second period including the highest category. During the first period the landless had sold 50 per cent of their land to the highest category but in the second period the percentage came down to 23. The landless accounted for 31 per cent of the land purchased by the category 5—10 acres in the first period but it declined to 19 per cent in the second period. The category of 2.5—5 acres purchased 48 per cent of its land from categories higher than itself in the first period but the same declined to 27 per cent

TABLE 6.9

Land Transfer Matrix in central U.P. according to Size Category of owned Holdings

Pre-Green Revolution Period

(Size and Area in acres)

	BUYERS				
SELLERS	Less than 2.5	2.5—5	5.0—10.0	10.0 & above	Total
1	2	3	4	5	6
Landless	—	4.13	14.93	26.63	45.69
	(0.00)	(9.04)	(32.68)	(58.28)	(100.00)
Less than 2.5	1.00	8.59	9.26	2.05	21.60
	(4.63)	(39.77)	(46.12)	(9.48)	(100.00)
2.5—5.0	—	8.05	4.42	13.03	25.50
	(0.00)	(31.56)	(17.34)	(51.10)	(100.00)
5.0—10.0	—	16.52	13.34	1.57	31.93
	(0.00)	(51.74)	(43.34)	(4.92)	(100.00)
10.0 & above	2.00	2.80	4.20	9.79	18.79
	(10.65)	(14.90)	(22.35)	(52.10)	(100.00)
Total	3.00	40.09	47.35	53.07	143.51
	(2.08)	(27.94)	(33.00)	(36.98)	(100.00)

	Post-Green Revolution Period				
Landless	12.06 (12.03)	24.89 (24.85)	44.48 (44.40)	18.76 (18.72)	100.19 (100.00)
Less than 2.5	23.69 (21.56)	55.04 (50.08)	20.43 (18.58)	10.75 (9.78)	109.91 (100.00)
2.5—5.0	12.17 (9.50)	58.05 (45.32)	46.92 (36.63)	10.95 (8 55)	128.09 (100.00)
5.0—10.0	4.07 (2.93)	42.00 (30.24)	77.23 (55.58)	15.63 (11 25)	138.93 (100.00)
10.0 & above	0.94 (1.20)	11.17 (14.30)	41.02 (52.50)	25.00 (32.00)	78.13 (100.00)
Total	52.93 (9.54)	191.15 (34.43)	230.08 (41.43)	81.09 (14.60)	555.25 (100.00)

N.B.— Figures in parentheses are percentages.

TABLE 6.10

Size Category-Wise Land Transfers as Percentage to total in Central U.P.

Pre-Green Revolution Period

SELLERS	BUEYRS				
	Less than 2.5	2.5—5 0	5.0—10.0	10.0 & above	Total
1	2	3	4	2	6
Landless		10.30	31.54	50.18	31.83
Less than 2.5	33.33	21.43	21.03	3.86	15.06
2.5—5 0	—	20.08	9.33	24.56	17.76
5.0—10.0	—	41.21	29.23	2.95	22.25
10.0 & above	66.67	6.98	8.87	18.45	13.10
Total	100.00	100.00	100.00	100.00	100.00
Post-Green Revolution Period					
Landless	22.78	13 03	19.33	23.14	18.04
Less than 2.5	44.76	28.80	8.88	13.25	19.80
2.5—5.0	23.00	30.36	20.40	13.51	23.06
5.0—10.0	7.68	21.97	33.56	19.28	25.02
10.0 & above	1.78	5.84	17.83	30.82	14.08
Total	100.00	100.00	100.00	100.00	100.00

in the second period. Similarly the lowest category of less than 2.5 acres had purchased two thirds of the land from the highest category in the first period but the share of the latter was only 2 per cent in the second period.

In western U.P. during the pre-green revolution period the highest category accounted for 55 per cent of the land purchased but in the post-green revolution period its share declined to 44 per cent (Table 6.11). There was a relative increase in the share of the 5-10 acre category whose share increased from 19 per cent in the first period to 20 per cent in the second period. There was a slight decline in the percentage share of the 2.5—5 category while there was a marginal improvement in the share of lowest category which increased from 6 per cent in the first period to 9 per cent in the second period.

During the first period the highest category of 10 acres and above accounted for 52 per cent of all the land sold (Table 6.12) but in the second period it accounted for only 19 per cent. The next lower category had sold no land during the first period but during the second they accounted for 22 per cent of the land sold. There was little change in the position of the 2.5—5 category which accounted for 12 per cent of the land sold in the first period and 14 per cent in the second period. Significantly landless accounted for 28 per cent of the land sold in the first period but their percentage increased to 35 in the second period. It means the tendency to dispose off the entire agricultural land was not weakened in western U.P. unlike eastern or central region during the post-green revolution period. It may be that because of greater diversification of the economy of this region many poorer households sold their entire land to take up new vocations.

In Bundelkhand (Table 6.13) during the pre-green revolution period the highest category accounted for 48 per cent of all the land purchased but unlike eastern, western or central regions its share increased to 64 in the post-green revolution period. There was marginal decline in the relative position of the next lower category of 5—10 acres as its share declined from 22 per cent in the first period to 19 per cent in the second period. There was a significant decline in the position of the 2 5—5 acre category as its share in the total land purchased

TABLE 6.11

Land Transfer Matrix in western U.P.

Pre-Green Revolution Period

(Size and Area in acres)

SELLERS	BUYERS Less than 2.5	2.5—5.0	5.0—10.0	10.0 & above	Total
1	2	3	4	5	6
Landless	— (0.00)	— (0.00)	2.97 (29.24)	7.19 (70.76)	10.16 (100.00)
Less than 2.5	0.60 (22.82)	—	2.03 (77.18)	—	2.63 (100.00)
2.5—5.0	1.40 (31.68)	2.39 (54.07)	0.63 (14.25)	—	4.42 (100.00)
5.0—10.0	--	—	—	—	—
10.0 & above	—	5.00 (26.20)	1.25 (6 72)	12.34 (66.36)	18.59 (100.00)
Total	2.00 (5.58)	7.39 (20.65)	6 88 (19.22)	19.53 (54.55)	35.80 (100.00)

Table 6.11 (*Contd.*)

	Post-Green Revolution Period				
Landless	10.83	37.25	50.07	147.13	245.28
	(4.42)	(15.18)	(20.42)	(59.98)	(100.00)
Less than 2.5	16.02	22.46	19.85	11.76	70.09
	(22.86)	(32.05)	(28.31)	(16.78)	(100.00)
2.5—5.0	13.96	46.33	23.36	15.85	99.50
	(14.03)	(45.56)	(23.48)	(15.93)	(100.00)
5.0—10.0	6.09	22.84	73.54	50.59	153.06
	(3.98)	(14.92)	(48.04)	(33.06)	(100.00)
10.0 & above	12.71	6.93	28.91	82.75	131.30
	(9.68)	(5.28)	(22.02)	(63.02)	(100.00)
Total	59.61	135.81	195.73	308.08	699.23
	(8.52)	(19.42)	(28.00)	(44.06)	(100.00)

N.B.— Figures in parentheses are percentages

TABLE 6.12

Size-wise land Transfer as Percentage to total in western U.P.

Pre-Green Revolution Period

SELLERS	BUYERS				
	Less than 2.5	2.5—5.0	5.0—10.0	10.0 & above	Total
1	2	3	4	5	6
Landless	—	—	43.17	36.82	28.38
Less than 2.5	30.00	—	29.50	—	7.35
2.5—5.0	70.00	32.34	9.16	—	12.35
5.0—10.0	—	—	—	—	—
10.0 & above	—	67.66	18.17	63.18	51.92
Total	100.00	100.00	100.00	100.00	100.00
Post-Green Revolution Period					
Landless	18.16	27.42	25.59	47.75	35.08
Less than 2.5	26.88	16.54	10.14	43.82	10.03
2.5—5.0	23.42	34.12	11.93	5.15	14.23
5.0—10.0	10.22	16.82	37.58	16.43	21.88
10.0 & above	21.32	5.10	14.76	26.85	18.78
Total	100.00	100.00	100.00	100.00	100.00

TABLE 6.13

Land Transfer Matrix in Bundelkhand According to Size Category of Owned Holding

Pre-Green Revolution Period

(Size and Area in acres)

SELLERS	BUYERS				
	Less than 2.5	2.5—5.0	5.0—10.0	10.0 & above	Total
1	2	3	4	5	6
Landless	—	3.60	2.00	1.25	6.85
	—	(52.56)	(29.20)	(18.24)	100.00
Less than 2.5	—	—	2.00	4.82	6.82
			(29.33)	(70.67)	(110.00)
2.5—5.0	—	0.80	—	0.60	1.40
		(57.15)		(42.85)	(100.00)
5.0—10.0	—	—	—	2.00	2.00
				(100.00)	(100.00
10.0 & above	—	1.00	—	—	1.00
		(100.00)			(100.00)
Total	—	5.40 (29.88)	4.00 (22.14)	8.67 (47.98)	18.07 (100.00)

Table 6.3 (*Contd.*)

Post-Green Revolution Period

Landless	0.98	1.52	7.75	2.72	12.97
	(7.55)	(11.72)	(59.75)	(20.98)	(100.00)
Less than 2.5	—	4.13	1.20	4.84	10.17
		(40.61)	(11.80)	(47.59)	(100.00)
2.5—5.00	1.95	2.80	9.90	17.69	32.34
	(6.02)	(8.66)	(30.62)	(54.70)	(100.00)
5.0—10.0	1.20	3.10	0.90	25.13	30.33
	(3.96)	(18.22)	(2.96)	(82.86)	(100.00)
10.0 & above	0.90	2 30	2.50	22.81	28.51
	(3.16)	(8.07)	(8.77)	(80.00)	(100.00)
Total	5.03	13.85	22.25	73.19	114.32
	(4.40)	(12.11)	(19.47)	(64.02)	(100.00)

N.B. —Figures in parentheses are percentages.

declined from 30 per cent in the first period to only 12 per cent in the second period and interestingly whereas the lowest category of less than 2.5 acres did not undertake any purchase of land in the first period it accounted for 4 per cent of the land purchased in the second period.

During the pre-green revolution period landless accounted for 38 per cent for the land sold while the same declined to 11 per cent in the post-green revolution period (Table 6.14). The less than 2.5 category accounted for 38 per cent of the land sold in the first period but its share also declined significantly to 9 per cent in the second period. The 2.5—5 category accounted for only 8 per cent of the land sold in the first period but its share rose to 28 per cent in the second period. The relative share of 5—10 acre category also increased from 11 per cent in the first period to 27 per cent in the second period. Surprisingly the highest category which accounted for only 5 per cent of the total land sold during the first period accounted for 25 per cent of the land sold during the second period but the fact remains that the highest category was the main purchaser of land and their purchased land was nearly three times the land sold by them.

In the Hill region the only category to purchase land was the 2.5—5 acre category in the pre-green revolution period but in the post green-revolution period purchases were more diffused. While the highest share (44 per cent) was purchased by the 5—10 acre category, the next lower category of 2.5-5 acres accounted for 37 per cent of the purchased land. Significantly the lowest category of less than 2.5 acres also accounted for 18 per cent of the purchased land in the latter period. It only testifies to an improvement in the conditions of the lower categories which has enabled them to emerge as buyers of land.

Taking the State as a whole (Table 6.15) it is worth noticing that whereas in the pre-green revolution period the largest category of 10 acres and above accounted for 46 per cent of all the land that was purchased its share fell to 27 per cent during the post-green revolution period. All the other categories gained in relative terms. Share of lowest category improved from 9 per cent to 12 per cent that of 2.5—5 category

TABL 6.14

Size-Wise Land Transfers in Bundelkhund Region as Percentage to total

Pre-Green Revolution Period

SELLERS	BUYERS				
	Less than 2.5	2.5—5.0	5.0—10.0	10.0 & above	Total
1	2	3	4	5	6
Landless	—	66.67	50.00	14.42	37.90
Less than 2.5	—	—	50.00	55.60	37.75
2.5 5.0	—	14.82	—	6.92	7.75
5.0—10.0	—	—	—	23.06	11.06
10.0 & above	—	18.51	—	—	5.54
Total	—	100.00	100.00	100.00	100.00
Post-Green Revolution Period					
Landless	19.48	10.98	34.84	3.72	11.35
Less than 2.5	—	29.82	5.40	6.62	8.90
2.5—5.0	38.76	20.22	44.50	24.17	28.28
5.0—10.0	23.86	22.38	4.04	34.33	26.53
10.0 & above	17.90	16.60	11.23	31.16	24.94
Total	100.00	100.00	100.00	100.00	100.00

N.B. — Figures in parentheses are percentages.

TABLE 6.15

Land Transfers Matrix in U.P. according to Size Category of Owned Holdings

Pre-Green Revolution Period

(Size and Area in acres)

SELLERS	BUYERS				
	Less than 2.5	2.5—5.0	5.0—10.0	10.0 & above	Total
1	2	3	4	5	6
Landless	45.32 (11.23)	33.15 (8.22)	140.40 (34.78)	184.70 (45.77)	403.57 (100.00)
Less than 2.5	5.70 (10.25)	16.95 (30.46)	22.11 (39.73)	10.89 (19.56)	55.65 (100.00)
2.5—5.0	6.45 (12.68)	15.01 (29.50)	15.34 (30.15)	14.08 (27.67)	50.88 (100.00)
5.0—10.0	2.85 (3.91)	25.21 (34.51)	26.75 (36.62)	18.24 (24.96)	73.05 (100.00)
10.0 & above	4.86 (3.87)	11.27 (8.98)	12.32 (9.80)	97.14 (77.35)	125.59 (100.00)
Total	65.18 (9.20)	101.59 (14.33)	216.92 (30.61)	325.05 (45.86)	708.74 (100.00)

Table 6.15 (*Contd.*)

	Post-Green Revolution Period				
Landless	42.62	136.00	205.97	193.78	578.40
	(7.38)	(23.52)	(35.60)	(33.50)	(100.00)
Less than 2.5	81.16	119.13	81.41	48.19	329.89
	(24.61)	(36.12)	(24.68)	(14.61)	(100.00)
2.5—5.0	55.41	162.67	125.66	58.67	402.41
	(13.76)	(40.43)	(31.23)	(14.58)	(100.00)
5.0—10.0	48.10	135.20	199.43	130.80	513.53
	(9.37)	(26.33)	(38.84)	(25.46)	(100.00)
10.0 & above	36.84	60.74	119.98	159.80	377.36
	(9.76)	(16.10)	(31.80)	(42.34)	(100.00)
Total	264.16	613.74	732.45	591.24	2201.59
	(12.00)	(27.88)	(33.26)	(26.86)	(100.00)

N.B.—Figures in parentheses are percentages.

from 14 to 28 per cent and that of 5–10 category from 31 per cent to 33 per cent. Thus the share of small and semi-medium farmers which accounted for 45 per cent of the total land purchased in the first period improved to 61 per cent in the second period. The most spectacular rise was in the case of 2.5—5 category which witnessed a two-fold rise in the percentage share. The larger categories may have relatively gained more through the new agricultural technology but the small and semi-medium farmers appear to be more keen to utilize their surplus in augmenting their land base.

During the first period the bigger categories, by and large, preferred their own category in land transactions but in the second period their transactions were more diffused towards lower categories although the preference for their own category continued.

The landless had preferred the larger categories in disposing off their land in both the periods. Category 2.5—5 acres had sold 58 per cent of its land to categories higher than itself during the first period but during the second period the share had declined to 46 per cent. The 5–10 acre category had sold 37% of the land to the same category and 25 per cent to the highest category during the first period and during the second period also there was little variation. The highest category had sold 77 per cent its land to the same category in the first period but it came down to 42 per cent during the second period.

It will be seen from Table 6.16 that during the first period landless accounted for 57 per cent of the total land that was sold but significantly such category accounted for only 26 per cent of the land sold during the second period. Thus the tendency to dispose off land altogether seems to have been weakened in the post-green revolution period due to rise in productivity and the fact that the new technology was size neutral. But all the same it is a matter of concern that despite the rapid gains in agricultural productivity the tendency persists in a significant manner as more than one-fourth of the alienated land in the second period belonged to persons who became landless. This only indicates that a process of proletarianisation is also simultaneously at work in the rural areas.

TABLE 6.16

Size-Wise Land Transfers in U.P. as Percentage to Total

Pre-Green Revolution Period

SELLERS	BUYERS				
	Less than 2.5	2.0—5.0	5.0—10.0	10.0 & above	Total
Landless	69.53	32.63	64.72	56.82	56.95
Less than 2.5	8.74	16.68	10.20	3.35	7.86
2.5—5.0	9.90	14.77	7.08	4.33	7.17
5.0—10.0	4.38	24.82	12.33	5.62	10.30
10.0 & above	7.46	11.10	5.67	29.88	17.72
Total	100.00	100.00	100.00	100.00	100.00
		Post-Green Revolution			
Landless	16.15	22.16	28.11	32.78	26.28
Less than 2.5	30.73	19.40	11.12	8.15	14.98
2.5—5.0	20.98	26.51	17.16	9.93	18.28
5.0—10.0	18.20	22.03	27.23	22.11	23.32
10.0 & above	13.94	9.90	16.38	27.03	17.14
Total	100.00	100.00	100.00	100.00	100.00

In both the periods the highest category accounted for 17 per cent of the land that was sold but whereas during the first period the lowest category had purchased 7 per cent of its land from the highest category, the share rose to 14 per cent during the second period. Likewise the 2.5—5 acre category had purchased nearly half of its land from categories that stood lower to it during the first period but their share marginally declined to 41 per cent during the second period. Similar was the case with 5—10 acre category which had purchased 82 per cent of its land from categories which stood lower to it in the first period but the same declined to 56 per cent during the second period. The highest category had purchased 57 per cent of the land from landless in the first period but the same declined to 33 per cent in the second period.

7

Income-Wise Land Transfers

Table 7.1 shows income-wise land transfer matrix in eastern U.P. during the reference period. It would be seen that households with gross income of less than Rs 5,000 accounted for 42 per cent of all the land sold. It was followed by households in the income size of Rs. 10,000 to Rs. 25,000 which accounted for 28 per cent of total land sold. Households in the income size of Rs 5,000 to 10,000 accounted for 18 per cent of total land sold and those in the income range of Rs 25,000 to 50,000 accounted for 10 per cent of land sold. The top income group of Rs 50,000 and above accounted for only 1 per cent of the land sold. It will thus be seen that the sellers generally belonged to the poorer strata of rural households.

As regards purchases of land the lowest income group accounted for 10 per cent of the land purchased while income group of Rs. 5,000 to 10,000 accounted for 34 per cent and income group of Rs 10,000 to 25,000 accounted for another 45 per cent of the land purchased. It will thus be seen that poorest peasants were net sellers of land and middle income groups were the main buyers of land. The net effect of transfer of land as between different categories is summarised in Table 7.2.

TABLE 7.1

Income-Wise Land Transfer Matrix in eastern U.P.

(Area in acres)

SELLERS	BUYERS Less than Rs 5,000	Rs 5,000 to to Rs 10,000	Rs 10,000 to Rs 25,000	Rs 25,000 to Rs 50,000	Rs 50,000 & above	Total	Land sold as % of total land sold
1	2	3	4	5	6	7	8
Less than 5000	80.78 (14.31)	246.09 (42.58)	213.78 (37.86)	23.02 (4.01)	0.97 (0.17)	564.64 (100.00)	42.21
Rs 5,000 to Rs 10,000	28.59 (11.96)	69.49 (29.07)	96.57 (40.40)	30.74 (12.86)	13.63 (5.70)	239.02 (100.00)	17.87
Rs 10,000 to Rs 25,000	16.16 (4.26)	104.59 (27.54)	191.65 (50.47)	52.56 (13.84)	14.76 (3.89)	379.72 (107.00)	28.40
Rs 25,000 to Rs 50,000	4.79 (3.48)	40.01 (29.04)	84.64 (61.44)	4.95 (3.59)	3.36 (2.44)	137.75 (100.00)	10.30
Rs 50,000 & above	2.70 (16.59)	1.25 (7.68)	11.80 (72.56)	—	0.52 (3.17)	16.27 (100.00)	1.22
Total	133.02 (9.95)	461.43 (34.50)	598.44 (44.75)	111.27 (8.32)	33.24 (2.48)	1337.40 (100.00)	100.00

N.B.—Figures in parentheses are percentages.

TABLE 7.2

Income-Wise net Effect of Land Transfers in eastern U.P.

(Area in acres)

Income group (Rs)	Land Sold	Land Purchased	Net gain or loss	At Percentage
1	2	3	4	5
Less than Rs 5,000	564.64	133.02	(—) 431.62	(—) 94.22
Rs 5,000—10,000	239.02	461.33	(+) 222.41	(+) 48.55
Rs 10,000—25,000	379.72	598.44	(+) 218.72	(+) 47.75
Rs 25,000—50,000	137.75	111.27	(—) 26.48	(—) 5.78
Rs 50,000 & above	16.27	33.24	(+) 16.97	(+) 3.70
Total	1337.40	1337.30	—	—

It would be seen that the lowest income category having income of less than Rs 5,000 was the biggest loser of land accounting to 94 per cent of the net loss. The group which increased its area through purchase was the one in the income size of Rs 5,000—25,000 which accounted for 96 per cent of the net gain.

Table 7.3 shows income-wise land transfer matrix in central U.P. It shows that households with less than an annual gross income of Rs 5,000 accounted for 23 per cent of all the land sold but this category purchased 9 per cent of all the alienated land. The income category of Rs 5,000—10,000 accounted for 29 per cent of all sold land and 35 per cent of all land purchased. The next higher categories of Rs 10,000—25,000 accounted for 42 per cent of all the land sold and 45 per cent of all land purchased. Thus this group can be said to be most active in the land market. The share of the next higher category of Rs 25,000—50,000 was only 5 per cent in total sales and 8 per cent in total land purchased. The corresponding share of the highest category was nil in sales and only 2 per cent in purchases. The net effect of land transaction on each category is summarised in Table 7.4. It will be seen that the lowest income category accounted for the entire loss. Significantly the Rs 5000—10,000 category accounted for one-third of the net gain.

In western U.P. the lowest income category of less than Rs 5,000 accounted for 20 per cent of the entire land sold in that region while this category purchased 8 per cent of the land (Table 7.5). Thus this category was a net loser of land. The next higher category of Rs 5,000—10,000 accounted for 30 per cent of the land sold but it purchased 16 per cent of the total land. Thus this category was also a net loser. Households in the income category of Rs 10,000—25,000 accounted for 31 per cent of all the sold land whereas their share in total purchased land was slightly higher at 33 per cent. The main gainers were the households in the income category of Rs 25,000—50,000 which accounted for 12 per cent of the land sold but significantly their share in the purchased land was nearly 30 per cent. Likewise the highest income group of

TABLE 7.3

Income-Wise Land Transfer Matrix in Central U.P.

(Area in acres)

SELLERS	BUYERS: Less than Rs 5,000	Rs 5,000 to Rs 10,000	Rs 10,000 to Rs 25,000	Rs 25,000 to Rs 50,000	Rs 50, 000 & above	Total	Land sold as % to total land sold
Less than Rs 5,000	35.27 (21.76)	63.93 (39.45)	46.09 (28.44)	16.76 (10.35)	—	162.05 (100.00)	23.30
Rs 5,000 to Rs 10,000	20.34 (9.91)	84.65 (41.24)	89.64 (43.67)	9.71 (4.73)	0.94 (0.45)	205.28 (100.00)	29.37
Rs 10,000 to Rs 25,000	6.65 (2.28)	78.92 (26.81)	168.42 (57.21)	24.42 (8.28)	16.00 (5.42)	294.41 (100.00)	42.13
Rs 25,000 to Rs 50,000	1.30 (3.51)	16.42 (44.35)	10.86 (29.34)	8.44 (22.80)	—	37.02 (100.00)	5.30
Rs 50,000 & above	—	—	—	—	—	—	—
Total	63.56 (9.10)	243.92 (34.90)	315.01 (45.09)	59.33 (8.48)	16.94 (2.43)	698.76 (100.00)	100.00

N.B.—Figures in parentheses are percentages.

TABLE 7.4

Income-Wise net Effect of land Transfers in Central U.P.

(Area in acres)

Income Category (Rs)	Land Sold	Land Purchased	Net gain (+) or loss (—)	As percentages
Less than 5,000	162.05	63.56	(—) 98.49	(—) 100.00
Rs 5,000 to 10,000	205.28	243.92	(+) 38.64	(+) 38.23
Rs 10,000 to 25,000	294.41	315.01	(+) 20.60	(+) 20.92
Rs 25,000 to 50,000	37.02	59.33	(+) 22.31	(+) 22.65
Rs 50,000 & above	—	16.94	(+) 16.94	(+) 17.20
Total	698.76	698.76	—	—

Rs 50,000 and above accounted for 7 and 13 per cent respectively of all the land sold and purchased.

Thus it can be seen that in western U.P. households upto income level of Rs 10,000 were net losers of land while there was a marginal positive gain in the income category of Rs 10,000—25,000. The main gainers were in the income categories of Rs 25,000 and above. Unlike eastern or central U.P. where middle income categories were the main gainers, comparatively larger income groups in western U.P. were significant gainers.

In Bundelkhand (Table 7.6) the lowest income category accounted for 28 per cent of all the land sold while their share in land purchased was only less than 3 per cent. Similarly the next income category of Rs 5000—10,000 accounted for 40 per cent of the land sold but its share in land purchased was 26 per cent. These two categories were the net losers of land. Households in the income size of Rs 10,000—25,000 accounted for 31 per cent of all land sold but their share in land purchased was much higher at 68 per cent. The other category to gain was the households in the income range of Rs 25,000—50,000 which accounted for 3 per cent of the land purchased but did not sell any land. It can be thus seen that in this region households with an income of less than Rs 10,000 were net losers of land and households in the income category of Rs 10,000—50,000 were the net gainers.

The lowest income category sold nearly 10 per cent of the land to the same category. Significantly the relatively larger category of Rs 25,000—50,000 accounted for only 5 per cent of their sold land and the remaining 85 per cent of their land was sold to the income category of Rs 5,000—25,000 Households in the income category of Rs. 5,000—10,000 sold 29 per cent of their land to the same income category while the remaining 71 per cent of the land was purchased by the next higher income category of Rs. 10,000—25,000. Households in the income category of Rs 10,000—25,000 sold nearly three-fourths of their land to the same income category.

In the Hill region the lowest income category accounted for half of the total land sold. Significantly this category accounted for 64 per cent of all the land purchased. Thus a different trend is witnessed in Hill region where contrary to the rest of the state

TABLE 7.5

Income-Wise land Transfer Matrix in Western U.P.

(Area in acres)

SELLERS	BUYERS: Less than Rs 5,000	Rs 5,000 to 10,000	Rs 10,000 to 25,000	Rs 25,000 to 50,000	Rs 50,000 & above	Total	Land sold as % of total land sold
Less than	25.43	37.84	43.20	36.49	3.75	146.71	19.95
Rs 5,000	(17.33)	(25.79)	(29.45)	(24.87)	(2.56)	(100.00)	
Rs 5,000 to	19.73	44.05	79.02	46.09	33.91	222.80	30.32
Rs 10,000	(8.86)	(19.77)	(35.47)	(20.69)	(15.22)	(100.00)	
Rs 10,000 to	7.75	25.72	102.67	76.16	12.85	225.15	30.63
Rs 25,000	(3.44)	(11.42)	(45.60)	(33.83)	(5.71)	(100.00)	
Rs 25,000 to	7.62	6.31	10.49	51.16	11.72	87.30	11.88
Rs 50,000	(8.73)	(7.23)	(12.02)	(58.60)	(13.42)	(100.00)	
Rs 50,000 &	1.34	5.06	9.25	7.43	29.99	53.07	7.22
above	(2.52)	(9.53)	(17.43)	(14.00)	(56.52)	(100.00)	
Total	61.87	118.98	244.63	217.33	92.22	735.03	100.00
	(8.42)	(16.18)	(33.28)	(29.57)	(12.55)	(100.00)	

N.B.—Figures in parentheses are percentages,

TABLE 7.6

Income-Wise Land Transfer Matrix in Bundelkhand

(Area in acres)

SELLERS	BUYERS					Total	Land sold as % of total land sold
	Less than Rs 5,000	Rs 5,000 to 10,000	Rs 10,000 25,000	Rs 25,000 to 50,000	Rs 50,000 & above		
Less than Rs, 5,000	3.60 (9.58)	10.11 (26.92)	21.75 (57.91)	2.10 (5.59)	— —	37.56 (100.00)	28.37
Rs 5,000 to Rs 10,000	— —	15.59 (29.11)	37.96 (70.89)	—	—	53.55 (100.00)	40.45
Rs 10,000 to Rs 25,000	—	8.60 (20.83)	30.18 (73.11)	2.50 (6.06)	...	41.28 (100.00)	31.18
Rs 25,000 to Rs 50,000	—	—	—	—	—	—	—
Rs 50,000 & above	—	—	—	—	—	—	—
Total	3.60 (2.72)	34.30 (25.90)	89.89 (67.90)	4.60 (3.48)	—	132.39 (100.00)	100.00

N.B.—Figures in parentheses are percentages.

the lowest income group was the net gainer of land. The next income group of Rs 5,000—10,000 accounted for 30 per cent of land sold but did not purchase any land. Thus it was net loser of land. The next higher income group accounted for the remaining 20 per cent of the sold land and 36 per cent of the land purchased. It was also a net gainer. While the lowest category had sold 70 per cent of its land to Rs. 10,000 to 25,000 category the remaining categories had sold their land to the lowest category.

Taking the state as a whole it will be seen that households with an income of less than Rs. 5,000 accounted for 31 per cent of all the sold land and 9 per cent of all land purchased (Table 7.7). Such households sold nearly one-sixth of their land to the same income category and roughly 40 per cent to the income category of Rs. 5,000 — 10,000 and another 35 per cent to the income category of Rs. 10,000 to 25,000. Thus three-fourths of their land was sold to income category of Rs. 5,000 to 25,000. Purchasers with an income of Rs. 25,000 and above accounted for only 9 per cent of their land.

The next income category of Rs. 5,000 to 10,000 accounted for 25 per cent of all land sold and 29 per cent of all land that was purchased. Roughly 10 per cent of their land was sold to the lowest category while roughly 30 per cent was sold to the same income category. About 42 per cent of the land was sold to the households in the income category of Rs 10,000 to 25,000 while 19 per cent was sold to the remaining higher categories. This category had purchased 42 per cent of the land from the lowest category, 25 per cent from the same category and rest from higher categories.

The income category of Rs. 10,000 to 25,000 accounted for nearly one-third of all land sold while this category accounted for 43 per cent of all land purchased. More than half of the land (52 per cent) was sold to the same income category. Significantly more than one-fourth of the land was sold to those who stood in lower income categories and 21 per cent of the land was sold to those who stood higher as compared to them in terms of income. Of the total land purchased by this category 25 per cent was purchased from the lowest category,

TABLE 7.7

Income-Wise Land Transfer Matrix in U.P.

(Area in acres)

SELLERS	BUYERS: Less than Rs, 5,000	Rs, 5,000 to 10,000	Rs, 10,000 to 25,000	Rs, 25,000 to 50.000	Rs, 50,000 & above	Total	Land sold as% of total land sold
Less than Rs, 5,000	146.08 (15.98)	357.97 (39.16)	327.22 (35.79)	78.37 (8.58)	4.72 (0.49)	914.36 (100.00)	31.41
Rs, 5,000 to Rs 10,000	70.66 (9.78)	213.78 (29.58)	303.19 (41.96)	86.54 (11.97)	48.48 (6.71)	722.65 (100.00)	24.83
Rs, 10,000 to Rs 25,000	31.91 (3.39)	271.83 (23.13)	492.92 (52.33)	155.64 (16.25)	43.61 (4.63)	941.91 (100.00)	32.36
Rs, 25,000 to Rs 50,000	13.71 (5.23)	62.74 (23.94)	105.99 (40.45)	64.55 (24.63)	15.08 (5.75)	262.07 (100.00)	9.01
Rs, 50,000 & above	4.04 (5.83)	6.31 (9.10)	21.05 (30.35)	7.43 (10.72)	30.51 (44.00)	69.34 (100.00)	5.39
Total	266.40 (9.15)	858.63 (29.50)	1250.37 (42.99)	392.53 (13.48)	142.40 (4.88)	2910.33 (100.00)	100.00

N.B.—Figures in parentheses are percentages.

24 per cent from Rs. 5,000 to 10,000 category and 39 per cent from that very category.

The income category of Rs. 25,0000—50,000 accounted for 9 per cent of land sold but this category purchased 13 per cent of the land thereby showing a positive balance. This category sold 5 per cent of the land to the lowest category, 24 per cent to the category of Rs. 5,000—10,000 and as high as 40 per cent to the category of Rs.10,000—25,000. Thus roughly 70 per cent of the land was sold to them who stood lower in terms of income while another one-fourth of the land was sold to the same income category and 6 per cent of the land was sold to those who stood in a higher category. Of the total land purchased by this income category 16 per cent was purchased from that very income category, 82 per cent from categories which stood lower to it and only 2 per cent from category that stood higher to it.

The highest category of Rs. 50,000 and above accounted for only 2 per cent of the sold land but it accounted for 5 per cent of the land that was purchased. Fourty four per cent of the land was sold to the same income category and nearly 15 per cent of their land was sold to the bottom two categories. Of the total land purchased by this category 21 per cent was purchased from that very income category and the rest obviously from categories which stood lower to it. The net effect of land transaction is summarised in Table 7.8.

It would be seen that the lowest income category alone has been net loser of land while all the other categories have gained at their cost. The largest gainers in terms of area have been the income category of Rs. 10,000—25,000 followed by income category of Rs. 5,000—10,000. The highest income group's gain in percentage terms has also been highest. The fact that the lowest income group is the net loser of land corroborates the hypothesis that the land market is working to the detriment of the poor.

TAALE 7.8

Income-Wise Net Effect of Land Transfers in U.P.

(Area in acres)

Income Category	Land sold	Land Purchased	Land purchased as % of land Sold	Net gain (+) or loss (—)	As Precentages
Less than Rs 5,000	914.36	266.40	29.13	(—) 647.96	(–) 1.00
Rs, 5,000- 10,000	722.65	858.63	118.54	(+) 135.98	(+) 20.89
Rs, 10,000—25,000	941.91	1250.37	132.74	(+) 308.46	(+) 47.60
Rs, 25,000—50,000	262.07	392.53	149.78	(+) 130.46	(+) 20.13
Rs, 50,000 & above	69.34	142.40	205.36	(+) 73.06	(—) 11.28
Total	2910.33	2910.33	100.00	—	—

8

Assets-Wise Land Transfers

Asset-wise land transfer in eastern Uttar Pradesh can be seen from Table 8.1. Nearly 40 per cent of the total alienated land was sold by asset category of less than Rs. 10,000 and the same group purchased less than 3 per cent of the land. The asset category of Rs. 10,000-25,000 sold nearly 6 per cent of the alienated land and the same group purchased nearly 10 per cent of such land. Nearly 30 per cent of the alienated land was accounted for by assets category of Rs. 25,000 to 1,00,000 and the same group purchased nearly 63 per cent of the transferred land. The highest asset category sold as well as purchased nearly one-fourth of the total land. It would further be seen that except the highest category all the other categories purchased maximum land from the lowest category and even in the case of largest category one-fifth of the land came for the lowest category. The net position of different asset groups in terms of land transferred is summarised in Table 8.2. It would be seen that the only asset group to lose was the lowest asset group which was a net seller of the land and all the other groups gained at its cost. This indicates a process of immiserisation of the poorest peasantry.

In western U.P. (Table 8.3) asset category of less than

TABLE 8.1

Assets-Wise Land Transfer Matix in Eastern U.P.

(Assets in Rs and Area in Acres)

SELLERS	BUYERS Less than Rs. 10,000	Rs. 10,000 to 25,000	Rs. 25,000 to 50,000	Rs. 50,000 to 1,00,000	Rs. 1,00,000 & above	Total	As percentage to total land sold
1	2	3	4	5	6	7	8
Less than Rs. 10,000	15.85 (2.96)	86.35 (16.17)	214.15 (40.11)	150.02 (28.10)	67.60 (12.66)	533.97 (100.00)	39.93
Rs. 10,000—25,000	1.00 (1.20)	9.90 (11.85)	18.41 (22.03)	20.83 (24.93)	33.41 (39.99)	83.55 (100.00)	6.24
Rs. 25,000—50,000	2,00 (1.09)	7.40 (4.05)	33.87 (18.53)	95.87 (52.45)	43.66 (23.88)	182.80 (100.00)	13.67
Rs. 50,000—1,00,000	11.78 (5.48)	9.43 (4.39)	53.29 (24.78)	72.99 (33.96)	67.47 (31.39)	214.96 (100.00)	16.08
Rs. 1,00,000 & above	1.88 (0.58)	14.75 (4.58)	58.83 (18.26)	119.38 (37.06)	127.28 (39.52)	322.12 (100.00)	24.08
Total	32.51 (2.43)	127.83 (9.56)	378.55 (28.30)	459.09 (34 33)	339.42 (25.38)	1337.40 (100.00)	100.00

N.B.—Figures in parentheses are percentages.

TABLE 8.2

Asset-Wise Net Effect of Land Transfer in eastern U.P.

(Area in acres)

Assets group (Rs)	Land Sold	Land Purchased	Net gain (+) or loss (—)	As Percentages
1	2	3	4	5
Less than Rs. 10,000	533.97	32.51	(—) 501.46	(—) 100.00
Rs. 10,000—25,000	83.55	127.83	(+) 44.28	(+) 8.83
Rs. 25,000—50,000	182.80	378.55	(+) 195.75	(+) 39.04
Rs. 50,000—1,00,000	214 96	459.09	(+) 244.13	(+) 48.68
Rs. 1,00,000 & above	322.12	339.42	(+) 17.30	(+) 3.35
Total	1337.40	1337.40	—	—

TACLE 8.3

Assets-Wise Land Transfer Matrix in western U.P.

(Assets in Rs. & Area in acres)

SELLERS	BUYERS						
	Less than 10,000	Rs. 10,000 to 25,000	Rs. 25,000 to 50,000	Rs. 50,000 to 1,00,000	Rs. 1 00,000 & above	Total	As percentage to total land sold
1	2	3	4	5	6	7	8
Less than Rs. 10,000	4.38 (1.76)	5.05 (2.03)	4.79 (1.92)	26.48 (10.62)	208.61 (83.67)	249.31 (100.00)	33.92
Rs. 10,000—25,000	—	0.06 (0.28)	6.87 (32.48)	1.88 (8.89)	12.34 (58.35)	21.15 (100.00)	2.88
Rs. 25,000 50,000	0.63 (0.96)	2.67 (4.05)	4.83 (7.33)	8.28 (12.56)	49.49 (75.10)	65.90 (100.00)	8.97
Rs. 50,000—1,00,000	—	2.78 (2.82)	14.14 (14.37)	12.64 (12.84)	63.86 (69.97)	98.42 (100.00)	13.38
Rs. 1,00,000 & above	0.01 (0.00)	2.42 (0.81)	8.49 (2.83)	33.96 (11.31)	255.37 (85.05)	300.25 (100.00)	40.84
Total	5.02 (0.68)	12.98 (1.76)	39.12 (5.33)	83.24 (11.33)	594.67 (80.90)	735.03 (100.00)	100.00

N.B.—Figures in parentheses are percentages.

Rs. 10,000 accounted for 34 per cent of the total land sold while this category accounted for only 0.7 per cent of the land purchased. The next category of Rs. 10,000—25,000 accounted for 3 per cent of the total land sold and about 2 per cent of the land purchased. The asset category of Rs. 25,000—1,00,000 accounted for 22 per cent of the land sold and 17 per cent of the land that was purchased while the highest category of Rs. 1,00,000 and above accounted for 41 per cent of the land sold and 81 per cent of the land purchased. Thus this asset group was the sole gainer.

What is significant about all the asset categories is the fact that these categories sold a large part of their land to highest asset category. For example, the lowest category of less than Rs. 10,000 sold 84 per cent of its alienated land to the highest category of 1,00,000 and above. The proportion was 58 per and 75 per cent respectively in the next two intermediate categories while it was 70 per cent in the asset category of Rs. 50,000—1,00,000 and was as high as 85 per cent in the highest category of 1 lakh and above. The net position of different asset groups is summarised in Table 8.4.

It will be seen that while the highest category cornered the entire gain the poorest category accounted for bulk of the loss (83 per cent). It shows that land is being cornered in a big way only by the highest assets category in western U.P. which is agriculturally prosperous and where green revolution has succeed in a big way. Green revolution has, no doubt, resulted in higher production but at the same time it has widened the disparities.

In central U.P. (Table 8.5) the lowest asset category accounted for 15 per cent of the alienated land while it accounted for only 1 per cent of the land purchased. Similarly the next higher category accounted for 10 per cent of the land sales and 5 per cent of the land purchased. The asset category of Rs. 25,000—50,000 accounted for one-fourth of all land sales and one-fifth of all land purchased while the next higher category of Rs. 50,000—1,00,000 accounted for one-third of the land sales and nearly 40 per cent of the land purchased. The highest category accounted for one-sixth of the land sales and nearly one-third of land purchased. Thus more than

TABLE 8.4

Asset-Wise Net Effect of Land Transfers in western U.P.

(Area in acres)

Asset Category	Ladd Sold	Land Purchased	Net gain (+) or loss (—)	As %
1	2	3	4	5
Less than Rs. 10,000	249.31	5.02	(—) 244.29	(—) 82.97
Rs. 10.000—25,000	21.15	12.98	(—) 8.17	(—) 2.77
Rs. 25,000—50,000	65.90	39.12	(—) 26.78	(—) 9.10
Rs. 50,000—1,00,000	98.42	83.24	(—) 15.18	(—) 5.16
Rs. 1,00,000 & above	300.25	594.67	(+) 294.42	(+) 100.00
Total	735.03	735.03	—	—

TABLE 8.5

Asset-Wise Land Transfer Matrix in central U.P.

(Asset in Rs. Area in acres)

SELLERS	BUYERS						
	Less than 10,000	Rs. 10,000—25,000	Rs. 25,000—50,000	Rs. 50,000—1,00,000	Rs. 1,00,000 & above	Total	As percentage to total land sold
1	2	3	4	5	6	7	8
Less than Rs. 10,000	—	5.54	23.61	30.32	42.43	101.90	14.59
		(5.44)	(23.17)	(29.75)	(41.64)	(100.00)	
Rs. 10,000—25,000	0.63	9.31	14.88	25.46	19.30	69.58	9.96
	(0.90)	(13.38)	(21.39)	(36.59)	(27.74)	(100.00)	
Rs. 25,000—50,000	1.72	14.28	64.90	68.25	25.53	174.68	24.99
	(0.98)	(8.17)	(37.16)	(39.07)	(14.62)	(100.00)	
Rs. 50,000—1,00,000	3.64	5.80	36.72	115.25	72.64	234.35	33.49
	(1.56)	(2.48)	(15.68)	(49.24)	(31.04)	(100.00)	
Rs. 1,00,000 & above	3.28	2.51	10.42	36.71	65.63	118.55	16.97
	(2.77)	(2.12)	(8.78)	(30.97)	(55.36)	(100.00)	
Total	9.27	37.44	150.53	275.99	225.53	698.76	100.00
	(1.33)	(5.36)	(21.54)	(39.49)	(32.28)	(100.00)	

N.B.—Figures in parentheses are percentages.

70 per cent of the land was purchased by asset group of Rs. 50,000 and above. Significantly they accounted for more than half of all land sold also.

As regard land purchased it will be seen that surprisingly the lowest category purchased three-fourths of the land from the two highest asset categories while the next higher category purchased the bulk of the land from middle categories. The asset category of Rs. 50,000—1,00,000 purchased 42 per cent of the land from the same category and the highest category purchased 29 per cent of the land from the highest category. The net position of different categories as affected by land transfers is summarised in Table 8.6.

It will be seen that the greatest loser was the lowest asset group of less than Rs. 10,000 and the largest gainer was the highest asset group of over 1 lakh which accounted for 72 per cent of the gains. Whereas bottom three categories lost land the highest two-asset categories gained at their cost. Thus in central U.P. also the land market seems to be working in favour of large asset groups which have increased their possession over land through land transactions.

In Bundelkhand (Table 8.7) the lowest asset category accounted for 14 per cent of all land sales but was nowhere in the land market as purchasers. The next higher category of Rs. 10,000—25,000 accounted for less than 2 per cent of the sales and less than 1 per cent of the land purchased. The asset category of Rs. 25,000—50,000 accounted for 17 per cent of the land sold and 7 per cent of land purchased and the same was 21 per cent and 11 per cent respectively in the next higher category of Rs. 50,000—1,00,000. The highest asset category of 1 lakh and above significantly accounted for 46 per cent of all land sold and 81 per cent of all land purchased. Thus it can be seen that in this region only biggest asset group has gained and all the other categories were net losers of land. All the categories sold between 70 to 90 per cent of their land to the highest category of 1 lakh and over.

In the Hill region asset group of Rs. 10,000—25,000 accounted for 36 per cent of the land sale and the remaining 64 per cent was accounted for by the highest asset group. Interestingly while the former asset group had

TABLE 8.6

Asset-Wise Net Effect of Land Transfers in Central U.P.

(Area in acres)

Asset Category Rs.	Land Sold	Land Purchased	Net gain (+) or loss (—)	As Percentage
1	2	3	4	5
Less than Rs. 10,000	101.90	9.27	(—) 92.63	(—) 62.20
Rs 10,000—25.000	69.58	37.44	(—) 32.14	(—) 21.58
Rs 25,000—50 000	174.68	150.53	(—) 24.15	(—) 16.22
Rs 50,000—1,00 000	234.05	275.99	(+) 41.94	(+) 28.16
Rs 1,00,000 & above	118.55	225.53	(+) 106.98	(+) 71.84
Total	698.76	698.76	—	—

TABLE 8.7

Assets-Wise Land Transfer Matrix in Bundelkhand

(Asset in Rs. and Area in acres)

SELLERS	BUYERS						
	Less than Rs 10,000	Rs 10,000—25.000	Rs 25,000—50,000	Rs 50,000—1,00,000	Rs 1,00,000—above	Total	As percentage to total land sold
1	2	3	4	5	6	7	8
Less than Rs 10,000	—	0.72 (3.92)	4.58 (24.90)	—	13.09 (17.18)	18.39 (100.00)	13.89
Rs 10,000—25,000	—	—	0.56 (21.88)	—	2.00 (78.13)	2.56 (100.00)	1.93
Rs 25,000—50,000	—	—	0.40 (1.76)	3.62 (15.94)	18.69 (82.30)	22.71 (100.00)	17.16
Rs 50,000—1,00.000	—	—	1.95 (6.96)	6.40 (22.86)	19.65 (70.18)	28.00 (100.00)	21.14
Rs 1,00,000 & above	—	—	2.10 (3.46)	4.30 (7.08)	54.33 (89.46)	60.73 (100.00)	21.58
Total	—	0.72 (0.54)	9.59 (7.24)	14.32 (10.82)	107.76 (81.39)	132.39 (100 00)	100.00

N.B.—Figures in parentheses are percentages.

purchased its entire land from the highest asset group the latter had purchased its entire land from the asset category of Rs. 10,000—25,000.

The asset category of Rs. 10,000 25,000 accounted for 15 per cent of all the purchased land while the next higher asset category of Rs. 25,000—50,000 accounted for 50 per cent of the purchased land. The highest category accounted for the remaining 35 per cent of the purchased land. It would be seen that the asset category of Rs. 10,000—25,000 and the highest category of 1 lakh and above were the net losers of land and the asset group of Rs. 25,000 – 50,000 gained at their cost.

Taking the state as a whole (Table 8.8) it will be seen that the lowest asset group of less than Rs. 10,000 accounted for 31 per cent of all the land sold while this category accounted for only less than 2 per cent of all the land purchased. This category had sold 36 per cent of its land to the highest category and the asset category Rs 25,000—1,00,000 accounted for half of its sold land. The next higher category of Rs. 10,000—25,000 accounted for only 6 per cent of the total sold land and its share in the purchased land was also to the same extent. It had sold 10 per cent of its land to the same asset category, 23 per cent of the land was sold to the next higher category, while the highest category accounted for 39 per cent of its sold land. Asset category of Rs. 25,000—50,000 accounted for 15 per cent of all sold land and its share in total land purchased was 20 per cent. It had also sold nearly one-fourth of the land to the same asset category while only 6 per cent of the land was sold to lower asset categories. The asset category of Rs. 50,000—1,00,000 accounted for 20 per cent of the total land sold and its share in the total land purchased was 29 per cent. More than one-third of the land was transferred to the same asset group while lower asset group claimed nearly one-fourth of the land. The share of the highest category was as high as 40 per cent. Significantly the highest category of 1 lakh and above accounted for 28 per cent of all the sold land but its share in the land purchased was quite high at 44 per cent. This category had sold nearly two-thirds of the land to the same category, and the next lower category

TABLE 8.8
Asset-Wise Land Transfer Matrix in U.P.

(Asset in Rs. & Area in acres)

SELLERS	BUYERS Less than Rs. 10,000	Rs. 10,000—25,000	Rs. 25.000—50,000	Rs. 50,000—1,00,000	Rs. 1,00,000 & above	Total	As percentage to total land sale
1	2	3	4	5	6	7	8
Less than Rs. 10,000	20.23 (2.24)	97.66 (10.81)	247.13 (27.35)	206.82 (22.89)	331.73 (36.71)	903.57 (100.00)	31.04
Rs. 10,000—25,000	1.63 (0.91)	19.27 (10.75)	40.72 (22.72)	48.17 (26.87)	69.45 (38.75)	179.24 (100.00)	6.16
Rs. 25,000—50,000	4.35 (0.98)	24.35 (5.46)	104.00 (23.31)	176.02 (39.46)	137.37 (30.79)	446.09 (100.00)	15.33
Rs. 50,000—1,00,000	15.42 (2.68)	18.01 (3.13)	106.10 (18.44)	207.28 (36.02)	228.62 (39.73)	575.43 (100.00)	19.78
Rs. 1,00,000 & above	5.17 (0.64)	20.68 (2.57)	83.19 (10.32)	194.35 (24.11)	502.61 (62.36)	806.00 (100.00)	27.69
Total	46.80 (1.60)	179.97 (6.18)	581.14 (19.96)	832.64 (28.63)	1269.78 (43.63)	2910.33 (100.00)	100.00

N.B.—Figures in parentheses are percentage.

accounted for 24 per cent. The lowest two categories accounted for only 3 per cent of the land sold.

Asset-wise land purchased as percentage to total land purchased is shown in Table 8.9. It will be seen that the lowest category purchased 43 per cent of the land from that very asset category. Significantly they had purchased more than one-tenth of the land from the highest category. In the asset category of Rs. 10,000—25,000 more than half of the land was purchased from the lowest asset category while the share of the same asset category only 11 per cent. The highest category also accounted for 11 per cent of the land. The lowest category accounted for 43 per cent of the land that was purchased by the households in the asset category of Rs. 25,000—50,000 while the share of the highest category was 14 per cent. One-fourth of the land in the asset category of Rs. 50,000—1,00,000 was purchased from the households in the lowest category and another one-fourth from the same asset category. The largest category also accounted for 23 per cent of the land purchased. It is significant to note that 26 per cent of the purchased land in the highest category came from the lowest category. About 40 per cent of the land was purchased from the same category. Thus 60 per cent of the land purchased by highest category belonged to the categories lower than that category. Asset category-wise net effect of land transactions in U.P. is summarised in Table 8.10.

It would be seen that the lowest asset category was the only category to lose land. All the other categories gained and the larger the asset category the greater was the gain. Thus whereas the share of the category of Rs. 10,000—25,000 was less than 0.1 per cent in the total gain the share of next category rose to 16 per cent. The gain of the next higher category of Rs. 50,000—1,00,000 was even more striking which accounted for 30 per cent of the total gain and the highest category of 1 lakh and over appropriated 54 percent of the gain.

It can only be a very disturbing and distressing trend that those who stand at the lowest level are constantly being pushed down and are being forced to sell their land while big are gaining at their cost and the biggest among them are commanding the bulk of the gains.

TABLE 8.9

Asset-Wise Percentage Distribution of Land Purchased in U.P.

(Asset in Rs)

SELLERS	BUYERS Less than Rs 10,000	Rs 10,000 to 25,000	Rs 25,000 to 50,000	Rs 50,000 to 1,00,000	Rs 1,000,000 & above	Total
1	2	3	4	5	6	7
Less than Rs 10,000	43.23	54.26	42.43	24.84	26.12	31.04
Rs 10,000—25,000	3.48	10.71	7.00	5.79	5.48	6.16
Rs 25,000—50,000	9.29	13.53	17.90	21.14	10.82	15.33
Rs 50,000 – 1,00,000	32.95	10.01	18.26	24.89	18.00	19.78
Rs 1,00,000 & above	11.05	11.49	14.31	23.34	39.58	27.69
Total	100.00	100.00	100.00	100 00	100.00	100.00

TABLE 8.10

Asset-Wise Net Effect of Land Transfers in U.P.

(Area in acres)

Asset category (Rs.)	Land Sold	Land Purchased	Net gain (+) or loss (—)	As percentage
1	2	3	4	5
Less than Rs 10,000	903.57 (31.04)	46.80 (1.61)	(—) 856.77	(—) 100. 0
Rs 10,000—25,000	179.24 (6.16)	179.97 (6.18)	(+) 0.73	(+) 0.08
Rs 25,000—50,000	446.09 (15.33)	581.14 (19.97)	(+) 135.05	(+) 15.76
Rs 50,000—1,00,000	575.43 (19.78)	832.64 (28.61)	(+) 257.21	(+) 30.03
Rs 1,00,000 & above	806.00 (27.69)	1269.78 (43.63)	(+) 463.78	(+) 54.13
Total	2910.33 (100.00)	2910.33 (100.00)	—	—

N.B.—Figures in parentheses are percentages.

9

Caste-Wise Land Transfers

Caste is an important social institution and it has determined many an aspect of village life. The high castes have been the privileged castes not only in terms of social hierarchy but they have also been the owners of the land. The lower castes and the Scheduled Castes had little access to land which reduced them economically to a dependency relationship. They generally depend on the high castes for their livelihood by working as tenants of leased-in land or as farm seivants and agricultural labourers. In the Zamindari days, the Zamindars hailed exclusively from high castes as well as Muslims. Despite many changes in the countryside the caste factor, if at all, has been reinforced because of certain socio-political factors mainly due to electoral politics. On account of its continued importance it was considered desirable to analyse the land transfers in U.P. in terms of the caste factor which is presented in the following pages.

Caste-wise transfer of land in eastern U.P. has been shown in Table 9.1. It will be seen that high caste Hindus accounted for half of the alienated land followed by Backward Castes whose share was 27 per cent. Muslims accounted for one-sixth of all alienated land and Scheduled Caste's share was 6 per cent.

TABLE 9.1

Caste-Wise Land Transfer Matrix in Eastern U.P.

Areas in acres

SELLERS	BUYERS High Caste Hindu	Backward Caste	Scheduled Caste	Muslims	Sikhs & others	Total	As percentage to total land sold
1	2	3	4	5	5	7	8
High Caste Hindu	277.25 (42.14)	321.99 (48.93)	44.03 (6.69)	14.73 (2.24)	—	658.00 (100.00)	49.20
Backward Caste	59.67 (16.22)	262.09 (71.25)	18.76 (5.10)	23.35 (6 35)	4.00 (1.08)	367.87 (100.00)	27.51
Scheduled Caste	23.07 (26.67)	33.54 (38.77)	29.30 (33.87)	0.60 (0.69)	—	86.51 (100.00)	6.47
Muslim	18.21 (8.09)	89.66 (39.85)	1.41 (0.63)	115.74 (51.43)	—	225.02 (100.00)	16.82
Sikh	—	—	—	—	—	—	—
Total	378.20 (28.28)	707.28 (52.88)	93.50 (6.99)	154.42 (11.55)	4.00 (0.30)	1337.40 (100.00)	100.00

N.B.—Figures in parentheses are percentages.

Significantly high caste Hindus had sold the bulk of their alienated land (49 per cent) to Backward Caste. Forty two per cent of their land was sold to their own caste group. Roughly 7 per cent of the land was sold to Scheduled Castes and 2 per cent to the Muslims.

Backward Castes had sold 71 per cent of the land to the same caste group, 16 per cent to high caste Hindus and 5 per cent to Scheduled Caste and 6 per cent to Muslims. The Scheduled Castes had sold 39 per cent of their land to Backward Castes, 34 per cent to Scheduled Castes, 27 per cent to high caste Hindus and less than 1 per cent to Muslims.

Muslims who accounted for 17 per cent of the alienated land had sold 40 per cent of their alienated land to Backward Castes. More than half of the land was sold to the same community of Muslims and 8 per cent was sold to high caste Hindus while Scheduled Castes accounted for less than 1 per cent of such land.

As regards purchases more than half of the land (53 per cent) was purchased by Backward Castes. The share of high castes Hindus was 28 per cent followed by Muslim (11 per cent) and Scheduled Caste (7 per cent). High Caste Hindus had purchased the bulk of the land from the same caste (73 per cent) while Backward Caste had purchased most of the land from high castes. Scheduled Castes had mainly purchased from high caste Hindus while Muslims preferred their own community. Caste-wise net gain or loss in terms of area is summarised in Table 9.2.

It would be seen that Backward Caste were the main gainers and they had increased their land holding considerably through land purchases. They accounted for 97 per cent of the net gain. Scheduled Caste also belonged, although marginally, to the same category. High Caste Hindus and Muslims were the main losers of land High Caste Hindus alone accounted for 80 per cent of the net loss.

In central U.P. (Table 9.3) high caste Hindus accounted for 42 per cent of the total alienated land followed by Backward Caste (35 per cent), Muslims (17 per cent), Scheduled Caste (6 per cent) and Sikhs (0.2 per cent). The high caste Hindus had sold nearly half of their alienated land to Backward Caste

TABLE 9.2

Caste-wise Net Effect of Land Transfers in eastern U.P.

(Area in acres)

Caste	Land Sold	Land Purchased	Net gain (+) or loss (—)	As percentage
1	2	3	4	5
High Caste Hindu	658.00	378.20	(—) 279.80	(—) 79.35
Backward Caste	367.87	707.28	(+) 339.41	(+) 96.86
Scheduled Caste	86.51	93.50	(+) 6.99	(+) 1.99
Muslim	225.02	154.42	(—) 70.60	(—) 20.15
Sikh	—	4.00	(+) 4.00	(—) 1.14
Total	1337.40	1337.40	—	—

TABLE 9.3

Caste-Wise Land Transfer Matrix in Central U.P.

(Area in acres)

SELLERS	BUYERS						
	High Caste Hindn	Backward Caste	Scheduled Caste	Muslim	Sikh	Total	As percentage to total land sold
1	2	3	4	5	6	7	8
High Caste Hindu	78.53 (26.98)	144.01 (49.48)	37.82 (12.99)	30.67 (10.54)	—	291.03 (100.00)	41.65
Backward Caste	59.36 (24.13)	137.05 (55.71)	16.63 (6.76)	32.96 (13.40)	—	246.00 (100.00)	35.21
Scheduled Caste	2.85 (6.97)	21.52 (52.68)	13.71 (33.56)	2.77 (6.78)	—	40.82 (100.00)	5.84
Muslim	12.97 (10.80)	35.10 (29.34)	5.50 (4.60)	66.09 (55.25)	—	119.62 (100.00)	17.12
Sikh	—	0.63 (50.00)	—	0.63 (50.00)	—	1.26 (100.00)	0.18
Total	153.67 (21.99)	338.31 (48.42)	73.66 (10.54)	133.12 (19.05)	—	698.76 (100.00)	100.00

N.B.—Figures in parentheses are percentages.

and more than one fourth (27 per cent) was sold to their own caste group. Significantly Scheduled Castes had purchased 13 per cent of their land and Muslims accounted for another 11 per cent.

The Backward Caste had preference for their own caste as 56 per cent of their sold land was transferred to the same caste while high caste Hindus accounted for another one-fourth of the land. The share of Muslims was 13 per cent followed by Scheduled Caste (7 per cent).

Scheduled Castes had favoured Backward Castes in land transactions as 53 per cent of their alienated land was in favour of the members of that caste while one-third of such land was transferred to their own caste. High Caste Hindu and Muslims accounted for 7 per cent each of their alienated land.

Muslims favoured their own community as 55 per cent of the alienated land was in favour of their own community. Backward caste came next with a share of 29 per cent followed by High Caste Hindus (11 per cent) and Scheduled Caste (5 per cent). Sikhs had favoured Backward Caste and Muslims equally as these two groups shared their total land that was sold. Table 9.4 summarises the caste-wise net effect of land transfers.

It would be seen that high caste Hindus were almost the exclusive net losers of land as they accounted for 99 per cent of the net loss. Sikh also had a negative balance. All the other castes had a positive balance. Backward Caste were the main gainers of land in this region also as they accounted for 67 per cent of the net gain. Significantly Scheduled Caste accounted for 24 per cent of the net gain.

In western U.P. (Table 9.5) high caste Hindus accounted for half of the alienated land followed by Backward Caste (17 per cent), Muslims (15 per cent), Scheduled Castes (10 per cent) and Sikh (7 per cent). A general feature observed in land transfers here as in other regions was the fact that caste groups preferred their own castes in the land transaction as the bulk of such transfers took place within the same caste group. High caste Hindus had sold nearly 60 per cent of their alienated land to the same caste group. Similarly Backward castes had

TABLE 9.4

Caste-wise Net Effect of Land Transfers in central U.P.

(Area in acres)

Caste Group	Land Sold	Land Purchased	Net gain (+) or loss (—)	As percentage
1	2	3	4	5
High Caste Hindu	291.03	153.67	(—) 137.36	(—) 99.09
Backward Caste	246.00	338.31	(+) 92.31	(+) 66.59
Scheduled Caste	40.85	73.66	(+) 32.81	(+) 23.67
Muslim	119.62	133.12	(+) 13.50	(+) 9.74
Sikh	1.26	—	(—) 1.26	(—) 0.91
Total	698.76	698.76	—	—

TABLE 9.5

Caste-Wise Land Transfer Matrix in Western U.P.

(Area in Acres)

SELLERS	BUYERS						
	High Caste Hindu	Backward Caste	Scheduled Caste	Muslim	Sikh	Total	As percentage to total land sold
1	2	3	4	5	6	7	8
High Caste Hindu	219.96	48 30	31.17	53.07	18.06	370.56	50.41
	(59.36)	(13.03)	(8.41)	(14.32)	(4.87)	(100.00)	
Backward Caste	14.46	68.34	12.12	12.24	21.00	128.16	17.44
	(11.28)	(53.32)	(9.45)	(9.55)	(16.38)	(100.00)	
Scheduled Caste	15.03	15.35	39.20	3.99	1.22	74.79	10.18
	(20.10)	(20.52)	(52.41)	(5.34)	(1.63)	(100.00)	
Muslim	5.37	9.35	2.82	89.46	1.87	108.87	14.81
	(4.93)	(8.59)	(2.59)	(82.17)	(1.72)	(100.00)	
Sikh	—	2.52	0.32	—	49.81	52.65	7.16
		(4.78)	(0.60)		(94.60)	(100.00)	
Total	254.82	143.86	85.63	158.76	91 96	735.03	100.00
	(34.67)	(19.57)	(11.65)	(21.60)	(12.51)	(100.00)	

N.B.—Figures in parentheses are percentages.

sold 53 per cent to the same caste group. Scheduled Castes had sold 52 per cent of such land to members of their own community and Muslims had sold 82 per cent of such land to fellow Muslims. Likewise Sikhs had sold 95 per cent of their sold land to their own community.

Of all the land that was purchased, high caste Hindus had purchased 35 per cent of it followed by Muslims (22 per cent), Backward Caste (19 per cent), Sikh and Scheduled Caste (12 per cent each). Thus the trend in western U.P. is different from eastern as also central U.P. in so far as Backward Castes are not so prominent as purchasers of land in this region while Muslims and to some extent Sikhs are quite conspicuous in the land market as purchasers. Caste-wise net gain or loss in land transactions is summarised in Table 9.6.

It would be seen that high Caste Hindus were the sole losers of land and all other caste groups had registered improvement in their position at their cost. Muslims accounted for 43 per cent of the net gain followed by Sikhs (34 per cent), Backward Caste (14 per cent) and Scheduled Caste (9 per cent).

In Bundelkhand (Table 9.7) it would be seen that high caste Hindus accounted for 74 per cent of all the land that was alienated by way of sale followed by Backward Castes (16 per cent), Scheduled Castes (8 per cent) and Muslim (2 per cent). High caste Hindus had preferred to sell their land to the same caste group as 77 per cent of their land was sold to that caste followed by Backward Caste (22 per cent) and Scheduled Caste (1 per cent).

The Backward Caste had favoured high caste Hindus as 77 per cent of the land was sold to them whereas Backward Castes accounted for 16 per cent of the land and Scheduled Castes for the remaining 7 per cent of the land. The Scheduled Caste too had sold 44 per cent of their alienated land to high caste Hindus followed by their own caste and Backward Caste (28 per cent each). Muslims had sold their land only to Backward Castes.

High caste Hindus had purchased 73 per cent of all the land that was alienated in this region. About 78 per cent of their purchased land belonged to that very caste followed by 17 per cent from Backward Castes. Backward Castes accounted

TABLE 9.6

Caste-wise Net Effect of Land Transfers in western U.P.

(Area in acres)

Caste group	Land Sold	Land Purchased	Net gain (+) or loss (+)	As Percentage
1	2	3	4	5
High Caste Hindu	370.56	254.82	(—) 115.74	(—) 100.00
Backward Caste	128.16	143.86	(+) 15.70	(+) 13.56
Scheduled Caste	74.79	85.63	(+) 10.84	(+) 9.37
Muslim	108.87	158.76	(+) 49.89	(+) 43.11
Sikh	52.65	91.96	(—) 39.31	(—) 33.96
Total	735.03	735.03	—	—

TABAE 9.7

Caste-wise Land Transfer Matrix in Bundelkhand

(Area in acres)

SELLERS	BUYERS						
	High Caste Hindu	Backward Caste	Scheduled Caste	Muslim	Sikh	Total	As percentage to total land sold
1	2	3	4	5	6	7	8
High Caste Hindu	74.98 (76.88)	21.25 (21.79)	1.30 (1.33)	—	—	97.53 (100.00)	73.68
Backward Caste	16.71 (76.69)	3.58 (16.43)	1.50 (6.88)	—	—	21.79 (100.00)	16.56
Scheduled Caste	4.65 (43.99)	2.92 (27.63)	3.00 (28.38)	—	—	10.57 (100.00)	7.98
Muslim	—	2.50 (100.00	—	—	—	2.50 (100.00)	1.88
Sikh	—	—	—	—	—	—	—
Total	96.34 (72.77)	30.25 (22.85)	5.80 (4.38)	—	—	132.39 (100.00)	100.00

N.B.—Figures in parentheses are percentages.

TABLE 9.8

Caste-wise Land Transfer Matrix in U.P.

(Area in acres)

SELLERS	BUYERS						
	High Caste Hinds	Backward Caste	Scheduled Caste	Muslim	Sikh	Total	As percentage to total land scld
1	2	3	4	5	6	7	8
High Caste Hindu	656.47 (46.10)	535.55 (37.61)	115.32 (8.10)	98.47 (6.92)	18.06 (1.27)	1423.87 (100.00)	48.92
Backward Caste	150.20 (19.66)	471.06 (61.68)	49.01 (6.42)	68.55 (8.97)	25.00 (3.27)	763.82 (100.00)	26.25
Scheduled Caste	45.60 (21.44)	73.33 (34.47)	85.21 (40.06)	7.36 (3.46)	1.22 (0.57)	212.72 (100.00)	7.31
Muslim	36.51 (8.01)	136.61 (29.96)	9.73 (2.13)	271.29 (59.49)	1.87 (0.41)	456.01 (100.00)	15.67
Sikh	—	3.15 (5.84)	0.32 (0.59)	0.63 (1.18)	49.81 (92.39)	53.91 (100.00)	1.35
Total	888.78 (30.54)	1219.70 (41.90)	259.59 (8.92)	446.30 (15.34)	95.96 (3.30)	2190.33 (100.00)	100.00

N.B.—Figures in parentheses are percentages,

for 23 per cent of the total purchased land which they had brought mainly from high caste Hindus. The latter accounted for 70 per cent of the land purchased by Backward Castes followed by the same caste group (12 per cent). The land purchased by Scheduled Castes formed 4 per cent of the total purchased land. Slightly more than half of their purchased land belonged to that very caste. The rest came from high caste Hindus and Backward Castes. It will thus be seen that while all the other castes were net losers of land, the Backward Caste accounted for the entire gain.

In the Hill region high caste caste Hindus were the sole sellers of land. Eighty five per cent of the sold land was transferred to that very caste and the rest to Scheduled Castes. No other caste group was found to be involved in land deals.

Taking the state as a whole (Table 9.8) it would be seen that high caste Hindus accounted for almost half (49 per cent) of the alienated land followed by Backward Castes (26 per cent), Muslims (16 per cent), Scheduled Castes (7 per cent), and Sikhs (2 per cent). High caste Hindus had sold 46 per cent of their alienated land to their own caste group. Backward Castes came next with 38 per cent and Scheduled Caste's share was 8 per cent. Muslims accounted for 7 per cent Sikhs for the remaining 1 per cent. Thus high caste Hindus and Backward Castes accounted for 84 per cent of their sold land.

Backward Castes had preferred their own caste in selling the land as 62 per cent of the alienated land was transferred by them to their own caste. Next came high caste Hindus with one-fifth of the land followed by Muslims (9 per cent), Scheduled Caste (6 per cent) and Sikh (3 per cent).

Scheduled Caste too preferred their own caste group in making land deals as 40 per cent of their aliented land was transferred to their own caste group followed by Backward Castes (35 per cent). High Caste Hindus came next with 21 per cent followed by Muslims (3 per cent), and Sikh 1 per cent).

Muslims too had a similar tendency as 59 per cent of their alienated land was transferred to members of the same community followed by Backward Castes (30 per cent), high caste

Hindus (8 per cent), Scheduled Caste (2 per cent) and Sikh (1 per cent). This was even more true for Sikhs as they transferred 92 per cent of their alienated land to that very community followed by Backward Castes (6 per cent). High Caste Hindus did not figure in their land deals. Thus the preference of the sellers of land for their own caste group in land transactions comes out in sharp relief as a universal phenomenon in this state.

The buyers of land also in most of the cases preferred their own caste group (Table 9.9). It would be seen that almost three-fourths of the land purchased by high caste Hindus was purchased from their own caste group while 17 per cent of their land was purchased from Backward Castes. The share of Scheduled Caste and Muslims was 5 per cent and 4 per cent respectively. Backward Caste had purchased 44 per cent of the land from high caste Hindus and 39 per cent from their own caste. Next came Muslims (11 per cent), followed by Scheduled Caste (6 per cent).

Significantly Scheduled Caste too had purchased largest chunk of land from high caste Hindus (44 per cent). Almost one-third of their land was purchased from the Scheduled Caste followed by Backward Caste (19 per cent). Muslims had preferred their own community as they had purchased 61 per cent of their land from among the Muslims. This was equally true for Sikhs. Net effect of the transactions is summarised in Table 9.10.

It would be seen that high caste Hindus were the main losers of land as the Backward Castes were the main gainers. High caste Hindus accounted for 90 per cent of the net loss while Backward caste accounted for 84 per cent of the net gains in land transactions.

TABLE 9.9

Caste-wise Percentage Distribution of Land Purchased in U.P.

SELLERS	BUYERS				
	High Caste Hindus	Backward Caste	Scheduled Caste	Muslims	Sikh
1	2	3	4	5	6
High Caste Hindu	73.86	43.91	44.42	22.06	18.82
Backward Caste	16.90	38.62	18.88	15.36	26.05
Scheduled Caste	5.13	6.01	32.82	1.65	1.27
Muslim	4.11	11.20	3.75	60.79	1.95
Sikh	—	0.26	0.13	0.14	51.91
Total	100.00	100.00	100.00	100.00	100.00

TABLE 9.10

Caste-Wise net Effect of Land Transfers in U.P.

(Area in acres)

Caste group	Land Sold	Land Purchased	Net gain + or loss	As Percentage
1	2	3	4	5
High caste Hindu	1423.87	888.78	(—) 535.09	(—) 98.22)
Backward caste	763.82	1219.70	(+) 455.88	(—) 83.68
Scheduled caste	212.72	259.59	(+) 46.87	(—) 8.60
Muslim	956.01	446.30	(+) 9.71	(—) 1.78
Sikh	53.91	95.96	(—) 42.05	(—) 7.72
Total	2910.33	2910.33	—	—

10

Caste and Size Category-Wise Land Transfers

An attempt was also made to analyse the land transfers in the different regions of the state on the basis of caste as also size category of holding of buyers and sellers. Table 10.1 shows the land transactions of high caste Hindus of eastern U.P. as buyers of land.

High Caste Hindus as Buyers Land in eastern U.P.

It will be seen that of the total land purchased by High Caste Hindus (HCH) from other high caste Hindus roughly 10 per cent was purchased by lowest category, another 26 per cent was purchased by 2.5—5 acre category. The share of 5—10 acre category was 24 per cent and that of the highest category was 40 per cent. Thus nearly two-thirds of the land was purchased by households having more than 5 acres of land.

As regards land purchased by high caste Hindus from Backward Caste (BC) it would be seen that 43 per cent of the land was purchased by 5—10 acre category and another 26 per cent was purchased by the highest category. The landless

TABLE 10.1

Caste and Size Category-Wise Distribution of land Purchased by High Caste Hindu in Eastern U.P.

(Area in acres)

SELLERS	HIGH CASTE HINDUS AS BUYERS				
	Less than 2.5	2.5—5	5—10	10 & above	Total
1	2	3	4	5	6
H.C.H.					
Landless	2.16	23.91	11.20	39.08	76.35
Less than 2.5	5.91	10.38	13.08	1.76	31.13
2.5—5.0	2.67	16.18	8.47	2.71	30.03
5.0—10.0	15.03	11.57	16.04	25.00	67.65
10.0 & above	2.38	9.66	18.40	41.65	72.09
Total	28.15 (10.15)	71.70 (25.86)	67.19 (24.33)	110.21 (39.75)	277.25 (100.00)
B.C.					
Landless	2.72	0.56	8.25	—	11.53
Less than 2.5	1.73	7.67	8.53	3.56	21.49
2.5—5.0	1.93	1.53	3.43	1.98	8.87
5.0—10.0	0.20	1.11	5.49	7.30	14.10
10.0 & above	0.40	0.40	0.08	2.80	3.68
Total	6.98 (11.70)	11.27 (18.89)	25.78 (43.10)	15.64 (26.21)	59.67 (100.00)

Table 10.1 (*Contd.*)

1	2	3	4	5	6
S.C.					
Landless	—	1.91	6.30	3.29	11.50
Less than 2.5	0.58	1.15	—	3.60	5.33
2.5—5.0	0.28	—	—	—	0.28
5.0—10.0	—	—	1.11	2.85	3.96
10.0 & above	—	—	—	2.00	2.00
Total	0.86 (3.73)	3.06 (13.26)	7.41 (32.12)	11 74 (50.89)	23.07 (100.00)
MUSLIM					
Landless	—	—	4.12	3.15	7.27
Less than 2.5	0.84	2.00	2.00	0.92	5.76
2.5—5.0	—	0.32	4.55	—	4.87
5.0—10.0	—	—	0.31	—	0.31
10.0 & above	—	—	—	—	—
Total	0.84 (4.61)	2.32 (12.74)	10.98 (60.30)	4.07 (22.35)	18.21 (100.00)
Grand Total	36.83 (9.73)	88.35 (23.36)	111.36 (29.43)	141.66 (37.48)	378.20 (100.00)

N.B. —Figures in parentheses are percentage.

and marginal farmers among Backward Caste accounted for 55 per cent of the land sold to high caste Hindus. It will thus be seen that higher categories among high caste Hindus accounted for the major portion of land that was purchased from Backward Castes.

As regards land purchased by high caste Hindus from Scheduled Caste (SC) a similar picture is discernible where the lower categories among Scheduled Castes sold land to higher categories among high caste Hindus.

Backward Castes as Buyers of Land in eastern U.P.

Table 10.2 shows the caste and size category-wise distribution of land purchased by Backward Castes in eastern U.P. It will be seen that less than 2.5 acre category accounted for 16 per cent of total land purchased by this caste. The 2.5—5 acre category and 5—10 acre category accounted for 25 and 33 per cent respectively of the land purchased while the largest category accounted for 26 per cent of the land. Thus small and marginal farmers among the Backward Caste have emerged as significant purchasers of land. The landless category among the sellers belonging to all the castes save the Scheduled Castes formed the largest chunk of sellers of land to the Backward Castes as they accounted for 44 per cent of the land sold to them.

Scheduled Castes as buyers of land in eastern U.P.

Land purchased by Scheduled Castes according to size category of owned holdings and caste is shown in Table 10.3. It will be seen that less than 2.5 category accounted for 38 per cent of the land purchased by Scheduled Caste in eastern U.P. The next two higher categories accounted for 30 and 27 per cent of the land respectively and the highest category accounted for only 5 per cent of the land purchased. Significantly the lowest category of less than 2.5 acres accounted for 30 per cent of all the land that was purchased from high caste Hindus, 51 per cent in case of Backward Caste, nearly 40 per cent in case of Scheduled Caste, and cent per cent in case of Muslims. Likewise the 2.5—5 acre category accounted for 35 per cent of the land that was purchased from high caste

TABLE 10.2

Caste and Size Category-Wise Distribution of land Purchased by by Backward Caste in eastern U.P.

(Area in acres)

SELLERS	BACKWARD CASTE AS BUYERS: Less than 2.5	2.5—5.0	5—10	10.0 & above	Total
1	2	3	4	5	6
H.C.H.					
Landless	4.92	7.77	31.39	27 05	71.13
Less than 2.5	9.45	7.88	12.27	2.61	32.21
2.5—5.0	6.73	17.66	17.69	1.96	44.04
5.0—10.0	8.89	35.46	15.52	14.38	74.25
10.0 & above	11.50	19.98	22.08	46.80	100.36
Total	41.49 (12.89)	88.75 (27.56)	98.95 (30.73)	92.80 (28.82)	321.99 (100.00)
B.C.					
Landless	2.44	38.46	86.48	38.32	165.70
Less than 2.5	8.11	7.57	3.19	5.45	24.32
2.5—5.0	6.40	7.11	7.13	5.73	26.37
5.0—10.0	2.39	9.01	11.04	2.20	24.64
10.0 & above	0.63	0.40	13.03	7.00	21.06
Total	19.97 (7.62)	62.55 (23.86)	120.87 (46.12)	58.70 (22.40)	262.09 (100.00)

Table 10.2 (*Contd.*)

1	2	3	4	5	6
S.C.					
Landless	—	2.36	0.46	—	2.82
Less than 2.5	1.53	3.39	0.60	2.16	7.68
2.5—5.0	1.76	7.60	1.26	1.05	11.67
5.0—10.0	—	3.15	6.64	1.58	11.37
10 & above	—	—	—	—	—
Total	3,29	16.50	8.96	4.79	33.54
	(9.82)	(49.19)	(26.71)	(14.28)	(100.00)
MUSLIM					
Landless	42.00	4.73	—	25.14	71.87
Less than 2.5	3.10	1.83	2.40	0.40	7.73
2.5—5.0	1.10	0.63	8.23	1.20	6.16
5.0—10.0	0.68	0.20	3.22	0.80	3.90
10.0 & above	—	—	—	—	—
Total	46.88	7.39	7.85	27.54	80.66
	(52.29)	(8.24)	(8.75)	(30.72)	(100.00)
SIKHS	—	—	—	—	—
Grand Total	111.63	175.19	236.73	183.83	707.28
	(15.78)	(24.77)	(33.46)	(25.99)	(100.00)

N.B.— Figures in parentheses are percentages.

TABLE 10.3

Caste and Size Category-wise Distribution of Land Purchased by Scheduled Caste in Eastern U.P.

(Area in acres)

SELLERS	SCHEDULED CASTE AS BUYERS				
	Less than 2.5	2.5—5.0	5.0—10.0	10,0 & above	Total
1	2	3	4	5	6
H.C.H.					
Landless	1.86	0.46	5.67	—	7.99
Less than 2.5	0.85	0.94	3.00	—	4.79
2.5—5.0	1.26	3.31	5.01	—	9.58
5.0—10.0	7.21	8.01	1.26	—	16.48
10.0 & above	2.19	2.69	0.31	—	5.19
Total	13.37 (30.37)	15.41 (35.03)	15.25 (34.63)	—	44.03 (100.00)
B.C.					
Landless	0.40	0.44	—	—	0.84
Less than 2.5	1.84	0.65	—	4.40	6.89
2.5—5.0	4.05	1.68	—	—	5.73
5.0—10.0	1.07	—	0.63	—	1.70
10.0 & above	2.29	1.31	—	—	3.60
Total	9.65 (51.43)	4.08 (21.75)	0.63 (3.35)	4.40 (23.47)	18.76 (100.00)

Table1 0.3 (*Contd.*)

1	2	3	4	5	6
S.C.					
Landless	2.90	4.41	8.82	—	16.13
Less than 2.5	6.51	1.15	0.12	—	7.78
2.5—5.0	0.89	3.24	—	—	4.13
5.0—10.0	—	—	—	—	—
10.0 & above	1.26	—	—	—	1.26
Total	11.50	8,80	8.94	—	29.30
	(39.45)	(30.03)	(30.52)		(100.00)
MUSLIM					
Landless	—	—	—	—	—
Less than 2.5	—	—	—	—	—
2.5—5.0	7.78	—	—	—	0.78
5.0—10.0	0.63	—	—	—	0.63
10.0 & above	—	—	—	—	—
Total	1.41	—	—	—	1.41
	(100.00)	—	—	—	(100.00)
SIKHS	—	—	—	—	—
Grand Total	35.99	28.29	24.82	4.40	93.50
	(38.59)	(30.24)	(26.53)	(4.75)	(100.00)

N.B.—Figures in parentheses are percentages.

Hindus, 22 per cent in case of Backward Castes and 30 per cent in case of Muslims. High caste Hindus accounted for more than 47 per cent of the land that was purchased by Scheduled Castes. Although the Scheduled Castes purchased land from all categories yet the landless and the marginal farmers among the sellers together accounted for 47 per cent of the land sold to them. Significantly the marginal as small farmers among Scheduled Castes purchased the largest chunk of land (68 per cent)

Muslims as Buyers of land in eastern U.P.

Table 10.4 shows the caste and size category-wise distribution of land purchased by Muslims in eastern U.P. It will be seen that the lowest category among them accounted for 14 per cent of the total land purchased. The next higher category of 2.5—5.0 acres accounted for 17 per cent and the 5—10 acres category accounted for as high as 44 per cent of the land purchased. The highest category accounted for one-fourth of the land purchased.

Of the total land purchased by Muslims the largest chunk came from Muslims (75 per cent) themselves followed by Backward Caste (15 per cent) and high caste Hindus (8 per cent). The landless among the sellers accounted for the bulk (76 per cent) of the land sold to Muslims.

High caste Hindus as Buyers of Land in central U.P.

Table 10.5 shows the caste and size category-wise distribution of land purchased by high caste Hindus in central U.P. It would be seen that 49 per cent of the land was purchased by 5—10 acres category and another 30 per cent was purchased by 10 and above category. Thus roughly 80 per cent of the land was purchased by high caste Hindus in the size category of 5 acres or more of owned land. The share of households in the size category of 2.5—5.0 land less than 2.5 acre was 18 per cent and 2 per cent respectively.

Of the total land purchased by high caste Hindus 51 per cent was purchased from high caste Hindus, 39 per cent from Backward Caste, 2 per cent from Scheduled Caste and 8 per cent from Muslims. Landless among the sellers accounted for nearly one-third of the land sold to high caste Hindus.

TABLE 10.4

Caste and Size Category-wise Distribution of Land Purchased by Muslims in eastern U.P.

(Area in acres)

SELLERS	MUSLIMS AS BUYERS				
	Less than 2.5	2.5—5.0	5.0—10.0	10.0 & above	Total
1	2	3	4	5	6
H.C.H.					
Landless	—	2.52	7.30	1.50	11.32
Less than 2.5	—	—	—	—	—
2.5—5.0	0.32	—	—	—	0.32
5.0—10,0	1.00	—	—	—	1.00
10.0 & above	1.20	0.37	0.52	—	2.09
Total	2.52 (17.11)	2.89 (19.62)	7.82 (53.09)	1.50 (10.18)	14.73 (100.00)
B.C.					
Landless	1.71	6.88	—	—	8.59
Less than 2.5	1.76	—	—	—	1.76
2.5—5.0	—	—	—	—	—
5.0—10.0	—	1.60	0.10	—	1.70
10.0 & above	3.30	8.00	—	—	11.30
Total	6.77 (28.99)	16.48 (70.58)	0.10 (0.43)	—	23.35 (100.00)

Table 10.4 (*Contd.*)

1	2	3	4	5	6
Landless	—	—	—	—	—
Less than 2.5	—	0.60	—	—	0.60
25—5.0	—	—	—	—	—
5.0—10.0	—	—	—	—	—
10.0 & above	—	—	—	—	—
Total	—	0.60 (100.20)	—	—	0.60 (100.00)
Landless	2.99	3.35	54.18	37.27	97.79
Less than 2.5	3.34	0.65	0.46	—	4.45
2.5—5.0	3.21	—	5.00	—	8.21
5.0—10.0	2.49	2.49	0.31	—	5 29
10.0 & above	—	—	—	—	—
Total	12.03 (10.39)	6.49 (5.61)	59.95 (51.80)	37.27 (32.20)	115.74 (100.00)
SIKHS	—	—	—	—	—
Grand Total	21.32 (13.80)	26.46 (17.14)	67.87 (43.95)	38.77 (25.11)	154.42 (100.00)

N.B.— Figures in parentheses are percentages.

TABLE 10.5

Caste and Size Category-Wise Distribution of Land Purchased by High Caste Hindu in central U.P.

(Area in acres)

SELLERS	HIGH CASTE HINDUS AS BUYERS Less than 2.5	2.5—5.0	5.0—10.0	10.0 & above	Total
1	2	3	4	5	6
H.C.H.					
Landless	—	2.21	11.69	16.88	30.78
Less than 2.5	0.63	4.59	1.18	—	6.40
2.5—5.0	1.25	7.74	10.19	1.00	20.18
5.0—10.0	—	1.77	11.51	3.94	17.22
10.0 & above	—	1.00	2.95	—	3.95
Total	1.88 (2.39)	17.31 (22.04)	37.52 (47.78)	21.82 (27.79)	78.53 (100.00)
B.C.					
Landless	—	0.49	12.61	5.23	18.33
Less than 2.5	0.49	3.66	5.44	1.60	11,19
2.5—5.0	0.20	5.23	4.73	12.05	22.21
5.0—10.0	—	—	5.75	1.00	6.75
10.0 & above	—	—	0.88	—	0.88
Total	0.69 (1.16)	9.38 (15.80)	29.41 (49.55)	19.88 (33.49)	59.36 (100.00)

Table 10.5 (*Contd.*)

1	2	3	4	5	6
S.C.					
Landless	—	—	—	—	—
Less than 2.5	—	1.45	1.40	—	—
2.5—5.0	—	—	—	—	—
5.0—10.0	—	—	—	—	—
10.0 & above	—	—	—	—	—
Total	—	1.45 (50.88)	1.40 (49.12)	—	2.85 (100.00)
MUSLIM					
Landless	—	—	—	—	—
Less thaa 2.5	—	0.24	5.00	1.40	6.64
2.5—5.0	—	—	0.43	1.00	1.43
5.0—10.0	—	—	1.92	—	1.92
10.0 & above	0.94	—	—	2.00	2.94
Total	0.94 (7.27)	2.24 (1.86)	7.35 (56.84)	4.40 (34.03)	12.93 (100.00)
SIKH					
Landless	—	—	—	—	—
Less than 2.5	—	—	—	—	—
2.5—5.0	—	—	—	—	—
5.0 - 10.0	—	—	—	—	—
10.0 & above	—	—	—	—	—
Total	—	—	—	—	—
Grand Total	3.51 (2.28)	28.38 (18.47)	75.68 (49.25)	46.10 (30.00)	153.67 (100.00)

N.B.— Figures in parentheses are parcentages.

Backward Caste as Buyers of Land in central U.P.

Table 10.6 shows caste and category-wise distribution of land purchased by Backward Caste in central U.P. It will be seen that 10 per cent of the land was purchased by less than 2.5 acre category while about 40 per cent of the land was purchased by 2.5—5 acres category. The share of the next two higher categories was 35 and 15 per cent respectively. Thus the small farmers and semi-medium farmers accounted for roughly three-fourths of the land purchased by Backward Castes in Central U.P.

Of the total land that was purchased by Backward Caste 43 per cent was purchased from high caste Hindus, 41 per cent from Backward Caste, 6 per cent from Scheduled Caste and 10 per cent from Muslims and Sikhs. Sellers of land were more evenly distributed and landless among them accounted for one-sixth of the land.

Scheduled Caste as Buyers of Land in central U.P.

Table 10.7 shows the caste and size-wise distribution of land purchased by Scheduled Caste in central U.P. It will be seen that 18 per cent of the land was purchased by the lowest category among Scheduled Caste and another 46 per cent was purchased by the next higher category of 2.5—5 acres. The 5—10 acre category accounted for 35 per cent and the highest category accounted for only 1 per cent of the land purchased. It is noteworthy that more than half (51 per cent) of the land was purchased by Scheduled Caste from high caste Hindus, another 23 per cent from Backward Caste while Scheduled Castes provided another 19 per cent and Muslims about 7 per cent of the land. Interestingly the landless were not the main sellers of land accounting for only 12 per cent of the land that was sold to Scheduled Caste. Small farmers accounted for 46 per cent of the land purchased by scheduled caste.

Muslims as Buyers of Land in central U.P.

Caste and size-wise distribution of land purchased by Muslims in central U.P. is shown in Table 10.8. It will be seen that the lowest category of less than 2.5 acres accounted for nearly 4 per cent of the land purchased by Muslims. The next two higher categories accounted for 26 per cent and

TABLE 10.6

Caste and Size-wise Distribution of Land Purchased by Backward Caste in central U.P.

(Area in acres)

SELLERS	BACKWARD CASTE AS BUYERS				
	Less than 2.5	2.5—5.0	5.0—10.0	10.0 & above	Total
1	2	3	4	5	6
H.C.H.					
Landless	0.63	10.77	5.29	5.00	21.69
Less than 2.5	1.65	5.57	—	2.39	9.61
2.5—5.0	6.03	20.21	15.25	7.70	49.29
5.0—10.0	1.17	11.99	16.51	5.13	34.80
10.0 & above	—	4.74	16.09	7.89	28.72
Total	9.48 (6.58)	53.28 (37.00)	53.14 (36.90)	28.11 (19.52)	144.01 (100.00)
B.C.					
Landless	9.80	5.30	8.64	1.88	25.62
Less than 2.5	9.06	18.82	2.60	4.21	34.69
2.5—5.0	1.32	11.47	8.45	1.60	22.84
5.0—10.0	0.63	12.89	18.95	0.63	33.10
10.0 & above	—	2.80	6.60	11.40	20.80
Total	20.81 (15.18)	51.28 (37.42)	45.24 (33.01)	19.72 (14.39)	137.05 (100.00)

1	2	3	4	5	6
S.C.					
Landless	—	1.00	3.97	—	4 97
Less than 2.5	0.45	6.74	3 60	—	10.79
2.5—5.0	—	2.99	—	—	2.99
5.0—10.0	—	1.00	1.77	—	2.77
10.0 & above	—	—	—	—	—
Total	0.45 (2.09)	11.73 (54.51)	9.34 (43.40)	—	21.52 (100.00)
MUSLIM					
Landless	1.00	3.00	—	—	4.00
Less than 2.5	1.80	0.89	—	1 60	4.29
2.5—5.0	—	3.90	2.32	—	6.22
5.0—10.0	0.80	8.89	3.30	2.60	15.59
10.0 & above	—	—	4.50	0.50	5.00
Total	3.60 (10.26)	16.68 (47.52)	10.12 (28.83)	4.70 (13.39)	35.10 (100.00)
SIKH					
Landless	—	—	—	—	—
Less than 2.5	—	—	—	—	—
2.5—5.0	—	—	—	—	—
5.0—10.0	—	0.63	—	—	0.63
10.0 & above	—	—	—	—	—
Total	—	0.63 (100.00)	— —	— —	0.63 (100.00)
Grand Total	34.34 (10.15)	133.60 (39.49)	117.84 (34.83)	52.53 (15.53)	338.31 (100.00)

N.B.—Figures in parentheses are percentages.

TABLE 10.7

Caste and Size-wise Distribution of Land Purchased by Scheduled Caste in central U.P.

(Area in acres)

SELLERS	SCHEDULED CASTE AS BUYERS				
	Less than 2.5	2.5—5.0	5.0—10.0	10.0 & above	Total
1	2	3	4	5	6
H.C.H.					
Landless	—	3.62	1.88	—	5.50
Less than 2.5	—	—	—	—	—
2.5—5.0	0.83	6.25	0.94	—	8.02
5.0—10.0	1.47	12.54	2.69	—	16.70
10.0 & above	2.00	2.40	3.20	—	7.60
Total	4 30 (11.37)	24.81 (65.60)	8.71 (23.03)	— —	37.82 (100.00)
B.C.					
Landless	0.63	—	2.50	—	3.13
Less than 2.5	3.69	4.04	0.60	—	8.33
2.5—5.0	1.85	—	0.32	—	2.17
5.0—10.0	—	—	3.00	—	3.00
10.0 & above	—	—	—	—	—
Total	6.17 (37.10)	4.04 (24 29)	6.42 (38.61)	— —	16.63 (100.00)

Table 10.7 (*Contd.*)

1	2	3	4	5	6
S.C.					
Landless	—	—	—	—	—
Less than 2.5	2.15	3.23	4.38	—	9.76
2.5—5.0	0.69	0.60	1.61	0.63	3.53
5.0—10.0	—	0.42	—	—	0.42
10.0 & above	—	—	—	—	—
Total	2.84 (20.71)	4.25 (31.00)	5.99 (43.69)	0.63 (4.60)	13.71 (100.00)
MUSLIM					
Landless	—	—	—	—	—
Less than 2.5	—	0.40	1.25	—	1.65
2.5—5.0	—	—	—	—	—
5.0—10.0	—	—	3.55	—	3.25
10.0 & above	—	0.60	—	—	0.60
Total	—	1.00 (18.18)	4.50 (81.82)	—	5.50 (100.00)
SIKH					
Landless	—	—	—	—	—
Less than 2.5	—	—	—	—	—
2.5—5.0	—	—	—	—	—
5.0—10.0	—	—	—	—	—
10.0 & above	—	—	—	—	—
Total	—	—	—	—	—
Grand Total	13.31 (18.07)	34.10 (46.29)	25.62 (34.78)	0.63 (0.86)	73.66 (100.00)

N.B.—Figures in parentheses are percentages.

TABLE 10.8

Caste and Size-wise Distribution of Land Purchased by Muslims in central U P.

(Area in acres)

SELLERS	MUSLIMS AS BUYERS				
	Less than 2.5	2.5—5.0	5.0—10.0	10.0 & above	Total
1	2	3	4	5	6
H.C.H.					
Landless	—	2.63	—	—	2.63
Less than 2.5	—	1.47	—	—	1.47
2.5—5.0	—	1.70	1.25	—	2.95
5.0—10.0	—	3.59	11.90	—	15.49
10.0 & above	—	0.63	7.50	—	8.13
Total	—	10.02 (32.67)	20.65 (67.33)	—	30.67 (100.00)
B.C.					
Landless	—	—	10.63	—	10.63
Less than 2.5	1.91	4.81	1.80	0.80	9.32
2.5—5.0	—	1.29	2.00	—	3.29
5.0—10.0	—	—	4.32	3.60	7.92
10.0 & above	—	1.80	—	—	1.80
Total	1.91 (5.79)	7.90 (23.97)	18.75 (56.89)	4.40 (13.35)	32.96 (100.00)

1	2	3	4	5	6
Landless	—	—	—	0.40	0 40
Less than 2.5	0.60	0.40	—	0.80	1.80
2.5—5.0	—	—	—	—	—
5.0—10.0	—	—	0.57	—	0.57
10.0 & above	—	—	—	—	—
Total	0.60 (21.66)	0.40 (14.44)	0.57 (20.58)	1.20 (43.32)	2.77 (100.00)
MUSLIM					
Landless	—	—	2.20	16.00	18 20
Less than 2.5	2.26	7.32	3.14	—	12.72
2.5—5.0	—	4.72	3.85	—	8.57
5.0—10.0	—	4.80	5.00	0.30	10.10
10.0 & above	—	—	3.53	13.00	16.50
Tctal	26 (3.42)	16.84 (25.48)	17.30 (26.77)	29.30 (44.33)	66.09 (100.00)
SIKH					
Land less	—	—	—	—	—
Less than 2.5	—	—	—	—	—
2.5—5.0	—	—	—	—	—
5.0—10.0	—	—	0.63	—	—
10.0 & above	—	—	—	—	—
Total	—	—	0.63 (100.00)	—	0.63 (100.00)
Grand Total	4.77 (3.58)	35.16 (26.41)	58.20 (43.79)	34.09 (26.22)	133.12 (100.00)

N.B.—Figures in parentheses ore percentages.

44 per cent of the purchased land respectively. The highest category accounted for 26 per cent of the land. High caste Hindus accounted for 23 per cent of the land purchased by Muslims. Backward Castes accounted for one-fourth of the land but Muslims accounted for half of the land purchased by Muslims. Sellers of land to Muslims were more evenly drawn from various categories. Landless accounted for nearly one-fourth of the land and the highest category also accounted for one-fifth of the land that was sold to them.

High caste Hindus as Buyers in western U.P.

Caste and category-wise distribution of land purchased by high caste Hindus in western U.P. is shown in Table 10.9. It will be seen that the respective share of high caste Hindus, Backward Castes, Scheduled Castes, Muslims and Sikhs was 86 per cent, 6 per cent, 6 per cent and 2 per cent in the total land purchased by high caste Hindu in western U.P.

Sellers in the size category of less than 2.5 acres including the landless among high caste Hindus accounted for about 40 per cent of the land that was sold to other high caste Hindus. Similarly the highest category among high caste Hindus accounted for 32 per cent of the land. Among the Backward Castes the bulk of the land was sold by 5—10 acres category to high caste Hindus while among the Scheduled Castes 57 per cent of the land was sold by landless and less than 2.5 acres category. Among the Muslims two-thirds of the land was sold by 2.5—5 acres category

Of all the land purchased by high caste Hindus more than 60 per cent was purchased by the highest category ; the 5—10 acre category came next with 24 per cent followed by 2.5—5 acre category (10 per cent). The lowest category accounted for only 5 per cent of the land. The landless accounted for one-third of the land that was sold and the highest category among the sellers accounted for 29 per cent of the land sold to high caste Hindus.

Backward Caste as Buyers in western U.P.

Caste and size-wise distribution of land purchased by Backward Caste in western U.P. is shown in Table 10.10. It

TABLE 10.9

Caste and Size-Wise Distribution of Land Purchased by High Caste Hindus in Western U.P.

(Area in Acres)

SELLERS	HIGH CASTE HINDUS AS BUYERS				
	Lesf than 2.5	2.5—5 0	5.0—10.0	10.0 & above	Total
1	2	3	4	5	6
H.C.H.					
Landless	2.18	0.63	6.87	70.30	79.98
Less than 2.5	2.53	1.56	1.38	1.25	6.72
2.5—5.0	0.20	3.38	11.22	5.72	20.52
5.0—10.0	0.58	6.79	26.76	9.12	43.25
10.0 & above	3.48	5.63	3.82	59.56	69.49
To:al	8.97	17.99	50.05	142.94	219.96
	(4.08)	(8.18)	(22.75)	(64.99)	(100.00)
B.C.					
Landless	—	—	—	—	—
Less than 2.5	—	0.25	—	0.38	0.63
2.5—5.0	—	3.99	—	—	3.99
5.0—10.0	0.92	—	2.75	1.04	9.21
10.0 & above	—	—	—	0.63	0.63
Total	0.92	4.24	7.52	2.05	14.46
	(6.36)	(29.32)	(50.14)	(14.18)	(100.00)

Table 10.9 (*Contd*).

1	2	3	4	5	6
S.C.					
Landless	—	—	—	3.44	3.44
Less than 2.5	0.93	0.70	3.59	—	5.22
2.5—5.0	—	0.75	—	—	0.75
5.0—10.0	—	—	—	3.75	3.75
10.0 & above	—	—	—	1.87	1.87
Total	0.93 (6.19)	1.45 (9.65)	3.59 (23.89)	9.06 (60.27)	15.03 (100.00)
MUSLIM					
Landless	—	—	—	—	—
Less than 2.5	—	0.60	—	—	0.60
2.5—5.0	2.18	1.34	—	—	3.52
5.0—10.0	—	—	—	—	—
10.0 & above	—	—	1.25	—	1.25
Total	2.18 (40.60)	1.94 (36.12)	1.25 (23.[illegible]8)	—	5.37 (100.00)
SIKH					
Landless	—	—	—	—	—
Less than 2.5	—	—	—	—	—
2.5—5.0	—	—	—	—	—
5.0—10.0	—	—	—	—	—
10.0 & above	—	—	—	—	—
Total	—	—	—	—	—
Grand total	13.00 (5.10)	25.62 (10.05)	62.14 (24.39)	154.06 (60.46)	254.82 (100.00)

N.B.—Figures in parentheses are percentages.

TABLE 10.10

Caste and Size-wise Distribution of Land Purchased by Backward Castes in Western U.P.

(Area in acres)

SELLERS	BACKWARD CASTE AS BUYERS				
	Less than 2.5	2.5—5.0	5.0—10.0	10.0 & above	Total
1	2	3	4	5	6
H.C.H.					
Landless	—	—	—	15.01	15.01
Less than 2.5	0.40	3.93	—	2.32	6.65
2.5—5.0	1.81	4.45	—	0.71	6.97
5.0—10.0	0.20	—	3.45	2.50	6.15
10.0 & above	1.34	1.25	3.33	7.60	13.52
Total	3.75	9.63	6.78	28.14	48.30
	(7.76)	(19.94)	(14.04)	(58.26)	(100.00)
B.C.					
Landless	—	2.50	10.39	4.38	17.27
Less than 2.5	0.36	1.27	—	—	1.63
2.5—5.0	2.09	9.08	1.76	—	12.93
5.0—10.0	—	3.83	5.85	2.15	11.83
10.0 & above	—	—	3.43	21.25	24.68
Total	2.45	16.68	21.43	27.78	68.34
	(3.59)	(24.40)	(31.36)	(40.65)	(100.00)

Table 10.10 (*Contd.*)

1	2	3	4	5	6
S.C.					
Landless	—	4.37	—	—	4.37
Less than 2.5	3.75	1.01	1.88	—	6.64
2.5—5.0	—	1.24	2 50	0.60	4.34
5.0—10.0	—	—	—	—	—
10.0 & above	—	—	—	—	—
Total	3.75 (24.43)	6.62 (43.13)	4.38 (28.53)	0.60 (3.91)	15.35 (100.00)
MUSLIM					
Landless	0.22	—	0.31	—	0.53
Less than 2.5	0.50	1.25	—	0.31	2.06
2,5—5.0	—	3.12	1.62	—	4.74
5.0—10.0	—	—	0.15	1.87	2.02
10.0 & above	—	—	—	—	—
Total	0.72 (7.70)	4.37 (46.74)	2.08 (22.24)	2.18 (23 .32)	9.35 (100.00)
SIRH					
Landless	—	—	—	—	—
Less than 2.5	—	—	—	—	—
2.5—5.0	—	—	—	—	—
5.0—10.0	—	0.32	—	1.10	1.42
10.0 & above	—	—	—	1.10	1.10
Total	—	0.32 (12.70)	—	2.20 (87.30)	2.52 (100.00)
Grand Total	10.67 (7.42)	37.62 (26.15)	34.67 (24.10)	60.90 (42.33)	143.86 (100.00)

N.B.—Figures in parentheses are percentages.

will be seen that the Backward Castes accounted for 47 per cent of the land that was purchased by the same caste followed by high caste Hindu (34 per cent). Scheduled Castes, Muslims and Sikh accounted for 11 per cent, 6 per cent and 2 per cent respectively of the total land purchased by Backwar d Caste.

The lowest category among the Backward Caste accounted for 7 per cent of the land purchased and the next two higher categories accounted for 26 per cent and 24 per cent respectively while the highest category accounted for 42 per cent of the land purchased. Land was sold by all the categories among sellers. The share of landless at 26 per cent was almost equal to that of medium and large farmers (27 per cent).

Scheduled Caste as Buyers in western U.P.

Table 10.11 shows the caste and size-wise distribution of land purchased by Scheduled Caste in western U.P. Interestingly high caste Hindus accounted for 36 per cent of the land purchased by Scheduled Caste. The share of Backward Castes, Scheduled Castes, Muslims and Sikh was 14 per cent, 46 per cent, 3 per cent and 1 per cent respectively. Thus Scheduled Caste also preferred their own caste in land deals.

Another noteworthy aspect of land purchased by Scheduled Caste was that almost three-fourths of the land was purchased by households with less than 5 acres. The respective share of other categories was 14 per cent in case of 5—10 acre category and 13 per cent in case of highest category of 10 acres and above. Landless among of the sellers accounted for 31 per cent of the land sold followed by small farmers (23 per cent) and semi-medium farmers (20 per cent).

Muslims as Buyers in western U.P.

Table 10.12 shows caste and size category-wise distribution of land purchased by Muslims in western U.P. It will be seen that high caste Hindus accounted for 33 per cent of the land that was purchased by Muslims. The share of Backward Caste, Scheduled Castes and Muslims was 8 per cent, 3 per cent and 56 per cent respectively.

Eleven per cent of the land was purchased by the lowest category among Muslims. The next higher category of 2.5—5

TABLE 10.11

Caste and Size-wise Distribution of Land Purchased by Scheduled Caste in Western U.P.

(Area in acres)

SELLERS	SCHEDULED CASTE AS BUYERS				
	Less than 2.5	2.5—5.0	5.0—10.0	10.0 & above	Total
1	2	3	4	5	6
H.C.H.					
Landless	2.00	10.00	—	—	12.00
Less than 2.5	—	2.50	0.63	—	3.13
2.5—5.0	2.54	—	—	—	2.54
5.0—10.0	0.40	3.13	—	8.91	12.44
10.0 & above	—	0.06	1.00	—	1.06
Total	4.94 (15.85)	15.69 (50.34)	1.63 (5.22)	8.91 (28.59)	31.17 (100.00)
B.C.					
Landless	0.72	0.25	—	—	0 97
Less than 2.5	—	0.34	—	—	0.34
2.5—5.0	0.99	2.41	0.35	—	3.75
5.0—10.0	0.86	2.77	—	—	3.63
10.0 & above	—	—	3.43	—	3.43
Total	2.57 (21.20)	5.77 (47.61)	3.78 (31.19)	—	12.12 (100.00)

Table 10.11 (*Contd.*)

1	2	3	4	5	6
S.C.					
Landless	1.51	8.13	2.35	0.63	12.62
Less than 2.5	3.41	3.86	2.03	—	9.30
2.5—5.0	3.77	9.22	0.31	0.25	13.55
5.0—10.0	0.63	—	—	—	0.63
10.0 & above	—	—	1.71	1.39	3.10
Total	9.32 (23.77)	21.21 (54.11)	6.40 (16.33)	2.27 (5.79)	39.20 (100.00)
MUSLIM					
Landless	1.26	—	—	—	1.26
Less than 2.5	—	—	—	—	—
2.5—5.0	—	—	—	—	—
10.0 & above	1.56	—	—	—	1.56
Total	2,82 (100.00)	—	—	—	2.82 (100.00)
SIKH					
Landless	—	—	—	—	—
Less than 2.5	—	—	—	—	—
2.5—5.0	—	—	—	—	—
5,0—10.0	0.32	—	—	—	0.32
10.0 & above	—	—	—	—	—
Total	0.32 (100.00)	—	—	—	0.32 (100.00)
Grand Total	19.97 (23.32)	42.67 (49.83)	11.81 (13.79)	11.18 (13.06)	85.63 (100.00)

N.B.—Figures in parentheses are parcentages.

TABLE 10.12

Caste and Size Category-wise Land Distribution of Land Purchased by Muslim in Western U.P.

(Area in acres)

SELLERS	MUSLIMS AS BUYERS				
	Less than 2.5	2.5—5.0	5.0—10.0	10.0 & above	Total
1	2	3	4	5	6
H.C.H.					
Landless	—	—	—	12.50	12.50
Less than 2.5	1.41	—	3.65	6.25	11.31
2.5—5.0	—	7.02	—	4.77	11.79
5.0—10.0	035	—	—	6.87	7.22
10.0 & above	1.88	—	7.00	1.37	10.25
Total	3.64 (6.86)	7.02 (13.23)	10.65 (20.07)	31.76 (59.84)	53.68 (100.00)
B.C.					
Less than 2.5	2.03	0.78	5.00	—	7 81
Less than 2.5	—	—	—	—	—
2.5—5.0	—	—	—	—	—
5.0—10.0	—	2.56	1.87	—	4.43
10.0 & above	—	—	—	—	—
Total	2.03 (16.58)	3.34 (27.29)	6.87 (56.13)	—	(12.24) (100.00)

Table 10.12 (*Contd.*)

1	2	3	4	5	6
S.C.					
Landless	—	1.09	—	2.50	3.59
Less than 2.5	—	0.40	—	—	0.40
2.5—5.0	—	—	—	—	—
5.0—10.0	—	—	—	—	—
10.0 & above	—	—	—	—	—
Total	—	1.49 (37.34)	—	2.50 (62.66)	3.99 (100.00)
MUSLIM					
Landless	0.47	9.37	10.24	2.42	22.50
Less than 2.5	3.33	4.79	—	1.25	9.37
2.5—5.0	1.78	2.72	2.13	3.80	10.43
5.0—10.0	1.83	3.13	18.84	9.84	33.64
10.0 & above	4.45	4.99	1.39	2.69	13.52
Total	11.86 (13.26)	25.00 (27.24)	32.60 (36.44)	20.00 (22.36)	89.46 (100.00)
SIKH					
Landless	—	—	—	—	—
Less than 2.5	—	—	—	—	—
2.5—5.0	—	—	—	—	—
5.0—10.0	—	—	—	—	—
10.0 & above	—	—	—	—	—
Grand Total	17.53 (11.04)	36.85 (23.21)	50.12 (31.57)	54.26 (34.18)	158.76 (100.00)

N.B —Figures in parentheses are percentages.

acres accounted for 23 per cent of the land whereas the 5—10 acre category accounted for 32 per cent of the land. The share of highest category was highest at 34 per cent. Thus it was the higher categories among Muslims which purchased the bulk of the land. Landless accounted for 29 per cent of the land and semi-medium farmers accounted for nearly the same percentage while medium and large farmers accounted for 15 per cent of the land sold to Muslims in this region.

Sikhs as Buyers in western U.P.

Out of the total land purchased by Sikhs 20 per cent of the land was purchased from high caste Hindus. The share of Backward Caste, Scheduled Caste, Muslim and Sikh was 23 per cent, 1 per cent, 2 per cent and 55 per cent respectively. It is also significant to note that almost the entire land was purchased by those who had 5 acre and above of land The share of the highest category was 51 per cent followed by 48 per cent in the next lower category. Distressingly two-thirds of the alienated land belonged to the landless category.

High Caste Hindus as Buyers in Bundelkhand

High caste Hinus purchased 79 per cent of the land from the same caste group in Bundelkhand. The share of Backward Caste, Scheduled Caste and Muslims was 17 per cent of 4 per-cent and nil respectively. It is significant to note that the lowest category did not purchase any land and the share of 2.5—5 acre category was only 7 per cent while 5-10 acre category accounted for 21 per cent of the land purchased. The bulk of the land was purchased by the highest category of 10 acres and above which accounted for 72 per cent of the total purchased land. All the categories sold land to high caste Hindus and landless did not constitute as high a per-centage as in some other cases. They accounted for only 14 per cent of the sold land. It is interesting to note that 29 per cent of the sold land belonged to the highest category among the sellers. Small farmers among sellers accounted for 26 per cent of the land followed by semi-medium farmers (18 per cent) and marginal farmers (13 per cent).

Backward Caste as Buyers in Bundelkhand

High caste Hindus accounted for 70 per cent of the land

purchased by Backward Caste in this region The share of Backward Caste, Scheduled Caste and Muslims was 12 per cent and 8 per cent respectively. The lowest category among the Backward Caste accounted for 17 per cent of the land purchased. The next higher category accounted for 26 per cent of the land purchased. The higher category accounted for the largest share at 37 per cent. Significantly 46 per cent of the land sold to Backward Caste belonged to 5—10 acre category and landless accounted for only 13 per cent of the land sold to Backward Caste.

Scheduled Caste as Buyers in Bundelkhand

High caste Hindus accounted for 52 per cent, Backward Caste 26 per cent, and Scheduled Caste accounted for 52 per cent of the land purchased by Scheduled Caste in Bundelkhand Significantly 83 per cent of the land was purchased by 2.5—5 acre category and the remaining 17 per cent by 10 and above category. No other category among Scheduled Caste purchased any land. Landless accounted for more than one-third of the land sold and marginal farmers accounted for more than one-fifth of the land sold.

Buyers in Hill Region

In the hill region high caste Hindus and Scheduled Caste alone purchased land ; the former accounted for 85 per cent of the land purchased and the latter remaining 15 per cent. Among the high caste Hindus 58 per cent of the land was purchased by 2.5—5.0 acre category and 42 per cent by the category of 5—10 acres. Among Scheduled Caste the land purchase was confined to less than 2.5 acre category. Of the total land purchased in Hill region half was purchased by 2.5—5 acre category and another 35 per cent by 5—10 acre category and 15 per cent by less than 2.5 acre category.

High Caste Hindus and Buyers in U.P.

For the State as a whole caste and category-wise distribution of land purchased by high caste Hindus is shown in Table 10.13. It will be seen that of the total land purchased by high caste Hindus, 6 per cent was purchased by the lowest category, another 17 per cent was purchased by 2.5—5.0 acre

TABLE 10.13

Caste and Size Category-wise Distribution of Land Purchased by High Caste Hindu in U.P.

(Area in acres)

SELLERS	HIGH CASTE HINDU AS BUYERS				Total
	Less than 2.5	2.5—5.0	5.0—10.0	10.0 & above	
1	2	3	4	5	6
H.C.H.					
Landless	4.34	26.75	35.76	126.26	193.11
Less than 2.5	9.07	17.23	18.94	8.01	53.25
2.5—5.0	4.12	29.10	31.48	25.27	89.97
5.0—10.0	15.61	23.48	55.21	52.70	147.00
10.0 & above	5.86	18.59	27.67	121.02	173.14
Total	39.00	115.15	169.06	333.26	656.47
	(5.94)	(17.54)	(25.75)	(50.71)	(100.00)
B.C.					
Landless	2.72	1.05	24.61	7.95	36.33
Less than 2.5	2.22	12.13	14.27	8.28	36.90
2.5—5.0	2.13	11.15	11.46	15.48	40.22
5.0—10.0	1.12	1.11	18.49	10.84	31.56
10.0 & above	0.40	0.40	0.96	3.43	5.19
Total	8.59	25.84	69.79	45.98	150.20
	(5.72)	(17.20)	(46.47)	(30.61)	(100.00)

Table 10.13 (*Contd.*)

1	2	3	4	5	6
S.C.					
Landless	—	1.91	6.30	7.98	16.19
Less than 2.5	1.51	3.30	5.99	5.20	16.00
2.5—5.0	0.28	1.55	—	—	1.83
5.0—10.0	—	—	1.11	6.60	7.71
10.0 & above	—	—	—	3.87	3.87
Total	1.79 (3.93)	6.76 (14.82)	13.40 (29.39)	23.65 (51.86)	45.60 (100.00)
MUSLIM					
Landless	—	—	4.12	3.15	7.27
Less than 2.5	0.84	2.84	7.00	2.32	13.00
2.5—5.0	2.18	1.66	4.98	1.00	9.82
5.0—10.0	—	—	2.28	—	2.23
10.0 & above	0.94	—	1.25	2.00	4.19
Total	3.96 (10.85)	4.50 (12.33)	19.58 (53.63)	8.47 (23.19)	36.51 (100.00)
SIKH					
Landless	—	—	—	—	—
Less than 2.5	—	—	—	—	—
2.5—5	—	—	—	—	—
5.0—10.0	—	—	—	—	—
10.0 & above	—	—	—	—	—
Total	—	—	—	—	—
Grand Total	53.34 (6.00)	152.25 (17.13)	271.83 (30.59)	411.36 (46.28)	888.78 (100.00)

N.B.—Figures in parentheses are percentages.

category. The two highest categories accounted for 31 per cent and 47 per cent of the land respectively. Thus the land was mainly purchased by higher categories. The share of different castes in the total land purchased by High caste Hindus was : high caste Hindus 74 per cent, Backward caste 17 per cent, Scheduled Caste 5 per cent and Muslims 4 per cent. The preference of high caste Hindus for their own Caste group in land transactions is unmistakable. It will further be seen that all the categories sold land to high caste Hindus. The landless accounted for 28 per cent of the sold land and the highest category among sellers accounted 21 per cent of the sold land.

Backward Caste as Buyers in U.P.

Caste and size-wise distribution of land purchased by Backward Caste in U.P. is shown in Table 10.14. It will be seen that 13 per cent of the land was purchased by lowest category of less than 2.5 acres and another 29 per cent was purchased by 2.5—5 acre category. The share of 5—10 acre category in the total purchases was 33 per cent while that of the highest category was 25 per cent. Thus the two highest categories accounted for 58 per cent of the purchased land. The percentage share of different castes in the total land purchased by Backward Caste was 44 per cent in case of high caste Hindus. The share of Backwgrd Caste was 39 per cent, that of Scheduled Castes 6 per cent and Muslims 11 per cent. It is quite significant that the Backward Caste purchased the largest area of land from high caste Hindus. The latter are generally non-agriculturists while the Backward Castes are generally agriculturists. It signifies a welcome feature in so far as land market is working in favour of Backward Castes which are traditionally agriculturists. All the category sold land to Backward Caste but the share of landless was highest who accounted for one-third of the sold land.

Scheduled Caste as Buyers in U.P.

Caste and size-wise distribution of land purchased by Scheduled Caste in U.P. is shown in Table 10.15. It will be seen that the lowest category among the Scheduled Castes accounted for 27 per cent of the land purchased while the share of 2.5—5 acre category was highest at 42 per cent. The

TABLE 10.14

Caste and Size Category-Wise Distribution of Land Purchased by Backward Caste in U.P.

(Area in acres)

SELLERS	BACKWARD CASTE AS BUYERS				
	Less than 2.5	2.5—5.0	5.0—10.0	10.0 & above	Total
1	2	3	4	5	6
H.C.H.					
Landless	5.55	18.54	36.68	47.06	107.83
Less than 2.5	11.50	17.38	12.27	7.32	48.47
2.5—5.0	15.52	42.92	36.94	10.37	105.75
5.0—10.0	11.46	49.05	35.48	33.01	129.00
10.0 & above	13.74	26.97	41.50	62.29	144.50
Total	55.77	154.86	162.87	160.05	535.55
	(10.79)	(28.92)	(30.41)	(29.88)	(100.00)
B.C.					
Landless	12.24)	46.24	105.51	44.58	208.59
Less than 2.5	17.53	29.24	5.79	9.66	62.22
2.5—5.0	10.81	27.66	18.34	7.33	64.14
5.0—10.0	3.02	25.73	35.84	4.98	69.57
10.0 & above	0.63	3.20	23.06	39.65	66.54
Total	44.23	132.09	188.54	106.20	471.06
	(9.39)	(28.04)	(40.02)	(22.55)	(100.00)

Table 10.14 (*Contd.*)

1	2	3	4	5	6
S.C.					
Landless	—	9.33	4 43	—	13.76
Less than 2.5	5.73	11.14	7.08	2.48	26.43
2.5—5.0	1.76	11.83	3.76	1.65	19.00
5.0—10.0	—	4.15	8.41	1.58	14.14
10.0 & above	—	—	—	—	—
Total	7.49 (10.21)	36.45 (49.71)	23.68 (32.29)	5.71 (7.79)	73.90 (100.00)
MUSLIM					
Landless	44.20	9.25	0.31	25.14	78.90
Less than 2.5	5.40	3.97	2.40	2.31	14.08
2.5—50	1.40	7.65	7.17	1.20	17.12
5.0—10.0	1.48	9.09	5.67	5.27	21.51
10.0 & above	—	—	4.50	0.50	5.00
Total	52.18 (38.20)	29.96 (21.93)	20.05 (14.67)	34.42 (25.20)	136.61 (100.00)
SIKH					
Landless	—	—	—	—	—
Less than 2.5	—	—	—	—	—
2.5—5.0	—	—	—	—	—
5.0—10.0	—	0.95	—	1.10	2.05
10.0 & above	—	—	-	1.10	1.10
Total	—	0.95 (30.16)	—	2.20 (69.84)	3.15 (100.00)
Grand Total	161.67 (13.25)	354.31 (29.05)	395.14 (32.40)	308.58 (25.30)	1219.70 (100.00)

N.B.—Figures in parentheses are percentages.

TABLE 10.15

Caste and Size Category-wise Distribution of land Purchased by Scheduled Caste in U.P.

(Area in acres)

SELLERS	SCHEDULED CASTE AS BUYERS Less than 2.5	2.5—5.0	5.0—10.0	10.0 & above	Total
1	2	3	4	5	6
H.C.H.					
Landless	3.86	14.08	7.55	—	25.49
Less than 2.5	0.85	3.74	3.63	—	8.22
2.5—5.0	5.63	9.56	5.95	1.00	22.14
5.0—10.0	9.08	23.68	3.95	8.91	45.62
10.0 & above	4.19	5.15	4.51	—	13.85
Total	23.61	56.21	25.59	9.91	115.32
	(20 48)	(48.74)	(22.19)	(8.59)	(100.00)
B.C.					
landless	1.75	0.69	2.50	—	4.94
Less than 2.5	5.53	5.03	0.60	4.40	15.56
2.5—5.0	6.89	4.09	0.67	—	11.65
5.0—10.0	1.93	4.27	3.63	—	9.83
10.0 & above	2.29	1.31	3.43	—	7.03
Total	18.39	15.39	10.83	4.40	49.01
	(37.52)	(31.40)	(22.10)	(8.98)	(100.00)

Table 10.15 (*Contd.*)

1	2	3	4	5	6
S.C.					
Landless	4.41	14.54	11.17	0.63	30.75
Less than 2.5	12.07	9.24	6.53	—	27.84
2.5—5.0	5.35	13.06	1.92	0.88	21.21
5.0—10.0	0.63	0.42	—	—	1.05
1.00 & above	1.26	—	1.71	1.39	4.36
Total	23.72 (27.84)	37.26 (43.73)	21.33 (25.03)	2.90 (3.40)	85.21 (100.00)
MUSLIM					
Landless	1.26	—	—	—	1.26
Less than 2.5	—	0.40	1.25	—	1.65
2.5—5.0	0.78	—	—	—	0.78
5.0—10.0	0.63	—	3.25	—	3.88
10.0 & above	1.56	0.60	—	—	2.16
Total	4.23 (43.47)	1.00 (10.28)	4.50 (46.25)	—	9.13 (100.00)
SIKH					
Landless	—	—	—	—	—
Less than 2.5	—	—	—	—	—
2.5—5.3	—	—	—	—	—
5.0—10.0	0.32	—	—	—	0.32
10.0 & above	—	—	—	—	—
Total	0.32 (100.00)	—	—	—	0.32 (100.00)
Grand Total	70.27 (27.07)	109.86 (42.32)	62.25 (23.98)	17.21 (6.63)	259.59 (100.00)

N.B.—Figures in parentheses are percentages.

share of 5—10 acre category was 24 per cent and the highest category accounted for only 7 per cent of the land purchased. Thus the bulk of the land was purchased by lower categories. It will be further seen that all the categories sold land to the Scheduled Castes. Landless among the sellers accounted for one-fourth of the sold land

Muslims as Buyers in U.P.

Caste and size category-wise distribution of land purchased by Muslims in U.P. is shaw in Table 10.16. It will be seen that Muslims purchased almost 61 per cent of the land from other Muslims followed by high caste Hindus (22 per cent), Backward Caste (15 per cent) and Scheduled Caste (2 per cent). The lowest category among Muslims accounted for 10 per cent of the land purchased. Size category of 2.5—5.0 acre accounted for 22 per cent of the land but the 5—10 acre category accounted for 40 per cent of the land purchased. The highest category accounted for 28 per cent of the land. Thus the cultivators in the size category of 2.5 to 10 acres accounted for 90 per cent of the land purchased. Landless among the seller accounted for 44 per cent of the alienated.

Sikhs as Buyers in U.P.

Caste and size-wise distribution of land purchased by the Sikhs in U.P. is shown in Table 10.17. It will be seen that the Sikhs purchased half of the land from their own community. Backward caste came next which accounted for more than one-fourth of the land purchased by the Sikhs followed by high caste Hindus who accounted for 19 per cent of the land. It is striking to note that it was the higher categories which accounted for almost the entire land purchased as 99 per cent of the land was purchased by households having more than 5 acres of land. The bulk of the land purchased was from those who sold their entire holding (landless)

CASTE AND SIZE-WISE DISTRIBUTION OF SOLD LAND

An analysis has been made in the following pages of the land sold by different caste and size categories in different regions of the state. It will be seen that landless among high

TABLE 10.16

Caste and size Category-Wise Distribution of land Purchased by Muslims in U.P

(Area in acres)

SELLERS	MUSLIM AS BUYERS				Total
	Less than 2.5	2.5—5.0	5.0—1.0	10.0 & above	
1	2	3	4	5	6
H.C.H.					
Landless	—	5.15	7.30	14.00	26.45
Less than 2.5	1.41	1.47	3.65	6.25	12.78
2.5—5.0	0.32	8.72	1.25	4.77	15.06
5.0—10.0	1.35	3.59	11.90	6.87	23.71
10.0 & above	3.08	1.00	15.02	1.37	20.47
Total	6.16 (6.26)	19.93 (22.24)	39.12 (39.73)	33.26 (33.77)	98.47 (100.00)
B.C.					
Landless	3.74	7.66	15.63	—	27.03
Less than 2·5	3.67	4.81	1.80	0.80	11.08
2.5—5.0	—	1.29	2.00	—	3.29
5.0—10.0	—	4.16	6.29	3.60	14.05
10.0 & above	3.30	9.80	—	—	13.10
Total	10.71 (15.62)	27.72 (40.44)	25.72 (37.52)	4.40 (6.42)	68.55 (100.00)

Table 10.16 (*Contd.*)

1	2	3	4	5	6
S.C.					
Landless	—	1.09	—	2.90	3.99
Less than 2.5	0.60	1.40	—	0.80	2.80
2.5—5.0	—	—	—	—	—
5.0—10.0	—	—	0.57	—	0.57
10.0 & above	—	—	—	—	—
Total	0.60 (8.15)	2.49 (33.83)	0.57 (7.75)	3.70 (50.27)	7.36 (100.00)
MUSLIM					
Landless	3.46	12.72	66.63	55.69	138.50
Less than 2.5	8.93	12.76	3.60	1.25	26.54
2.5—5.0	4.99	7.44	10.97	3.80	27.20
5.0—10.0	4.32	10.42	24.15	10.14	49.03
10.0 & above	4.45	4.99	4.89	15.69	30.02
Total	26.15 (9.64)	48.33 (17.82)	110.24 (40.63)	86.57 (31.91)	271.29 (100.00)
SIKH					
Landless	—	—	—	—	—
Less than 2.5	—	—	—	—	—
2.5—5.0	—	—	—	—	—
5.0—10.0	—	—	0.63	—	0.63
10.0 & above	—	—	—	—	—
Total	—	—	0.63 (100.00)	—	0.63 (100.00)
Grand Total	43.62 (9.77)	98.47 (22.06)	175.28 (39.50)	127.93 (28.67)	446.30 (100.00)

N.B.—Figures in parentheses are percentaggs.

TABLE 10.17

Caste and Size-Wise Distribution of Land Purchased by the Sikhs in U.P.

(Area in acres)

SELLERS	SIKH AS BUYERS Less than 2.5	2.5—5.0	5.0—10.0	10.0 & above	Total
1	2	3	4	5	6
H.C.H.					
Landless	—	—	—	4.16	4.16
Less than 2.5	—	—	4.53	—	4.53
2.5—5.0	—	—	—	—	—
5.0—10.0	—	—	9.37	—	9.37
10.0 & above	—	—	—	—	—
Total	—	—	13.90 (76.97)	4.16 (23.03)	18.06 (100.00)
B.C.					
Landless	—	—	—	12.50	12.50
Less than 2.5	—	—	—	—	—
2.5—5.0	—	—	3.76	—	3.76
5.0—10.0	—	—	—	0.31	0.31
10.0 & above	—	—	3.80	4.63	8.43
Total	—	—	7.56 (30.24)	17.44 (69.76)	25.00 (100.00)

Table 10.17 (*Contd.*)

S.C.					
Landless	0.44	—	—	—	0.44
Less than 2.5	—	—	0.44	—	0.44
2.5—50	—	—	0.34	—	0.34
5.0—10.0	—	—	—	—	—
10.0 & above	—	—	—	—	—
Total	0.44 (36.07)	—	0.78 (63.93)	—	1.22 (100.00)
MUSLIM					
Landless	—	—	—	—	—
Less than 2.5	—	—	1.87	—	1.87
2.5—5.0	—	—	—	—	—
5.0—10.0	—	—	—	—	—
10.0 & above	—	—	—	—	—
Total	— —	— —	1.87 (100.00)	— —	1.87 (100.00)
SIKH					
Landless	—	0.13	17.88	26.48	44.49
Less than 2.5	—	—	1.88	—	1.88
2.5—5.0	—	—	—	—	—
5.0—10.0	—	0.31	—	3.13	3.44
10.0 & above	—	0.44	19.76	29.61	49.81
Total	—	(0.88) —	(39.67) —	(59.45) —	(100.00) —
Grand Total	0.44 (0.46)	0.44 (0.46)	43.87 (45.72)	51.21 (53.36)	95.96 (100.00)

caste Hindu accounted for 27 per cent of the total land that was sold in eastern U.P. (Table 10.18) to other high caste Hindus. Landless among high caste Hindus accounted for 22 per cent of the land sold to Backward Castes and 77 per cent of the land sold to Muslims. Significantly medium and large farmers among the sellers accounted for the highest percentage of land sold (27 per cent) followed by landless (25 per cent). Semi-medium farmers accounted for 24 per cent of the land sold and the share of small and marginal farmers was 13 per cent and 11 per cent respectively.

Landless accounted for 51 per cent of the land that was sold by Backward Caste in Eastern U.P. (Table 10.19) followed by marginal farmers (15 per cent). The medium and large farmers, semi-medium farmers and small farmers accounted for 12 per cent, 11 per cent and 11 per cent respectively of the land that was sold.

Landless accounted for 35 per cent of the land sold by Scheduled Caste in eastern U.P. (Table 10.20) followed by marginal farmers (25 per cent). Small farmers accounted for 18 per cent of the land while semi-medium, medium and large farmers accounted for 18 per cent and 4 per cent respectively of the land sold.

Landless accounted for 79 per cent of the total land sold by Muslims in this region (Table 10.21) followed by small farmers (9 per cent). The share of marginal and semi-medium farmers was 8 percent and 4 percent respectively. There was no seller of land among medium and large farmers.

Landless accounted for 21 per cent of the total land sold by high caste Hindus in central U.P. (Table 10.22) Semi-medium farmers among the sellers accounted for 29 per cent of the land sold followed by small farmers (27 per cent), medium and large farmers (17 per cent) and marginal farmers (6 per cent).

Landless accounted for 23 per cent of the land sold by Backward Caste in central U.P. (Table 10.23). The marginal farmers among the Backward Caste were the largest sellers of land accounting for 26 per cent of the land. Semi-medium farmers and small farmers accounted for 21 per cent and 20 per cent of the land sold by them whereas the share of medium and large farmers was only 10 per cent.

TABLE 10.18

Caste and Size category-wise Distribution of Land sold by High Caste Hindus in eastern U.P.

(Area in Acres)

BUYERS	HIGH CASTE HINDUS AS SELLERS					Total
	Landless	Less than 2.5	2.5—5.0	5.0—10.0	10.0 & above	
1	2	3	4	5	6	7
H C.H.						
Less than 2.5	2.16	5.91	2.67	15.03	2.38	28.15
2.5—5.0	23.91	10.38	16.18	11.57	9.66	71.70
5.0—10.0	11.20	13.08	8.47	16.04	18.40	67 19
10.0 & above	39.08	1.76	2.71	25.01	41.65	110.21
Total	76.35	31.13	30.03	67.65	72.09	277.25
	(27.54)	(11.23)	(10.83)	(24.40)	(26.00)	(100.00)
B.C.						
Less than 2.5	4.92	9.45	6.73	8.89	11.50	41.49
2.5—5.0	7.77	7.88	17.66	35.46	19.98	88.75
5.0—10.0	31.39	12.27	17.69	15.52	22.08	98.95
10.0 & above	27.05	2,61	1.96	14.38	46.80	92.80
Total	71.13	32.21	44.04	74.25	100.36	321.99
	(22.09)	(10.00)	(13.68)	(23.06)	(31.17)	(100.00)

Table 10.18 (*Contd.*)

1	2	3	4	5	6	7
S.C.						
Less than 2.5	1.86	0.85	1.26	7.21	2.19	13.37
2.5—5.0	0.46	0.94	3.31	8.01	2.69	15.41
5.0—10.0	5.67	3.00	5.01	1.26	0.31	15.25
10.0 & above	—	—	—	—	—	—
Total	7.99	4.79	9.58	16.48	5.19	44.03
	(18.15)	(10.88)	(21.76)	(37.43)	(11.78)	(100.00)
MUSLIM						
Less than 2.5	—	—	0.32	1.00	1.20	2.52
2.5—5.0	2.52	—	—	—	0.37	2.89
5.0—10.0	7.30	—	—	—	0.52	7.82
10.0 & above	1.50	—	—	...	—	1.50
Total	11.32	—	0.32	1 00	2.09	14.73
	(76 85)	—	(2.17)	(6.79)	(14.19)	(100.00)
SIKHS	—	—	—	—	—	—
Grand Total	166.79	68.13	83.97	159.38	179.73	658.00
	(25.34)	(10.35)	(12.76)	(24.33)	(27.32)	(100.00)

N.B.—Figures in parentheses are percentages.

TABLE 10.19

Category-wise Distribution of Land Sold by Backward Caste in eastern U.P.

(Area in acres)

BUYERS	BACKWARD CASTE AS SELLERS					Total
	Landless	Less than 2.5	2.5—5.0	5.0—10.0	10.0 & above	
1	2	3	4	5	6	7
H.C.H.						
Less than 2.5	2.72	1.73	1.93	0.20	040	6.98
2.5—5.0	0.56	7.67	1.53	1.11	0.40	11.27
5.0—10.0	8.25	8.53	3.43	5.49	0.08	25.78
10.0 & above	—	3.56	1.98	7.30	2.80	15.64
Total	11.53 (19.3)	21.49 (36.01)	8.87 (14.87)	14.10 (23.63)	3.68 (6.17)	59.67 (100.00)
B.C.						
Less than 2.5	2.44	8.11	6.40	2.39	0.63	19.97
2.5—5.0	38.46	7.57	7.11	9.01	0.40	62.55
5.0—10.0	86.48	3.19	7.13	11.04	13.03	120.87
10.0 & above	38.32	5.45	5.73	2.20	7.00	58.70
Total	165.70 (63.22)	24.32 (9.28)	26.37 (10.05)	24.64 (9.40)	21.06 (8.04)	262.09 (100.00)

Table 10.19 (*Contd.*)

1	2	3	4	5	6	7
S.C.						
Less than	0.40	1.48	1.05	1.07	2.29	9.65
2.5—5.0	0.44	0.65	1.68	—	1.31	4.08
5.0—10.0	—	—	—	0.63	—	0.63
10.0 & above	—	4.40	—	—	—	4.40
Total	0.84 (4.48)	6.89 (36.73)	5.73 (30.54)	1.70 (9.06)	3.60 (19.19)	18.76 (100.00)
MUSLIM						
Less than 2.5	1.71	1.76	—	—	3.30	6.77
2.5—5.0	6.88	—	—	1.60	8.00	16.48
5.0—10.0	—	—	—	0.10	—	0.10
10.0 & above	—	—	—	—	—	—
Total	8.59 (36.79)	1.76 (7.54)	—	1.70 (7.28)	11.30 (48.39)	23.35 (100.00)
SIKHS	—	—	—	—	4.00 (9.17)	4.00 (1.09)
[illegible]	186.66 [illegible]	54.46 (14.81)	40.97 (11.14)	42.14 (11.46)	43.64 (11.86)	367.87 (100.00)

TABLE 10.20

Caste and Size Category-Wise Distribution of Land Sold by Scheduled Caste in eastern U.P.

(Area in acres)

BUYERS	SCHEDULE CASTE AS SELLERS					Total
	Landless	Less than 2.5	2.5—5.0	5.0—10.0	10.0 & above	
1	2	3	4	5	6	7
H.C.H.						
Less than 2.5	—	0.58	0.28	—	—	0.86
2.5—5.0	1.91	1.15	—	—	—	3.06
5.0—10.0	6.30	—	—	1.11	—	7.41
10.0 & above	3.29	3.60	—	2.85	2.00	11.74
Total	11.50 (49.85)	5.33 (23.10)	0.28 (1.21)	3.96 (17.17)	2.00 (8.67)	23.07 (100.00)
B.C.						
Less than 2,5	—	1.53	1.76	—	—	3.29
2.5—5.0	2.36	3.39	7.60	3.15	—	16.50
5.0—10.0	0.46	0.60	1.26	6.64	—	8.96
10.0 & above	—	2.16	1.05	1.58	—	4.79
Total	2.82 (8.41)	7.68 (22.90)	11.67 (34.79)	11.37 (33.90)	—	33.54 (100.00)

Table 10.20 (*Contd.*)

1	2	3	4	5	6	7
S.C.						
Less than 2.5	2.90	6.51	0.89	—	1.26	11.56
2.5—5,0	4.41	1.15	3.24	—	—	8.80
5.0—10.0	8.82	0.12	—	—	—	8.94
10.0 & above	—	—	—	—	—	—
Total	16.13 (55.05)	7.78 (26.55)	4.13 (14.10)	—	1.26 (4.36)	29.30 (100.00)
MUSLIM						
Less than 2.5	—	—	—	—	—	—
2.5—5.0	—	0.60	—	—	—	0.60
5.0—10.0	—	—	—	—	—	—
10.0 & above	—	—	—	—	—	
Total	—	0.60 (100.00)	—	—		0.60 (100.00)
SIKHS	—	—	—	—	—	—
Grand Total	30.45 (35.20)	21.39 (24.73)	16.08 (18.58)	15.33 (17.72)	3.26 (3.77)	86.15 (100.00)

N.B.—Figures in parentheses are percentages.

TABLE 10.21

Caste and Size Category wise Distribution of Land Sold by Muslim in eastern U.P.

(Area in Acres)

BUYERS	MUSLIMS AS SELLERS					Total
	Landless	Less than 2.5	2.5—5.0	5.0—10.0	10.0 & above	
1	2	3	4	5	6	7
H.C.H.						
Less than 2.5	—	0.84	—	—	—	0.84
2.5—5.0	—	2.00	0.32	—	—	2.32
5.0—10.0	4.12	2.00	4.55	0.31	—	10.98
10.0 & above	3.15	0.92	—	—	—	4.07
Total	7.27 (39.92)	5.76 (31.63)	4.87 (26.75)	0.31 (1.70)	—	18.21 (100.00)
B.C.						
Less than 2.5	42.00	3.10	1.10	0.68	—	46.88
2,5—5.0	4.73	1.83	0.63	0.20	—	7.39
5.0—10.0	—	2.40	3.23	2.22	—	7.85
1.00 & above	25.14	0.40	1.20	0.80	—	27.54
Total	71.87 (80.16)	7.73 (8.62)	6.16 (6.87)	3.90 (4.35)	—	89.66 (100.00)

Table 10.21 (*Contd.*)

1	2	3	4	5	6	7
S.C.						
Less than 2.5	—	—	0.78	0.63	—	1.41
2.5—5.0	—	—	—	—	—	—
5.0—10.0	—	—	—	—	—	—
10.0 & above	—	—	—	—	—	—
Total	—	—	0.78	0.63	—	1.41
			(55.32)	(44.68)		(100.00)
MUSLIM						
Less than 2.5	2.99	3.34	3.31	2.49	—	12.03
2.5—5.0	3.35	0.65	—	2.49	—	6.49
5.0—10.0	54.18	0.46	5.00	0.31	—	59.95
10.0 & above 4	37.27	—	—	—	—	37.27
Total	97.79	4.45	8.21	5.28	—	115.74
	(84.49)	(3.85)	(7.09)	(4.57)		(100.00)
SIKHS	—	—	—	—	—	—
Grand Total	176.93	17.94	20.02	10.13	—	225.02
	(78.62)	(7.97)	(9.80)	(4.51)		(100.00)

N.B.—Figures in parentheses are percentages.

TABLE 10.22

Caste and Size Category-wise Distribution of Land Sold by High Caste Hindus in central U.P.

(Area in aeres)

BUYERS	HIGH CASTE HINDUS AS SELLERS					Total
	Landless	Less than 2.5	2.5—5.0	5.0—10.0	10.0 & above	
1	2	3	4	5	6	7
H.C.H.						
Less than 2.5	—	0.63	1.25	—	—	1.88
2.5—5.0	2.21	4.59	7.74	1.77	1.00	17.31
5.0—10.0	11.69	1.18	10.19	11.51	2.95	37.52
10.0 & above	16.88	—	1.00	3.94	—	21.82
Total	30.78 (39.20)	6.40 (8.15)	20.18 (25.70)	17.22 (21.93)	3.95 (502)	78.53 (100.00)
B.C.						
Less than 2.5	0.63	1.65	6.03	1.17	—	9.48
2.5—5.0	10.77	5.57	20.21	11.99	4.74	53.28
5.0—10.0	5.29	—	15.25	16.51	16.09	53.14
10.0 & above	5.00	2.29	7.70	5.13	7.89	28.11
Total	21.69 (15.06)	9.61 (6.67)	49.19 (34.16)	34.80 (24.16)	28.72 (19.95)	144.01 (100.00)

Table 10.22 (*Contd.*)

1	2	3	4	5	6	7
Less than 2.5	—	—	0.83	1.47	2.00	4.30
2.5—5.0	3.62	—	6.25	12.54	2.40	24.81
5.0—10.0	1.88	—	0.94	2.69	3.20	8.71
10.0 & above	—	—	—	—	—	—
Total	5.50 (14.54)	—	8.02 (21.20)	16.70 (44.16)	7.60 (20.10)	37.82 (100.00)
Less than 2.5	—	—	—	—	—	—
2.5—5.0	2.63	1.47	1.70	3.59	0.63	10.02
5.0—10.0	—	—	1.25	11.90	7.50	20.65
10.0 & above	—	—	—	—	—	—
Total	2.63 (8.58)	1.47 (4.79)	2.95 (9.62)	15.49 (50.50)	8.13 (26.51)	30.67 (100.00)
SIKHS	—	—	—	—	—	—
Grand Total	60.60 (20.83)	17.48 (6.01)	80.34 (27.60)	84.21 (28.93)	48.40 (16.63)	291.03 (100.00)

N.B.—Figures in parentheses are percentages.

TABLE 10.23

Caste and Size Category-wise Distribution of Land Sold by Backward Caste in central U.P.

(Area in acres)

BUYERS	BACKWARD CASTE AS SELLERS					Total
	Landless	Less than 2.5	2.5–5.3	5.0—10.0	10.0 & above	
1	2	3	4	5	6	7
H.C.H.						
Less than 2.5	—	0.49	0.20	—	—	0.69
2.5—5.0	0.49	3.66	5.23	—	—	9.38
5.0—10.0	12.61	5.44	4.73	5.75	0.88	29.41
10.0 & above	5.23	1.60	12.05	1.00	—	19.88
Total	18.33 (30.88)	11.19 (18.85)	22.21 (37.42)	6.75 (11.37)	0.88 (1.48)	59.36 (100.00)
B.C.						
Less than 2,5	9.80	9.00	1.32	0.63	—	20.81
2.5—5.0	5.30	11.82	18.47	12.89	2.80	51.28
5.0—10.0	8.64	2.60	8.45	18.95	6.60	45.24
10.0 & above	1.88	4.21	1.60	0.63	11.40	19.72
Total	25.62 (18.69)	34.69 (28.31)	22.84 (16.67)	33.10 (24.15)	20.80 (15.18)	137.05 (100.00)

Table 10.23 (*Contd.*)

1	2	3	4	5	6	7
S.C.						
Less than 2.5	0.63	3.69	1.85	—	—	6.17
2.5—5.0	—	4.04	—	—	—	4.04
5.0—10.0	2.50	0.60	0.32	3.00	—	6.42
10.0 & above	—	—	—	—	—	—
Total	3.13	8.33	2.17	3.00	—	16.63
	(18.82)	(50.09)	(13.05)	(18.04)		(100.00)
MUSLIM						
Less than 2.5	—	1.91	—	—	—	1.91
2.5—5.0	—	4.81	1.29	—	1.80	7.90
5.0—10.0	10.63	1.80	2.00	4.32	—	18.75
10.0 & above	—	0.80	—	3.60	—	4.40
Total	10.63	9.32	3.29	7.92	1.80	32.96
	(32.25)	(28.28)	(9.98)	(24.03)	(5.46)	(100.00)
SIKHS	—	—	—	—	—	—
Grand Total	57.71	63.53	50.51	50.77	23.48	246.00
	(23.45)	(25.85)	(20.54)	(20.63)	(9.55)	(100.00)

N.B.—Figures in parentheses are percentages.

Landless accounted for 13 per cent of total land sold by Scheduled Caste in central U.P. (Table 10.24) but significantly marginal farmers were the largest sellers of land among Scheduled Caste as they accounted for 62 per cent of the land followed by small farmers (16 per cent) and semi-medium farmers (9 per cent).

Landless accounted for 18 per cent of the land sold by Muslims in central U.P. (Table 10.25) Semi-medium farmers among Muslims accounted for 26 per cent of the land sold followed by marginal farmers (21 per cent), medium and large farmers (21 per cent) and small farmers (13 per cent). Among the Sikhs in central U.P. semi-medium farmers were the sole sellers of land.

In western U.P (Table 10.26) out of the total land sold by high caste Hindus landless accounted for the largest proportion of land accounting for 33 per cent of the land followed by medium and large farmers (26 per cent), semi-medium farmers (21 per cent), small farmers (11 per cent) and marginal farmers (9 per cent).

Of the total land sold by Backward Caste in this region (Table 10.27) landless among the sellers accounted for the largest percentage of land sold accounting for 30 per cent of the land followed by medium and large farmers (26 per cent), semi-medium farmers (23 per cent), small farmers (19 per cent) and marginal farmers (2 per cent).

Of the total land sold by Scheduled Caste in this region (Table 10.28) landless among the sellers accounted for the highest share (33 per cent) followed by marginal farmers (29 per cent), small farmers (25 per cent), medium and large farmers (7 per cent) and semi-medium farmers (6 per cent).

Significantly the semi-medium farmers were the largest sellers of land among Muslims in this region (Table 10.29) as 33 per cent of the land was sold by them followed by landless (22 per cent), small farmers (17 per cent), medium and large farmers (15 per cent) and marginal farmers (13 per cent).

Of the total land sold by Sikhs in this region significantly the landless among them accounted for 84 per cent of the land sold followed by semi-medium farmers (10 per eent), marginal farmers (4 per cent) and medium and large farmers (2 per cent).

TABLE 10.24

Caste and Size Category-wise Distribution of land Sold by Scheduled Caste in central U.P.

(Area in acres)

BUYERS	SCHEDULE CASTE AS SELLERS					Total
	Landless	Less than 2.5	2.5—5.0	5.0—10.0	10.0 & above	
1	2	3	4	5	6	7
H.C.H.						
Less than 2.5	—	—	—	—	—	—
2.5—5.0	—	1.45	—	—	—	1.45
5.0—10.0	—	1.40	—	—	—	1.40
10.0 & above	—	—	—	—	—	—
Total	—	2.85 (100.00)	—	—	—	2.85 (100.00)
B.C.						
Less than 2.5	—	0.45	—	—	—	0.45
2.5—5.0	1.00	6.74	2.99	1.00	—	11.73
5.0—10.0	3.97	3.60	—	1.77	—	9.34
10.0 & above	—	—	—	—	—	—
Total	4.97 (23.09)	10.79 (50.14)	2.99 (13.90)	2.77 (12.87)	—	21.52 (100.00)

Table 10.24 (*Contd.*)

S.C.						
Less than 2.5	—	2.15	0.69	—	—	2.84
2.5—5.0	—	3.23	0.60	0.42	—	4.25
5.0—10.0	—	4.38	1.61	—	—	5.99
10.0 & above	—	—	0.63	—	—	0.63
Total	—	9.76 (71.19)	3.53 (25 75)	0 42 (3.06)	—	13.71 (100.00)
MUSLIM						
Less than 2.5	—	0.60	—	—	—	0.60
2.5—5.0	—	0.40	—	—	—	0.40
5.0—10.0	—	—	—	0.57	—	0.57
10.0 & above	0.40	0.80	—	—	—	1.20
Total	4.40 (14.44)	1.80 (64.98)	—	0.57 (20.58)	—	2.77 (100.00)
SIKHS	—	—	—	—	—	—
Grand Total	5.37 (13.15)	25.20 (61.68)	6.52 (15.96)	3.76 (9.21)	—	40.85 (100.00)

N.B.—Figures in parentheses are percentages.

TABLE 10.25

Caste and Size Category-wise Distribution of Land Sold by Muslims in central U.P.

(Area in acres)

BUYERS	MUSLIMS AS SELLERS					Total
	Landless	Less than 2.5	2.5—5.0	5.0—10.0	10.0 & above	
1	2	3	4	5	6	7
H.C.H.						
Less than 2.5	—	—	—	—	0.94	0.94
2.5—5.0	—	0.24	—	—	—	0.24
5.0—10.0	—	5.00	0.43	1.92	—	7.35
10.0 & above	—	1.40	1.00	—	2.00	4.40
Total	—	6.64 (51.35)	1.43 (11.06)	1.92 (14.85)	2.94 (22.74)	12.93 (100.00)
B.C.						
Less th in 2.5	1.00	1.80	—	0.80	—	3.60
2.5—5.0	3.00	0.89	3.90	8.89	—	16.68
5.0—10.0	—	—	2.32	3.30	4.50	10.12
10.0 & above	—	1.60	—	2.60	0.50	4.70
Total	4.00 (11.40)	4.29 (12.22)	6.22 (17.72)	15.59 (44.41)	5.00 (14.24)	35.10 (100.00)

Table 10.25 (*Contd.*)

S.C.						
Less than 2.5	—	0.40	—	—	0.60	1.00
2.5—5.0	—	1.25	—	3.25	—	4.50
5.0—10.0	—	—	—	—	—	—
10.0 & above	—	—	—	—	—	—
Total	—	1.65 (30.00)	—	3.25 (59.09)	0.60 (10.91)	5.50 (100.00)
MUSLIM						
Less than 2.5	—	2.26	—	—	—	2.26
2.5—5.0	—	7.32	4.72	4.80	—	16.84
5.0—10.0	2.20	3.14	3.85	5.00	3.50	17.69
10.0 & above	16.00	—	—	0.30	13.00	29.30
Total	18.20 (27.54)	12.72 (19.25)	8.57 (12.97)	10.10 (15.28)	16.50 (24.96)	66.09 (100.00)
SIKHS	—	—	—	—	—	—
Grand Total	22.20 (18.55)	25.30 (21.15)	16.22 (13.56)	30.86 (25.80)	25.04 (20.94)	119.62 (100.00)

N.B.—Figures in parentheses are percentages.

TABLE 10.26

Caste and Size Category-wise Distribution of Land Sold by High Caste Hindu in western U.P.

(Area in Acres)

BUYERS	HIGH CASTE HINDUS AS SELLERS					Total
	Landless	Less than 2.5	2.5—5.0	5.0—10.0	10.0 & above	
1	2	3	4	5	6	7
H.C.H.						
Less than 2.5	2.18	2.53	0.20	0.58	3.48	8.97
2.5—5.0	0.63	1.56	3.28	6.79	5.63	17.99
5.0—10.0	6.87	1.38	11.22	26.76	3.82	50.05
10.0 & above	70.30	1.25	5.72	9.12	56.66	142.95
Total	79.98 (36.36)	6.72 (31.59)	20.52 (9.33)	43.25 (19.66)	69.49 (3.06)	219.96 (100.00)
B.C.						
Less than 2.5	—	0.40	1.81	0.20	1.34	3.75
2.5—5.0	—	3.93	4.45	—	1.25	9.63
5.0—10.0	—	—	—	3.45	3.33	6.78
10.0 & above	15.01	2.32	0.71	2.50	7.60	28.14
Total	15.01 (31.08)	6.65 (13.77)	6.97 (14.43)	6.15 (12.73)	13.52 (27.99)	48.30 (100.00)

Table 10.26 (*Contd*))

1	2	3	4	5	6	7
S.C.						
Less than 2.5	2.00	—	2.54	0.40	—	4.94
2.5 – 5.0	1.00	2.50	—	3.13	0.06	15.69
5.0 – 10.0	—	0.63	—	—	1.00	1,63
10.0 & above	—	—	—	8.91	—	8.91
Total	12.00 (38.50)	3.13 (10.04)	2.54 (8.15)	12.44 (39.91)	1.06 (3.40)	31.17 (100.00)
MUSLIM						
Less than 2.5	—	1.41	—	0.35	1.88	3.64
2.5—5.0	—	—	7.02	—	—	7.02
5.0—10.0	—	3.65	—	—	7.00	10.65
10.0 & above	12.50	6.25	4.77	6.87	1.37	31.76
Total	12.50 (23.54)	11.31 (21.31)	11.79 (22.22)	7.22 (13.61)	10.25 (19.32)	53.07 (100.00)
SIKH						
Less than 2.5	—		—	—	—	—
2.5—5.0	—	—	—	—	—	—
5.0—10.0	—	4,53	—	9.37	—	13.90
10.0 & above	4.16	—	—	—	—	4.16
Total	4.16 (23.03)	4.53 (25.08)	—	9.37 (51.89)	—	18.06 (100.00)
Grand Total	123.65 (33.37)	32.34 (8.74)	41.82 (11.28)	78.43 (21.17)	94.32 (25.45)	370.56 (100.00)

N.B.—Figures in parentheses are percentages,

Of the total land sold by high caste Hindus in Bundelkhand significantly the medium and large farmers acoounted for 31 per cent of the land that was sold followed by semi-medium farmers (30 per cent), small farmers (26 per cent), marginal farmers (7 per cent) and landless (6 per cent). There was thus a positive relationship between the size of holding and area sold.

Of the total land sold by the Backward Caste in this region small farmers accounted for 33 per cent of the land followed by landless (29 per cent), marginal farmers (24 per cent) and semi-medium farmers (14 per cent).

Of the total land sold by Scheduled Caste in this region marginal farmers accounted for 47 per cent of the land followed by landless (46 per cent) and small farmers (7 per cent). Significantly the landless among the Muslims were the sole sellers of land in this region.

In the Hill region the land was sold only by high caste Hindus. Marginal and semi-medium farmers were the sellers of land among them in equal measures.

In the State as a whole (Table 10.30) out of the total land sold by high Caste Hindus, landless, semi-medium and medium and large farmers were the largest groups of sellers of land and they accounted for 25 per cent each of land sold while the share of small and marginal farmers was 16 per cent and 9 per cent respectively.

Of the total land sold by Backward Caste (Table 10.31) in the State landless accounted for the largest share of land (38 per cent) followed by marginal farmers (17 per cent), semi-medium farmers and small farmers (16 per cent each) and medium and large farmers (13 per cent).

Of the total land sold by Scheduled Caste (Table 10.32) in the State marginal farmers accounted for 34 per cent of the land followed by landless (31 per cent), small farmers (20 per cent) semi-medium farmers (11 per cent) and medium and large farmers (4 per cent).

Of the total land sold by Muslims (Table 10.33) landless accounted for the largest share of land (50 per cent) followed by semi-medium farmers (17 per cent), marginal farmers (12

TABLE 10.27

Caste and Size Category-wise Distribution of Land Sold by Backward Caste in western U.P.

(Area in acres)

BUYERS	BACKWARD CASTE AS SELLERS					Total
	Landless	Less than 2.5	2.5—5.0	5.0--10.0	10.0 & above	
1	2	3	4	5	6	7
H.C.H.						
Less than 2.5	—	—	—	0.92	—	0,92
2.5—5.0	—	0.25	3.99	—	--	4.24
5.0—10.0	—	—	—	7.25	—	7.25
10.0 & above	—	0.38	—	1.04	0.63	2.05
Total	—	0.63 (4.36)	3.99 (27.59)	9.21 (63.69)	0.63 (4.36)	14.46 (100.00)
B.C.						
Less than 2.5	.	0.36	2.09	—	—	2.45
2.5—5.0	2.50	1.27	9.08	3.83	—	16.68
5.0—10.0	10.39	—	1.76	5.85	3,43	21.43
10.0 & above	4.38	—	—	2.15	21.25	27.78
Total	17.27 (25.27)	1.63 (2.39)	12.93 (18.92)	11.83 (17.31)	24.68 (36.11)	68.34 (100.00)

Table 10.27 (*Contd.*)

1	2	3	4	5	6	7
S.C.						
Less than 2.5	0.72	—	0,99	0.86	—	2.57
2.5—5.0	0.25	0.34	2.41	2.77	—	5.77
5.0—10.0	—	—	0.35	—	3.43	3.78
10.0 & above	—	—	—	—	—	—
Total	0.97 (8.00)	0.34 (2.81)	3.75 (30.94)	3.63 (29.95)	3.43 (28.30)	12.12 (100.00)
MUSLIM						
Less than 2.5	2.03	—	—	—	—	2.03
2.5—5.0	0.78	—	—	2.56	—	3.34
5.0—10.0	5.00	—	—	1.87	—	6.87
10.0 & above	—	—	—	—	—	—
Total	7.81 (63.81)	—	—	4.43 (36.19)	—	12.24 (100.00)
SIKH						
Less than 2,5	—	—	—	—	—	—
2.5—5.0	—	—	—	—	—	—
5.0—10.0	—	—	3.76	—	3.80	7.56
10.0 & above	12.50	—	—	0.31	0.63	13.44
Total	12.50 (59.52)	—	3.76 (17.90)	0.31 (1.48)	4.43 (21.10)	21.00 (100.00)
Grand Total	38.55 (30.08)	2.60 (2.03)	24.43 (19.06)	29.41 (22.95)	33.17 (25.88)	128.16 (100.00)

N.B.—Figures in parentheses are percentages.

TABLE 10.28

Caste and Size Category-wise Distribution of Land Sold by Scheduled Caste in western U.P.

(Area in acres)

BUYERS	SCHEDULED CASTE AS SELLERS					Total
	Landless	Less than 2.5	2.5—5.0	5.0—10.0	10.0 & above	
1	2	3	4	5	6	7
H.C.H.						
Less than 2.5	—	9.93	—	—	—	0.93
2.5—5.0	—	0.70	0.75	—	—	1.45
5.3—10.0	—	3.59	—	—	—	3.59
10.0 & above	3.44	—	—	3.75	1.87	9.06
Total	3.44 (22.89)	5.22 (34.73)	0.75 (4.99)	3.75 (24.95)	1.87 (12.44)	15.03 (100.00)
B.C.						
Less than 2.5	—	3.75	—	—	—	3.75
2.5—5.0	4.37	1.01	1.24	—	—	6.62
5.0—10.0	—	1.88	2.50	—	—	4.38
10.0 & above	—	—	0.60	—	—	0.60
Tctal	4.37 (28.47)	6.64 (43.26)	4.34 (28.27)	—	—	15.35 (100.00)

Table 10.28 (*Contd.*)

1	2	3	4	5	6	7
S.C.						
Less than 2.5	1.51	3.41	3.77	0.63	—	9.32
2.5—5.0	8.13	3.86	9.22	—	—	21.21
5.0—10.0	2.35	2.03	0.31	—	1.71	6.40
10.0 & above	0.63	—	0.25	—	1.39	2.27
Total	12.62 (32.19)	9.30 (23.72)	13.55 (34.57)	0.63 (1.61)	3.10 (7.91)	39.20 (100.00)
MUSLIM						
Less than 2.5	—	—	—	—	—	—
2.5—5.0	1.09	0.40	—	—	—	1.49
5.0—10.0	—	—	—	—	—	—
10.0 & above	2.50	—	—	—	—	2.50
Total	3.59 (89.97)	0.40 (10.03)	—	—	—	3.99 (100.00)
SIKH						
Less than 2.5	0.44	—	—	—	—	0.44
2.5—5.0	—	—	—	—	—	—
5.0—10.0	—	0.44	0.34	—	—	0.78
10.0 & above	—	—	—	—	—	—
Total	0.44 (36.07)	0.44 (36.07)	0.34 (27.86)	—	—	1.22 (100.00)
Grand Total	24.46 (32.70)	22.00 (29.42)	18.98 (25.38)	4.38 (5.86)	4.97 (6.64)	74.79 (100.00)

N.B.—Figures in parentheses are percentages.

TABLE 10.29

Caste and Size Category-wise Distribution of Land Sold by Muslims in Western U.P.

(Area in acres)

BUYERS	MUSLIM AS SELLERS					Total
	Landless	Less than 2.5	2.5—5.0	5.0—10.0	10.0 & above	
1	2	3	4	5	6	7
H.C.H.						
Less than 2.5	—	—	2.18	—	—	2.18
2.5—5.0	—	0.60	1.34	—	—	1.94
5.0—10.0	—	—	—	—	1.25	1.25
10.0 & above	—	—	—	—	—	—
Total	—	0.60 (11.17)	3.52 (65.55)	—	1.25 (23.28)	5.37 (100.00)
B.C.						
Less than 2.5	0.22	0.50	—	—	—	0.72
2.5—5.0	—	1.25	3.12	—	—	4.37
5,0—10.0	0.31	—	1.62	0.15	—	2.08
10.0 & above	—	0.31	—	1.87	—	2.18
Total	0.53 (5.67)	2.06 (22.03)	4.74 (50.70)	2.02 (21.60)	—	9.35 (100.00)

Table 10.29 (*Contd.*)

1	2	3	4	5	6	7
S.C.						
Less than 2.5	1.26	—	—	—	1.56	2.82
2.5—10.0	—	—	—	—	—	—
5.0—10,0	—	—	—	—	—	—
10.0 & above	—	—	—	—	—	—
Total	1.26 (44.68)	—	—	—	1.56 (55.32)	2.82 (100.00)
MUSLIM						
Less than 2.5	0.47	3.33	1.78	1.83	4.45	11.86
2.5—5.0	9.37	4.79	2.72	3.13	4.99	25.00
5.0—10.0	10.24	—	3. 13	18.84	1.39	32.60
10.0 & above	2.42	1.25	3.80	9.84	2.69	20.00
Total	22.50 (25.13)	9.37 (10.47)	10.43 (11.66)	33.64 (37.60)	13.52 (15.12)	89.46 (100.00)
SIKH						
Less than 2.5	—	—	—	—	—	—
2.5—5.0	—	—	—	—	—	—
5.0—10.0	—	1.87	—	—	—	1.87
10.0 & above	—	—	—	—	—	—
Total	—	1.87 (100.00)	—	—	—	1.87 (100.00)
Grand Total	24.29 (22.31)	13.90 (12.76)	18.69 (17.17)	35.66 (32.26)	16.33 (15.00)	108.87 (100.00)

N.B. —Figures in parentheses are percentages.

TABLE 10.30

Caste and Size Castegory-wise Distribution of Land Sold by High Caste Hindus in U.P.

BUYERS	HIGH CASTE HINDUS AS SELLERS					
	Land less	Less than 2.5	2.5—5.0	5.0—10.0	10.0 & above	Total
1	2	3	4	5	6	7
H.C.H.						
Less than 2.5	4.35	9.07	4.12	15.61	5.86	39.00
2.5—5.0	26.75	17.23	29.10	23.48	18.59	115.15
5.0—10.0	35.76	18.94	31.48	55.21	67.67	169.06
10.0 & above	126.26	8.01	25.27	52.70	121.02	333.26
Total	193.11 (29.42)	53.25 (8.11)	89.97 (13.71)	147.00 (22.29)	173.14 (26.47)	656.47 (100.00)
B.C.						
Less than 2.5	5.55	11.50	15.52	11.46	13.74	57.77
25.—5.0	18.54	17.38	42.92	49.05	26,97	154.86
5.0—10.00	36.68	12.27	36.94	35.48	41.50	162.87
10.0 & above	47.06	7.32	10.37	33.01	62.29	160.05
Total	107.83 (20.13)	48.47 (9.05)	105.75 (19.75)	129.00 (24.09)	144,50 (26.98)	535.55 (100.00)

Table 10.30 (*Contd.*)

1	2	3	4	5	6	7
S.C.						
Less than 2.5	3.86	0.85	5.63	9.08	4.19	23.61
2.5—5.0	14.08	3.74	9.56	23.68	5.15	56.21
5.0—10.00	7.55	3.63	5.95	3.95	4.51	25.59
10.0 above	—	—	1.00	8.91	—	9.91
Total	25.49	8.22	22.14	45.62	13.85	115.32
	(22.10)	(7.13)	(19.20)	(39.56)	(12.01)	(100.00)
MUSLIM						
Less than 2.5	—	1.41	0.32	1.35	3.08	6.16
2.5—5.0	5.15	1.47	8.72	3.59	1.00	19.93
5.0—10.0	7.30	3.65	1.25	11.90	15.02	39.12
10.0 & above	14.00	6.25	4.77	6.87	13.7	33.26
Total	26.45	12.78	15.06	23.71	20.47	98.47
	(26.86)	(12.98)	(15.29)	(24.08)	(20.79)	(100.00)
SIKH						
Less than 2.5	—	—	—	—	—	—
2.5—5.0	—	—	—	—	—	—
5.0—10.0	—	4.53	—	9.37	—	13.90
10.0 & above	4.16	—	—	—	—	4.16
Total	4.16	4.53	—	9.37	—	18.06
	(23.03)	(25.08)		(51.89)		(100.00)
Grand Total	375.04	127.25	232.92	354.70	351.96	1423.87
	(25.08)	(8.94)	(16.36)	(24.90)	(24.72)	(100.00)

N.B.—Figures in parentheses are percentages.

TABLE 10.31

Caste and Size Category-Wise Distribution of Land Sold by Backward Caste in U.P.

(Area in acres)

BUYERS	BACKWARD CASTE AS SELLERS					
	Land less	Less than 2.5	2.5—5.0	5.0—10.0	10.0 & above	Total
1	2	3	4	5	6	7
H.C.H.						
Less than 2.5	2.72	2.22	2.13	1.12	0.40	8.59
2.5—5.0	1.05	12.13	11.15	1.11	0.40	25.84
5.0—10.0	24.61	14.27	11.46	18.49	0.96	69.79
10.0 & above	7.95	8.28	15.48	10.84	3.43	45.98
Total	36.33 (24.18)	36.90 (24.57)	40.22 (26.78)	31.56 (21.01)	5.19 (3.46)	150.20 (100.00)
B.C.						
Less than 2.5	12.24	17.53	10.81	3.02	0.63	44.23
2.5—5.0	46.26	29.24	27.66	25.73	3.20	132.09
5.0—10.0	105.51	5.79	18.34	35.84	23.06	188.54
10.0 & above	44.58	9.66	7.33	4.98	39.65	106.20
Total	208.59 (44.28)	62.22 (13.20)	64.14 (13.62)	69.57 (14.77)	66.54 (14.13)	471.06 (190.00)

Table 10.31 (*Contd.*)

1	2	3	4	5	6	7
S.C.						
Less than 2.5	1.75	5.53	6.89	1.93	2.29	18.39
2.5—5.0	0.69	5.03	4.09	4.27	1.31	15.39
5.0—10.0	2.50	0.60	0.67	3.63	3.43	10.83
10.0 & above	—	4.40	—	—	—	4.40
Total	4.94 (10.08)	15.56 (31.75)	11.65 (23.77)	9.83 (20.06)	7.03 (14.34)	49,01 (100.00)
MUSLIM						
Less than 2.5	3.74	3.67	—	—	3.30	10 71
2.5—5.0	7.66	4.81	1,29	4.16	9.80	27.72
5.0—10.0	15.63	1.80	2.00	6.29	—	25.72
10.0 & above	—	0.80	—	3.60	—	4.40
Total	27.03 (39.43)	11.08 (16.16)	3.29 (4.80)	14.05 (20.50)	13.10 (19.11)	68.55 (100.00)
SIKH						
Less than 2.5	—	—	—	—	—	—
2.5—5.0	—	—	—	—	—	—
5.0—10.0	—	—	3.76	—	3.80	7.56
10.0 & above	12.50	—	—	0.31	4.63	17.44
Total	12.50 (50.00)	—	3.76 (15.04)	0.31 (1.24)	8.43 (33.72)	25.00 (100.00)
Grand Total	289.39 (37.88)	125.76 (16.47)	123.06 (16.11)	125.32 (16.41)	100.29 (13.13)	763.82 (100.00)

N.B.—Figures in parentheses are percentages.

TABLE 10.32

Caste and Size Category-Wise Distribution of Land Sold by Scheduled Caste in U.P.

(Area in acres)

BUYERS	SCHEDULED CASTE AS SELLERS					
	Land less	Less than 2.5	2.5—5.0	5.0—10.0	10.0 & above	Total
1	2	3	4	5	6	7
H.C.H.						
Less than 2.5	—	1.51	0.28	—	—	1.79
2.5—5.0	1.91	3.30	1.55	—	—	7.76
5.0—10.0	6.30	5.99	—	1.11	—	13.40
10.0 & above	7.98	5.20	—	6.60	3.87	23.65
Total	10.19 (35.50)	16.00 (35.09)	1.83 (4.01)	7.71 (16.91)	3.87 (8.49)	45.60 (100.00)
B.C.						
Less than 2.5	—	5.73	1.76	—	—	7.49
2.5—5.0	9.33	11.14	11.83	4.15	—	36.45
5.0—10.0	4.43	7.08	3.76	8.41	—	23.68
10.0 & above	—	2.48	1.65	1.58	—	5.71
Total	13.76 (18.76)	26.43 (36.04)	19.00 (25.91)	14.14 (19.29)	—	73.33 (100.00)

Table 10.32 (*Contd.*)

1	2	3	4	5	6	7
S.C.						
Less than 2.5	4.41	12.07	5.35	0.63	1.26	23.72
2.5—5.0	14.54	9 24	13.06	0.42	—	37.26
5.0—10.0	11.17	6.53	1.92	—	1.71	21.33
10.0 & above	6.63	—	0.88	—	1.39	2.90
Total	30.75 (36.09)	27.84 (32.67)	21.21 (24.89)	1.05 (1.23)	4.36 (5.12)	85.21 (100.00)
MUSLIM						
Less than 2.5	—	0.60	—	—	—	0.60
2.5—5.0	1.09	1.40	—	—	—	2.49
5.0—10.0	—	—	—	0.57	—	0.57
10.0 & above	2.90	0.80	—	—	—	3.70
Total	3.99 (54.22)	2.80 (38.04)	—	0.57 (7.74)	—	7.36 (100.00)
SIKH						
Less than 2.5	0.44	—	—	—	—	0.44
2.5—5.0	—	—	—	—	—	—
5.0—10.0	—	0.44	0,34	—	—	0.78
10.0 & above	—	—	—	—	—	—
Total	0.44 (36.06)	0.44 (36,06	0.34 (27.88)	—	—	1.22 (100.00)
Grand Total	65.13 (30.62)	73.51 (34.56)	42.38 (19.92)	23.47 (11.03)	8.23 (5.87)	212.72 (100.00)

N.B.—Figures in parentheses are percentages.

TABLE 10.33

Caste and Size Category-Wise Distribution of Land Sold by Muslims in U.P.

(Areas in acrās)

BUYERS	MUSLIMS AS SELLERS					
	Land-less	Less than 2.5	2.5 5.0	5.0—10 0	10.0 & above	Total
1	2	3	4	5	6	7
H.C H.						
Less than 2.5	—	0.84	2.18	—	0.94	3.96
2.5—5 0	—	2.84	1.66	—	—	4.50
5.0—10,0	4.12	7.00	4.98	2.23	1.25	19.59
10 0 & above	3.15	2,32	1.00	—	2.00	8.47
Total	7.27 (19.91)	13.00 (36.61)	9.82 (26.90)	2.23 (6.11)	4,19 (11.47)	36,51 (100.00)
B.C.						
Less than 2.5	44.20	5.40	1.10	1.48	—	52.18
2.5—5.0	9.25	3.97	7.25	9.00	—	29.96
5,0—10.0	0.31	2.40	7,17	5.67	4,50	20.05
10,0 & above	25.14	2.31	1.20	5.27	0.50	34.42
Total	78,90 (57.76)	14.08 (10.31)	17.12 (12.53)	21.51 (15.74)	5.00 (3.66)	136.61 (100.00)

Table 10.33 (*Contd.*)

1	2	3	4	5	6	7
S.C.						
Less than 2,5	1.26	—	0 78	0.63	1.56	4.23
2,5—5,0	—	0.40	—	—	0.60	1.00
5,0—10,0	—	1.25	—	3.25	—	4.50
10,0 & above	—	—	—	—	—	—
Total	1.26 (12.95)	1.65 (16.96)	0.78 (8.02)	3.88 (39 88)	2.16 (22.19)	9.73 (100.00)
MUSLIM						
Less than 2,5	3.46	8.93	4.99	4.32	4.45	26.15
2,5— 5.0	12.72	12 76	7.44	10.42	4.99	48.33
5,0—10,0	66.63	3.60	10.97	24.15	4.89	110.24
10,0 & above	55.69	1.25	3 80	10.14	15·69	86.57
Total	138.50 (51.05)	26.54 (9.78)	27.20 (10.03)	49.03 (18.07)	30.02 (11.07)	271.29 (100.00)
SIKH						
Less than 2,5	—	—	—	—	—	—
2,5—5,0	—	—	—	—	—	—
5,0—10,0	—	1.87	—	—	—	1.87
10.0 —above	—	—	—	—	—	—
Total	—	1.87 (100.00)	—	—	—	1.87 (100.00)
Grand Total	225.93 (49.55)	57.14 (12.53)	54.92 (12 04)	76.65 (16.81)	41.37 (9.07)	465.01 (100.00)

N.B.—Figures in parentheses are percentages.

TABLE 10.34

Caste and Size Category-Wise Distribution of Land Sold by Sikhs in U.P.

(Area in acres)

BUYERS	SIKHS AS SELLERS					
	Land less	Fess than 2.5	2.5—5.0	5.0—10.0	10.0 & above	Total
1	2	3	4	5	6	7
H.C.H.						
Less than 2.5	—	—	—	—	—	—
2.5—5.0	—	—	—	—	—	—
5.0—10.0	—	—	—	—	—	—
10.0 & above	—	—	—	—	—	—
Total	—	—	—	—	—	—
B.C.						
Less than 2.5	—	—	—	—	—	—
2.5—5.0	—	—	—	0.95	—	0.95
5.0—10.0	—	—	—	—	—	—
10.0 & above	—	—	—	1.10	1.10	2.20
Total	—	—	—	2.05 (65.08)	1.10 (34.92)	3.15 (100.00)

Table 10.34 (*Contd.*)

1	2	3	4	5	6	7
S.C.						
Less than 2,5	—	—	—	0.32	—	0.32
2,5—5,0	—	—	—	—	—	—
5,0—10,0	—	—	—	—	—	—
10,0 & above	—	—	—	—	—	—
Total	—	—	—	0.32 (100.00)	—	0.32 (100.00)
MUSLIM						
Less than 2,5	—	—	—	—	—	—
2,5—5,0	—	—	—	—	—	—
5,0—10,0	—	—	—	0.63	—	0.63
10,0 & above	—	—	—	—	—	—
Total	—	—	—	0.63 (100.00)	—	0.63 (100.00)
SIKH						
Less than 2,5	—	—	—	—	—	—
2,5—5,0	0.13	—	—	0.31	—	0.44
5,0—10,0	17.88	1.88	—	—	—	19.76
10,0 & above	26.48	—	—	3.13	—	29.61
Total	44.49 (89.32)	1.88 (3.77)	—	3.44 (6.91)	—	49.81 (100.00)
Grand Total	44.49 (82.53)	1.88 (3.48)	—	6.44 (11.95)	1.10 (2.04)	53.91 (100.00)

N.B.—Figures in parentheses are percentages.

per cent), small farmers (12 per cent) and medium and large farmers (9 per cent).

Of the total land sold by Sikhs in the State (Table 10.34) landless accounted for 83 per eent of the land followed by semi-medium farmers (12 per cent). Marginal and medium and large farmers accounted for 3 per cent and 2 per cent respectively of the land that was sold.

Land sold and purchased by different castes and size categories in U.P. is summarised in the following tables. Table 10.35 shows the size-wise distribution of land sold and purchased by high caste Hindus in U.P.

TABLE 10.35

Size Wise Distribution of Land Sold and Purchased by High Caste Hindus in U.P.

(acres)

Size category (acres)	Land Sold	Land Purchased	Net gain (+) or loss (—)
Landless	357.04	—	(—) 357.04
Less than 2.5	127.25	53.34	(—) 73.91
2.5—5.00	232.92	152.25	(—) 80.67
5.00—10.00	354.70	271.83	(—) 82.87
10 & above	351.96	411.36	(+) 59.40
Total	1423.87	888.78	(—) 535.09

It is observed that as a caste group, high caste Hindus were net losers of land. All the categories among them were losers except the largest ones. Landless were the biggest losers of land.

TABLE 10.36

Size-Wise Distribution of Land Sold and Purchased by Backward Caste in U.P.

(acres)

Size category (acres)	Land Sold	Land Purchased	Net gain (+) or loss (–)
1	2	3	4
Landless	289.39	—	(—) 289.39
Less than 2.5	125.76	161.67	(+) 35.91
2.5—5.00	123.06	354.31	(+) 231.25
5.00—10.00	125.32	395.14	(+) 269.82
10 & above	100.29	308.58	(+) 208.29
Total	763.82	1219.70	(+) 455.88

As far as Backward Castes are concerned (Table 10.36) it will be observed that as a caste group they were net gainers of land. Excepting the landless category among them all the other categories purchased more land than they sold and the gain of small, semi-medium and large farmers was substantial.

TABLE 10.37

Size-Wise Distribution of Land Sold and Purchased by Scheduled Caste in U.P.

(acres)

Size-category (Acres)	Land Sold	Land Purchased	Net gains (+) or loss (—)
1	2	3	4
Landless	65.13	—	(—) 65.13
Less than 2.5	73.51	70.27	(—) 3.24
2.5 to 5.00	42.38	109.86	(+) 67.48
5.00—10.00	23.47	62.25	(+) 38.78
10 & above	8.23	17.21	(+) 3.98
Total	212.72	259.59	(+) 46.87

Scheduled Caste too were significantly net gainers of land in U.P. (Table 10.37). While landless among them were the main losers of land the small and semi-medium farmers were the main gainers of land.

TABLE 10.38

Size-wise Distribution of Lond sold and Purchased by Muslim in U.P.

(acres)

Size category (acres)	Land sold	Land purchased	Net gain (+) or Loss (—)
1	3	3	4
Landless	225.93	—	(—) 225.93
Less than 2.5	57.14	43.62	(—) 13.52
2.5 to 5.00	54.92	98.47	(+) 43.55
5.00 to 10.00	76.65	176.28	(+) 99.63
10 & above	41.37	127.93	(+) 86.56
Total	456.01	446.30	(—) 9.71

Muslims were net losers of land (Table 10.38) in the State. Among them the main losers of land were the landless and to some extent the marginal farmers. Small farmers, semi-medium farmers and medium and large farmers were the main gainers of land among Muslims.

TABLE 10.39

Size-wise Distribution of Land Sold and Purchased by Sikhs in U.P.

(Acres)

Size category (Acres)	Land Sold	Land Purchased	Net gain (+) or loss (—)
1	2	3	4
Landless	44.49	—	(—) 44.49
Less than 2.5	1.88	0.44	(—) 1.44
2.5 to 5.00	—	0.44	(+) 0.44
5.00 to 10.00	5.44	43.87	(+) 37.43
10 and above	1.10	51.21	(+) 50.11
Total	53.91	95.96	(+) 42.05

Sikhs were also net gainers of land (Table 10.39). Landless among them were the main losers but semi-medium and medium and large farmers were almost exclusive gainers.

11

Reasons for Land Alienation

One of the major objectives of the study was to discern the reasons for land alienation among different categories of land owners. In the following pages an attempt has been made to analyse this factor. Table 11.1 shows the distribution of number of cases of land transfers according to reason in different regions. It will be seen that in eastern U.P. 25 per cent of the cases of land alienation was attributable to marriage. "Left the village" or total migration accounted for 16 per cent of the cases of land sales in this region. Significantly "purchase of other land" accounted for nearly the same percentage. 'Treatment of diseases' accounted for 1 per cent of the total cases of land alienation, a factor which speaks both about the lack of public health system or its inadequacy as also about general poverty wherein people have to sell land to meet medical expenses. It is quite distressing to find that 13 per cent of the cases of land alienation was due to repayment of old debts. Marriage and domestic consumption accounted for 16 per cent and 28 per cent respectively of all cases of land sale which was undertaken towards repayment of old debts. Another distressing aspect of the matter is that 4 per cent of such cases was for repayment of debts incurred for purchase of

TABLE 11.1

Reason-Wise Number of Cases of Land Alienation in Different Regions of U.P.

(No.)

S. No.	Reason for sale of land	Eastern	Central	Western	Bundel-khand	Hill	U.P.
1	3	3	4	5	6	7	8
1	**Marriage**	210 (25.42)	171 (35.92)	88 (25.81)	43 (32.58)	—	512 (28.78)
2	**Education**	11 (1.33)	3 (0.63)	3 (0.88)	2 (1.51)	—	19 (1.07)
3.	**Treatment of diseases**	85 (10.29)	66 (13.87)	42 (12.32)	20 (15.15)	—	213 (11.97)
4.	**Purchase of other land**	132 (15.98)	34 (7.14)	26 (7.62)	6 (4.54)	—	198 (11.13)
5.	**Left the village for good**	136 (16.40)	56 (11.78)	43 (12.61)	2 (1.51)	—	237 (13.32)
6.	**Land was given on lease**	20 (2.42)	4 (0.84)	3 (0.88)	1 (0.76)	—	28 (1.57)
7.	**Repayment of old debts incurred towards :—**						
	(a) construction of house	1 (0.12)	—	—	—	—	**1** (0.06)

Table 11.1 (*Contd.*)

1	2	3	4	5	6	7	8
	(b) opening of shop	—	—	—	—	—	—
	(c) marriage	18 (2.18)	7 (1.47)	5 (1.47)	5 (3.80)	—	35 (1.97)
	(d) purchase of fertilizers	44 (5.33)	52 (10.92)	2 (0.59)	33 (25.00)	—	131 (7.36)
	(e) sewing machine	1 (0.12)	1 (0.21)	—	—	—	2 (0.11)
	(f) tube-wells	14 (1.70)	—	2 (0.59)	—	—	16 (0.90)
	(g) chaff cutter	2 (0.24)	1 (0.21)	—	1 (0.76)		4 (0.22)
	(h) consumption needs	31 (3.75)	—	48 (14.07)	11 (8.33)	—	90 (5.06)
	(i) Miscellaneous	—	16 (3.36)	9 (2.64)	6 (4.54)	—	31 (1.74)
8.	House construction	5 (0.61)	4 (0.84)	5 (1.47)	—	—	14 (0.79)
9.	To clear the debts on mortgaged land	73 (8.84)	36 (7.56)	9 (2.64)	—	—	118 (6.64)
10.	Shop	—	3 (0.63)	1 (0.29)	—	—	4 (0.22)
11.	Gambling	—	1 (0.21)	—	—	—	1 (0.06)
12.	Construction of wells	1 (0.12)	—	—	—	—	1 (0.06)

1	2	3	4	5	6	7	8
13.	Domestic consumption	3 (0.36)	8 (1.68)	12 (3.52)	—	—	23 (1.28)
14.	To evade ceiling laws	—	—	3 (0.88)	—	—	3 (0.17)
15.	Installation of tube-well	7 (0.85)	7 (1.47)	4 (1.17)	—	—	18 (1.01)
16.	To purchase tractor	2 (0.24)	—	3 (0.88)	—	—	5 (0.28)
17.	No issue	2 (0.24)	—	14 (4.10)	—	3 (75.00)	19 (1.07)
18.	Litigation	—	3 (0.63)	3 (0.88)	—	—	6 (0.34)
19.	Purchase of animal	—	3 (0.63)	1 (0.29)	2 (1.52)	—	6 (0.34)
20.	Land was with Harijan	—	—	—	—	1 (25.40)	1 (0.06)
21.	Purchase of taxi	2 (0.24)	—	—	—	—	2 (0.11)
22.	Far away from residence	25 (3.03)	—	—	—	—	25 (1.41)
23.	Land was infertile	1 (0.12)	—	—	—	—	1 (0.06)
24.	Miscellaneous	—	—	15 (4.40)	—	—	15 (0.84)
Total		826 (100.00)	476 (100.00)	341 (100.00)	132 (100.00)	4 (100.00)	1779 (100.00)

N.B —Figures in parentheses are percentages.

fertilizers. The cooperatives advance loans for purchase of fertilizers and in case of default the interest goes on multiplying. Poor farmers find it difficult to repay the loans and many a time have to sell land to repay the loans from cooperatives. It is also significant to note that 9 per cent of the cases of land alienation was connected with the sale of mortgaged land.

Land sold to meet capital expenditure formed only an insignificant portion of the total number of land sales. Such items formed less than 4 per cent of the total cases if we exclude the item of 'purchase of other land'. If we include the latter the percentage rises to 20. Still on the whole the bulk of the cases were connected with consumption need and the like.

In central U.P. also marriage accounted for 6 per cent of the cases of land sales. Significantly 'treatment of diseases' accounted for 14 per cent of the cases of land alienation. "Left the village" or total migration accounted for 12 per cent of the same. Nearly 8 per cent of the cases of land alienation was due to the fact that the land was given on mortgage and was subsequently sold. Repayment of old debts accounted for 17 per cent of the total cases of land alienation. Surprisingly out of 77 cases of land sales in order to repay old debts as many as 52 cases were connected with liquidation of old debts incurred to purchase fertilizers. Number of cases of land alienation to finance capital expenditure formed 4 per cent of such cases in the region if we exclude "land sold to purchase other land." After including it the same goes up to 11 per cent.

In western U.P. also marriage accounted for the highest percentage (26 per cent) of land alienation followed by total migration (13 per cent). Treatment of diseases accounted for 12 per cent of the cases. Repayment of old debts accounted for about 20 per cent of such cases. Surprisingly out of 66 cases of land alienation to repay old debts as many as 48 cases were connected with debts undertaken to meet consumption needs. Number of cases of land alienation to finance capital expenditure excluding 'purchase of other land' also formed less than 5 per cent of such cases. After including it the same rises to 12 per cent.

In Bundelkhand also one-third of the cases of land alienation was related to marriage. Significantly treatment of disease accounted for 15 per cent of the cases of land alienation. Curiously total migration was an insignificant factor (less than 2 per cent). Out of total cases of 56 to liquidate old debts as many as 33 were connected with purchase of fertilizers and 11 cases were connected with domestic consumption. Purchase of other land accounted for less than 5 per cent of the cases. Land sale to finance capital expenditure excluding purchase of other land accounted for 2 per cent of the cases. If we include the latter it rises to 7 per cent of the total cases of land alienation.

In the Hill Region out of 4 cases of land alienation 3 were related to there being no issue and the other was due to the fact that land was with a Harijan who could not be evicted and consequently the land was sold to him.

Taking the State as a whole, 29 per cent of the cases of land alienation was due to marriage. Next came total migration which accounted for 13 per cent of the cases of land sales. Treatment of diseases and purchase of other land accounted for 12 per cent and 11 per cent respectively of such cases. Repayment of old debts accounted for 17 per cent of the same, the bulk of which was taken for purchase of fertilizers and to meet consumption needs. Significantly 7 per cent of the total cases related to sale of mortgaged land. Cases of land sale to meet capital expenditure like construction of wells, installation of tube-wells, purchase of tractor transport equipment, animals, construction of shops and residential buildings *etc.*, accounted for only 4 per cent of total cases of land alienation if we exclude 'purchase of other land' and 15 per cent if we include it. Thus it can be inferred that land was sold in this State primarily to meet various types of consumption needs.

A reason-wise distribution of area of land sold in different regions of U.P. is shown in Table 11.2. It is significant to note that in eastern U.P. the single biggest cause for land sales was the fact that the sellers left the village after selling their entire landholding. It accounted for 42 per cent of the alienated land in this region. Such persons were generally small land owners.

TABLE 11 2

Reason-Wise Distribution of Land Sold in Different Regions of U.P.

(Area in acres)

S. No.	Reason	Eastern U.P.	Central U.P.	Western U.P.	Bundel-khand	Hill	All U.P.
1	2	3	4	5	6	7	8
1.	Marriage	192.94 (14.44)	176.14 (25.20)	84.69 (11.52)	41.06 (31.01)	— —	494.84 (17.00)
2.	Education	6.31 (0.47)	7.19 (1.02)	2.51 (0.34)	0.80 (0.60)	—	16.81 (0.58)
3.	Treatment of diseases	35.72 (2.67)	61.63 (8.82)	25.06 (3.41)	22.46 (16.97)	--	144.87 (4.98)
4.	To purchase other land	135.05 (10.10)	34.58 (4.95)	28.72 (3.91)	18.85 (14.24)	—	221.14 (7.60)
5.	Left the village for good	558.88	169.66	158.96	6.75	—	894.58
6.	Repayment of old debts incurred towards	(41.79)	(24 32)	(21.63)	(5.10)		(30.73)
	(a) Construction of house	—	3.93 (0.56)	—	—		3.93 (0.14)
	(b) Opening a shop	0,20 (0.01)	14.80 (2.12)	—	—	—	15.00 (0.52)
	(c) Marriage	40.91 (3.06)	30.54 (4.37)	15.44 (2.10)	5.32 (4.02)	—	92.21 (3.17)
	(d) Purchase of fertilizer	33.75 (2.52)	31.41 (4.50)	17.46 (2.38)	26.35 (19.90)	—	108.97 (3.74)

Table 11.2 (*Contd.*)

1	2	3	4	5	6	7	8
	(e) Sewing machine	1.20 (0.09)	0.40 (0.06)	—	—	—	1.60 (0.05)
	(f) Tube-wells	32.88 (2.46)	30.57 (4.37)	67.19 (9.14)	—	—	130.64 (4.48)
	(g) Chaff cutter	0.30 (0.02)	0.20 (0.03)	—	—	—	0.50 (0.02)
	(h) Consumption needs	46.49 (3.48)	35.20 (5.04)	154.91 (21.08)	6.48 (9.89)	—	243.08 (8.35)
7.	To clear embezzlement	0.40 (0.03)	—	5.00 (0.68)	—	—	5.40 (0 19)
8.	House construction	7.27 (0.54)	—	15.03 (2.04)	—	—	22.30 (077)
9.	To clear the debt on mortgaged land	57.25 (4.28)	38.54 (5.52)	3.12 (0.42)	—	—	98.91 (3.40)
10	Shop	2.12 (0 16)	—	1.43 (0.19)	—	—	3.55 (0.12)
11.	Gambling	—	7.80 (1.12)	0.31 (0.04)	—	—	8.11 (0.28)
12.	Construction of well	3.51 (0.26)	3.75 (0.54)	—	—	—	7,26 (0.25)
13.	Domestic Consumption	93.49 (7.40)	9.78 (1.40)	12 01 (1.63)	0.50 (0.38)	—	111.84 (3.84)
14.	To evade ceiling laws	—	12.00 (1.72)	4.69 (0.64)	—	—	16.69 (0.57)
15,	Installation of tube-wells	12,71 (0,95)	—	1149 (1,56)	—	—	24.20 (0.83)

Table 11.2 (*Contd.*)

1	2	3	4	5	6	7	8
16.	To purchase Tractor	8.61 (0.64)	12.66 (1.81)	8.13 (1.11)	—	—	29.40 (1.01)
17.	No issue	9.03 (0.68)	3.00 (0.43)	103.55 (14.09)	—	5.75 (85.10)	121.33 (4.17)
18.	Litigation	—	1.10 (0.16)	11.39 (1.55)	—	—	12.49 (0.43)
19.	Purchase of animal	0.53 (0.04)	1.10 (0.14)	0.25 (0.03)	2.62 (1.98)	—	4.40 (0.15)
20.	Land was with Harijan	—	—	—	—	1.00 (14.81)	1.00 (0.03)
21.	Far away from residence	36.35 (2.72)	12.55 (1.80)	3.06 (0.42)	1.20 (0.91)	—	53.16 (1.83)
22.	Purchase of Taxi	16.50 (1.23)	—	—	—	—	16.50 (0.57)
23.	Infertile Land	4.56 (0.34)	—	0.63 (0.09)	—	—	5.19 (0.18)
24.	Family Quarrel	0.44 (0.03)	—	—	—	—	0.44 (0.02)
	Total	1337.40 (100.00)	698.76 (100.00)	735.03 (100.00)	132.39 (100.00)	6.75 (100.00)	2910.33 (100.00)

B.N.—Figures in parenthcses are percentages.

who could not manage to make both ends meet in the villages and migrated to cities to undertake some odd job in the informal sector. Relatively rapid urbanisation seems to have abetted this process of out-migration. It is worth noting that this was an important factor in central and western U.P. as well where one-fourth and one-fifth of the land respectively was sold due to this reason. Only in Bundelkhand it was a minor factor accounting for only 5 per cent of land alienation. For the State as a whole it accounted for as high as 31 per cent of the total alienated land.

Next to it marriage has been the biggest reason for land sales. It accounted for 14 per cent of the land sold in western U.P., 14 per cent in eastern U.P., 24 per cent in central U.P. and 31 per cent in Bundelkhand. No land was sold in Hill region to perform marriage ceremony. For the State as a whole marriage accounted for 17 per cent of the total land alienation. It is also worth noting that when land was sold to clear old debts marriage was an important factor and it accounted for 15 per cent of all such land sold to clear old debts in the state. Repayment of old debts was responsible for 20 per cent of all the land sold in the state and it will be seen that more than 6 per cent of such land was alienated to meet consumption needs. It may also be noted that more than 3 per cent of the total alienated land was accounted for by those who were unable to repay the debt for which land was mortgaged and the land passed into the ownership of the creditors. Another noteworthy thing in this connection is that more than 4 per cent of the total alienated land in the state was accounted for by the fact that loan that was incurred to install tube-wells could not be cleared and recourse had to be taken to sell the land to repay it. This is naturally a distressing aspect of the situation where people have to sell land to repay the loan taken for installation of tube-wells. Anyone who reads vernacular papers will be familiar that frequently there are notices to the farmers through newspapers that the land of the defaulters in paying the instalment on such loans taken from the Land Development Bank will be auctioned and surprisingly such names run into hundreds at the branch level. Not all succeed in repaying the loans and many are forced to sell a part of the land to repay the instalment farmers also sell land to install tube-well. One per cent of the total land in the state was sold to install one's own tube-well. This incidentally illustrates the keenness of the farmers to take advantage of the new agricultural technology and if they find a particular proposition profitable they will even go to the extent of selling the land to acquire it. This is also indirectly reflected in the phenomenon where farmers sell a part of their land to purchase some other land which may be more fertile or adjacent to their land. Incidentally the magnitude of such land sale was as high as 8 per cent of the total alienated land in the state. Roughly 2 per cent of the aliented land was sold as it was at a from the residence. Domestic consumption accounted for another 4 per cent of the alienated land eastern U.P. had the largest proportion (7.4 per cent) on this count followed by western U.P. (1.6 per cent). Significantly 4 per cent of the alienated land was sold in the state as there was no issue in the family. Surprisingly this factor was responsible for 14 per cent of the land sold western U.P. Land sold for meeting medical expenses constituted 5 per cent of the total alienated land in the State. In view of utter lack of medical facilities particularly in the rural areas and the low income it is not surprising that people have to sell land to avail of medical facilities. In Bundelkhand 17 per cent of the land was sold on this count. Education also accounted for 0.6 per cent of the land sold in the state as a whole. Litigation is common in the countryside and this also accounted for about half per cent of the land sold. It will thus be seen that marriage, migration and repayment of old debts together accounted for 70 per cent of the land alienation in the state.

Land was sold for a variety of reasons but cases were not wanting when it was sold for productive purposes. For purchase of tractors, 29 per cent acres of land was sold which accounted for 1 per cent of the total land sold. Similarly as mentioned earlier about 1 per cent of the land was sold to install tube-wells and another 02.5 per cent to construct wells. Some people were also taking to new non-agricultural activities by selling the land and using the sale proceeds for the new activity. More than 16 acres of land was sold in the state accounting for 0.6 per cent of the total alienated land to purchase taxi for public transport. Likewise nearly 4 acres of land was sold to open shops and for purchase of animal each.

Land sold to meet capital expenditure accounted for 6.4 per cent of the alienated land in eastern U.P. excluding land sold to purchase other land. If the same is included the percentage rose to 16.5 In central U.P. the respective percentages were 9.6 and 14 5 while in western U.P. the respective percentages were 14 and 18. In Bundelkhand the respective percentages were 3 and 17. For the state as a whole the respective percentages were 8 and 16. Thus capital expenditure accounted for a small part of land alienation.

There were also some curious cases of land sale. Some 8 acres of land was sold in central U.P. for gambling purposes. About 17 acres of land (12 acres in central U.P. and 5 acres in Bundelkhand) was sold to evade ceiling laws. More than 5 acres was sold to clear embezzlement. Family quarrels also resulted in disposal of the land although the area involved was less than half an acre.

Size-Wise Analysis of Reasons for Land Alienation

Reason-wise land transfers in eastern U.P. according to size category of owned holding presented in Table 11.3 shows some interesting features. It will be seen that for the landless category the main reason for land alienation was total migration as such households sold their entire holding. Eighty per cent of their alienated land was due to this factor alone. Repayment of old debts accounted for 4 per cent of the alienated land and marriage accounted for slightly more than 2 per cent. Domestic consumption was an insignificant factor and accounted for 1 per cent of the alienated land. The share of medicine was slightly lower at 0.7 per cent.

For those who were in the size category of less than 2.5 acres, repayment of old debts was the most important reason for land alienation as it accounted for 29 per cent of such land. Next in importance was marriage (18 per cent) followed by medicine (12 per cent) and surprisingly purchase of other land (9 per cent).

TABLE 11.3

Reason-wise Land Transfers in Eastern U.P. According to Size Category of Land Holding

(Area in acres)

Size Category (acres)	Marriage	Education	Medicine	Purchase of other land	Left the village	Repayment of old debts
1	2	3	4	5	6	7
Landless	12.64	0.19	3.86	—	493.99	22.46
	(2.25)	(0.03)	(0.69)		(88.06)	(4.00)
Less than 2.5	28.81	1.23	19.41	14.90	12.24	46.18
	(17.81)	(0.76)	(12.00)	(9.21)	(7.57)	(28.55)
2.5—5.0	49.34	3.25	4.20	18.72	14.02	22.49
	(30.64)	(2.02)	(2.61)	(11.62)	(8.71)	(13.96)
5—10	49.43	0.66	2.91	42.65	36.75	25.61
	(21.77)	(0.29)	(1.28)	(18.79)	(16.19)	(11.28)
10 & above	52.72	0.98	5,34	58.78	1.88	38.99
	(23.26)	(0.43)	(2.36)	(25.94)	(0.83)	(17.21)
Total	192.94	6.31	35.72	135.05	558.88	155.73
	(14.44)	(0.47)	(2.67)	(9.69)	(41.79)	(11.64)

Table 11.3 (*Contd.*)

	Purchase of Machinery & equipment	House construction	Domestic consumption	Miscellancous	Total
1	8	9	10	11	12
Landless	2.53 (0.46)	—	6.14 (1.09)	19.18 (3.42)	560.99 (100.00)
Less than 2.5	3.62 (2.24)	1.20 (0.74)	9.58 (5.92)	24.59 (15.20)	161.76 (100.00)
2.5—5.0	3.90 (2.42)	2.00 (1.24)	24.14 (14.99)	18.98 (11.79)	161.04 (100.00)
5—10	8.98 (3.96)	4.07 (1.79)	29.37 (12.94)	26.57 (11.71)	227.00 (100.00)
10 & above	2.29 (1.01)	—	24.26 (10.71)	41.37 (18.25)	226.61 (100.00)
Total	21.32 (1.60)	7.27 (0.54)	93.49 (7.40)	130.69 (9.76)	1337.40 (100.00)

N.B.—Figures in parentheses are percentages.

TABLE 11.4

Reason-Wise Land Transfer in Central U.P. According to Size Category Owned Holdings

(Area in acres)

Size Category	REASONS Marriage	Education	Medicine	Purchase of other land	Left the village	Repayment of old debts
1	2	3	4	5	6	7
Landless	0.75 (0.51)	—	2.05 (1.40)	—	98.35 (67.42)	17.84 (12.23)
Less than 2.5	28.11 (21.37)	1.26 (0.96)	21.17 (16.10)	4.67 (3.55)	19.46 (14.80)	49.37 (37.54)
2.5—5.0	53.70 (34.96)	—	12.27 (7.99)	17.99 (11.71)	12.21 (7.95)	36 86 (24.00)
5—10	55.62 (32.55)	—	19.86 (11.63)	10.32 (6.04)	30.57 (17.89)	32.80 (19.20)
10 & above	37.96 (39.17)	5.93 (6.12)	6.28 (6.48)	1.40 (1.44)	9.40 (9.70)	10.18 (10.50)
Total	176.14 (25.21)	7.16 (1.03)	61.63 (8.82)	34.38 (4,81)	169.99 (24,33)	147.05 (21,04)

Table 11.4 (*Contd.*)

	REASONS				
	Purchase of machinery & equipment	House construction	Domestic consumption	Miscellaneous	Total
1	8	9	10	11	12
Landless	1.06 (0.73)	—	2.43 (1.67)	23.40 (16.04)	145.88 (100.00)
Less than 2.5	0.90 (0.68)	—	3.21 (2.44)	3.36 (2.56)	131.51 (100.00)
2.5—5	3.67 (2.39)	—	—	16.89 (11.00)	153.59 (100.00)
5—10	0.04 (0.02)	—	4.34 (2.54)	17.31 (10.13)	170.86 (100.00)
10 & above	6.99 (7.21)	—	—	18.78 (19.38)	96.92 (100.00)
Total	12.66 (1.81)	—	9.98 (1.54)	79.74 (11.41)	698.76 (100.00)

N.B.—Figures in parentheses are percentages.

In the 2.5—5 acre category marriage occupied the top position among the reasons for land alienation. It accounted for 31 per cent of the total alienated land. Purchase of other land also accounted for 12 per cent of the alienated land. Repayment of debts accounted for 14 per cent as against 29 per cent in the preceding category. Surprisingly domestic consumption accounted for 15 per cent of alienated land as against 6 per cent in the preceding category.

In the size-category of 5—10 acres marriage accounted for 22 per cent of the alienated land followed by purchase of other land (19 per cent). Curiously "left the village" accounted for 16 per cent of the alienated land in this category as against 9 per cent in the preceding category. Equally intriguing was the fact that even in this higher category 13 per cent of the alienated land was sold to meet domestic consumption needs. Repayment of old debts accounted for 11 per cent of the alienated land.

In the highest category of 10 acres and above roughly 26 per cent of the alienated land was due to the factor of "purchase of other land." Marriage was also an important factor accounting for 23 per cent of the total alienated land. Repayment of old debts also occupied an important place and the same accounted for 17 per cent of the alienation of land. Purchase of agricultural equipment which accounted for 4 per cent of the alienated land in the size category of 5—10 acres dropped down to 1 per cent in the highest category. Education accounted for less than half per cent and medicine more than 2 per cent of the alienated land. Intriguingly domestic consumption accounted for 11 per cent of the alienated land in this category also.

Broadly speaking marriage was an important cause for land alienation among all the landed categories more so in the higher ones. The factor of 'left the village' was mostly confined to poorer households but other categories were also affected by it. Repayment of old debts as a reason for land alienation was an important factor among all the landed categories. Surprisingly domestic consumption as a factor for land alienation was more marked among higher categories as against the lower ones. This cannot be explained in conventional terms.

May be the demonstration effect of urban consumption standards might have something to do with this phenomenon.

Reason-wise land transfers in central U.P. according to size of owned holdings is shown in Table 11 4. It will be seen that more than two-thirds of the alienated land of landless was due to their total migration from the village. Next in importance was the factor of repayment of old debts which accounted for 12 per cent of the alienated land. Domestic consumption accounted for less than 2 per cent of the land alienation. Marriage was of no consequence among them as a cause for land alienation. It was responsible for only 0.5 per cent of the alienated land. Treatment of disease accounted for nearly 1.5 per cent of land alienation. Purchase of machinery and equipments also accounted for nearly 1 per cent of the alienated land.

As the size category increases marriage assumes importance as a factor responsible for land alienation. In the size category of less than 2.5 acres 21 per cent of the alienated land was due to this factor although the largest percentage (38 per cent) of land alienation among them was due to repayment of old debts Domestic consumption also led to the alienation of land which accounted for slightly more than 2 per cent of such land. Migration was responsible for 15 percent of the alienated land. Purchase of other land accounted for about 4 per cent of alienation, but strictly speaking it was not land alienation.

In the size category of 2.5—5 acres marriage occupied the top place as a cause for land alienation. It accounted for 35 per cent of the alienated land. Repayment of old debts came next and accounted for 24 per cent of the alienation. Migration and medicine were responsible for 8 per cent each of the total alienation of land in this category. Purchase of other land as a factor stood higher at 12 per cent.

In the size category of 5—10 acres marriage again accounted for 33 per cent of the alienated land. The share of repayment of old debts was lower at 19 per cent. Surprisingly "left the village" accounted for 18 per cent of the land alienation in this category. It was only next to that of the landless. Nearly 12 per cent of the alienated land was due to medical expenses.

and purchases of other land accounted for 6 per cent of the alienated land.

In the highest category marriage accounted for as high as 39 per cent of the alienated land. "Left the village" as a factor for land sales accounted for 10 per cent while repayment of old debts was responsible for 11 per cent of the land alienation in this category. Purchase of agricultural machinery and equipment was highest in this category accounting for 7 per cent of their alienated land.

Broadly it can be said that marriage, migration and repayment of old debts were the leading factors for land alienation in central U.P. While marriage was important in case of land owning groups migration was a common factor in all the categories. Similarly land was sold by all categories to repay old debts and even the highest category was not immune from it

In western U.P. also quite understandably "left the village" was the most important reason for land alienation among the landless as will be evident from Table 11.5. About 55 per cent of their alienated land was due to this reason. Repayment of old debts also accounted for 15 per cent of the alienated land. Significantly marriage was of little consequence as less than 1 per cent of the land was alienated on this count. Similarly domestic consumption was also not an important factor as only 2 per cent of the land was alienated because of this factor.

In the size category of less than 2.5 acres, repayment of old debts was the biggest factor for land alienation as more than half the alienated land was due to this factor. Marriage also emerged as a significant factor in this category as 13 per cent of the alienated land was due to it. Significantly medicine, "left the village" and house construction accounted for 8 per cent each of the land alienation in this category. Purchase of other land was also a facts or with the farmers belonging to this category. Nearly 3 per cent of the alienated land was so involved, but as noted earlier this was no alienation as such.

In the 2.5—5.0 acre categry again, repayment of old debts accounted for 52 per cent of the alienated land followed by marriage which accounted for 16 per cent of the alienated

TABLE 11.5

Reason-wise Land Transfers in Western U.P. According to Size of Land Holdings

(Area in acres)

Size Category	REASONS					
	Marriage	Education	Medicine	Purchase of other land	Left the village	Repayment of old debts
1	2	3	4	5	6	7
Landless	1.47 (9.57)	—	2.63 (1.03)	—	139.88 (54.77)	39.04 (15.28)
Less than 2.5	9.34 (12.84)	—	6.12 (8.42)	1.80 (2.48)	6.09 (8.37)	37.43 (51 47)
2.5—5	16.46 (15.84)	1.26 (1.21)	5.65 (5.44)	9.01 (8.67)	2.34 (2.25)	53.69 (51.67)
5—10	41.32 (27.00)	1.25 (0.82)	8.75 (5.72)	13.12 (8.57)	4.12 (2.69)	49.62 (32.42)
10 & above	16.10 (10.74)	—	1.91 (1.27)	3.54 (2.36)	6.53 (4.36)	75.22 (50.18)
Total	84.69 (11.52)	5.51 (0.34)	25.06 (3.41)	27.47 (3.42)	158.96 (21.63)	255.00 (34.69)

Table 11.5 (*Contd.*)

Size Category	REASONS				
	Purchase of Machinery & equipment	House construction	Domestic consumption	Miscellaneous	Total
1	8	9	10	11	12
Landless	7.60 (2.97)	1.09 (0.43)	5.08 (1.99)	58.65 (22.96)	255.44 (100.00)
Less than 2.5	—	6.25 (8.59)	—	5.69 (7.83)	72.72 (100.00)
2.5—5	2.25 (2.16)	1.87 (1.80)	1.17 (1.13)	10.22 (9.83)	103.92 (100.00)
5—10	3.33 (2.18)	4.03 (2.63)	2.50 (1.63)	25.02 (16.34)	153.06 (100.00)
10 & above	6.44 (4.30)	1.79 (1.20)	4.51 (3.01)	33.85 (22.58)	149.80 (100.00)
Total	19.62 (2.67)	15.03 (2.05)	13.26 (2.12)	133.43 (18.15)	735.03 (100.00)

N.B.—Figures in parentheses are percentages.

land of this category. Purchase of other land was also of importance as 9 per cent of the alienated land was due to this factor. Purchase of machinery and equipment accounted for 2 per cent of the alienated land, a phenomenon conspicuous by its absence in the preceding category. Significantly medicine accounted for 5 per cent of land alienation and the share of education was slightly more than 1 per cent. Domestic consumption accounted for nearly the same percentage while house construction accounted for slightly less than 2 per cent of the alienated land.

In the 5—10 acre category it was repayment of old debts again which occupied the most important place among the reasons for land alienation as nearly one-third of the alienated land was due to this factor. Marriage came close to it and it accounted for 27 per cent of alienated land of this category. Purchase of other land also accounted for nearly 9 per cent of such alienation. Purchase of machinery and equipment and house construction accounted for 2 and 3 per cent respectively of the alienated land. Domestic consumption accounted for nearly 2 per cent of the alienated land—slightly higher than what it was in the preceding category.

In the highest category of 10 acres and above repayment of old debts again accounted for half the land alienation. Interestingly marriage accounted for 11 per cent of the alienated land—a figure which was lowest amongst all the land owning groups. The share of purchase of machinery and equipment was highest for any group at 4 per cent. But what was most curious was the fact that 3 per cent of the alienated land was due to the factor of domestic consumption. This was the highest percentage among all the categories. The phenomenon of "left the village" was not confined to landless and poorer households as even in the highest category it accounted for 4 per cent of the alienated land. It is well known that the pull effect of urban life is quite strong and cases are not wanting where even bigger landed households opt for urban living. Purchase of other land was not as important in this category as in the preceding categories. Only 2 per cent of the alienated land was due to it and house construction accounted for 1 per cent of the alienated land.

Broadly it can be said that repayment of old debts, total migration and marriage were prominant factors for land atienated in this region.

In Bundelkhand (Table 11.6) repayment of old debts accounted for 36 per cent of the alienated land of the landless followed by migration which accounted for another 34 per cent of the alienated land. The plight of the landless seems acute in this region as more than one-third of the land alienation was due to clearance of old debts. Medicine and marriage accounted for 23 per cent and 8 per cent respectively of the alienated land of the landless.

The households in the size category of less than 2.5 acres were still more weighted down by repayment of old debts as it accounted for 57 per cent of their alienated land. The share of marriage and medicine was 16 per cent and 11 per cent respectively of their alienated land. Significantly 10 per cent of the alienated land was due to purchase of other land.

Marriage emerged as the biggest factor in case of households in the size category of 2.5—5 acres as nearly 39 per cent of their alienated land was due to this factor. Repayment of old debts followed closely at 35 per cent. Medicine accounted for 17 per cent of their alienated land while purchase of other land was nominal at less than 2 per cent.

Marriage again was the biggest cause for land alienation among households in the size category of 5—10 acres as it accounted for 42 per cent of their alienated land. The share of medicine and repayment of old debts was 25 per cent and 22 per cent respectively. Purchase of other land also accounted for 8 per cent of the alienated land while miscellaneous reasons and domestic consumption accounted for the remaining 2 per cent.

In the highest category interestingly it was the purchase of other land which accounted for 47 per cent of the alienated land. Marriage came next accounting for 35 per cent of the alienated land. The share of repayment of old debts, medicine and education was 8 per cent, 7 per cent and 3 per cent respectively.

In the Hill region land was sold for miscellaneous reasons

TABLE 11.6

Reason-wise Land Transfers in Bundelkhand According to Size Category of Landholdings

(Area in acres)

Size Category	REASONS					
	Marriage	Education	Medicine	Purchase of other land	Left the village	Repayment of old debts
1	2	3	4	5	6	7
Landless	1.50 (7.57)	—	4.52 (22.80)	—	6.75 (34.06)	7.05 (35.57)
Less than 2.5	2.72 (16.01)	—	1.90 (11.18)	1.74 (10.24)	—	9.71 (57.15)
2.5—5	13.01 (38.56)	—	5.93 (17.58)	0.51 (1.51)	—	11.89 (35.24)
5—10	13.59 (42.03)	—	8.14 (25.18)	2.60 (8.04)	—	7.00 (21.65)
10 & above	10.24 (34.70)	0.80 (2.71)	1.97 (6.68)	14.00 (47.44)	—	2.50 (8.47)
Total	41.06 (31.01)	0.80 (0.60)	22.46 (16.97)	18.85 (14.25)	6.75 (5.10)	38.15 (28.82)

Table 11.6 (*Contd.*)

Size Category	REASONS				
	Purchase of machinery & equipment	House construction	Domestic consumption	Miscellaneous	Total
	8	9	10	11	12
Land less	—	—	—	—	19.82 (100.00)
Less than 2.5	—	—	—	0.92 (5.42)	16.99 (100.00)
2.5—5	—	—	—	2.40 (7.11)	33.74 (100.00)
5—10	—	—	0.50 (1.55)	0.50 (1.55)	32.33 (100.00)
10 & above	—	—	—	—	29.51 (100.00)
Total	—	—	0.50 (0.38)	3.82 (2.88)	132.39 (100.00)

N.B.—Figures in parentheses are percentages.

only and it was confined among less than 2.5 acres to 5—10 acre categories.

Reason-wise land transfers according to size category of owned holdings for the state as a whole have been presented in Table 11.7. It will be seen that for the category of landless total migration was the main reason for land alienation as it accounted for three-fourths of their alienated land. Repayment of old debts came next which accounted for 9 per cent of the alienated land. Marriage did not occupy an important place and accounted for less than 2 per cent of such land.

In the size category of less than 2.5 acres repayment of old debts was the biggest factor accounting for 37 per cent of the alienated land. Marriage emerged as an important factor and accounted for 18 per cent of the alienated land. Significantly medicine accounted for 13 per cent of the alienated land. Total migration also accounted for 10 per cent of such land while purchase of other land accounted for 6 per cent of the alienated land.

In the 2.5—5 acre category marriage occupied the first place accounting for 29 per cent of the alienated land followed by repayment of old debts (28 per cent), purchase of other land (10 per cent), total migration and medicine (6 per cent each). Domestic consumption also accounted for 6 per cent of the alienated land. Education accounted for only 1 per cent of such land. Purchase of machinery and equipment accounted for 2 per cent of the alienated land.

In the 5—10 acre category marriage again was the biggest factor for land alienation as 27 per cent of the alienated land was to be accounted for by this factor. Repayment of old debts accounted for another 20 per cent of the alienated land. Significantly total migration accounted for 12 per cent of such land. Purchase of other land was nearly of the same magnitude while medicine accounted for 7 per cent of the alienated land. Domestic consumption accounted for 6 per cent of the alienated land while miscellaneous reasons accounted for 12 per cent of such land.

In the highest category of 10 acres and above repayment of old debts was the biggest factor accounting for one-fourth of the alienated land. Marriage closely followed with a share of

TABLE 11.7

Reason-Wise Land Transfer in U.P. according to Size Category of owned Holdings

(Area in acres)

Size Category	REASONS					
	Marriage	Education	Medicine	Purchase of other land	Left the village	Repayment of old debts
1	2	3	4	5	6	7
Landless	16.36 (1.67)	0.19 (0.02)	13.06 (1.33)	—	738.97 (75.24)	86.39 (8.80)
Less than 2.5	68.98 (17.90)	2.49 (0.65)	48.60 (12.61)	23.11 (6.00)	37.79 (9.80)	142.66 (37.03)
2.5—5	132.51 (29.23)	4.51 (1.00)	28.05 (6.19)	46.23 (10.20)	28.57 (6.30)	124.93 (27.56)
5—10	159.96 (27.27)	1.91 (0.33)	39.66 (6.76)	68.69 (11.71)	71.44 (12.18)	115.03 (19.61)
10 & above	117.02 (23.27)	7.71 (1.53)	15.50 (3.08)	77.72 (15.45)	17.81 (3.54)	126.89 (25.23)
Total	494.83 (17.00)	16.81 (0.58)	144.87 (4.98)	215.75 (7.40)	894.58 (30.74)	595.93 (20.48)

Table 11.7 (*Contd.*)

Size Category	REASONS				
	Purchase of machinery & equipment	House construction	Domestic consumption	Miscellaneous	Total
1	8	9	10	11	12
Landless	11.19 (1.14)	1.09 (0.11)	13.65 (1.39)	101.23 (10.30)	982.13 (100.00)
Less than 2.5	4.25 (1.17)	7.45 (1.93)	12.79 (3.32)	36.96 (9.59)	385.38 (100.00)
2.5—5	9.82 (2.17)	3.87 (0.85)	25.31 (5.58)	40.49 (10.92)	453.29 (100.00)
5—10	12.35 (2.10)	8.10 (1.38)	36.71 (6.26)	72.75 (12.40)	586.60 (100.00)
10 & above	15.72 (3.13)	1.79 (0.36)	28.77 (5.72)	94.00 (18.69)	502.93 (100.00)
Total	53.60 (1.84)	22.30 (0.77)	117.23 (4.03)	345.43 (12.18)	2910.33 (100.00)

N.B.—Figures in parentheses are percentages.

23 per cent. Purchase of other land accounted for as high as 15 per cent of the alienated land which was highest for any category. Domestic consumption accounted for 6 per cent of the alienated land. Total migration among the highest category also accounted for nearly 4 per cent of the alienated land.

Briefly it can be said that poorer households are selling land largely because they are migrating for good while better-off households are selling land largely to meet marriage expenses and to repay old debts.

Caste and Size-wise Analysis of Reasons for Land Alienation

An attempt was made to analyse the reasons for land transfers on caste as well as category-wise basis also. The results for eastern U.P. are presented in Table 11.8.

It will be seen that marriage accounted for 18 per cent of the land transferred by high caste Hindus and its share among Backward Caste was lower at 13 per cent but was again higher at 17 per cent among Scheduled Caste while it was lowest among Muslims at less than 5 per cent. Among the high caste Hindu households in the size category of 2.5—5.0 acres the incidence was highest as almost one-third of their alienated land was due to this factor. In the other two higher categories it accounted for nearly one-fifth of the alienated land. Among the Backward Caste the highest category was particularly afflicted by it as 42 per cent of the land transfer in this category was on account of marriage. Significantly marriage was a big factor among the higher categories of Scheduled Castes also as more than one-third of the land in categories of above 2.5 acres was transferred due to the marriage factor. This was equally true for Muslims in the size category of 2.5 to 10 acres where also nearly 30 per cent of the land was transferred due to this reason. Thus the burden of marriage appears to be a big factor for land alienation in eastern U.P. and upper categories among all the castes are particularly affected by it.

The incidence of total migration was most marked among Muslims as 81 per cent of the total land alienation was due to this factor. Among the Backward Caste it accounted for more than half of the land alienation while among the Scheduled

TABLE 11.8

Reason-wise Distribution of Land Transfers in Eastern U.P. According to Size Category of Landholding and Caste

(Area in Acres)

Size Category	Marriage	Education	Medicine	Purchase of other land	Left the village	Repayment of old debts
1	2	3	4	5	6	7
H.C.H.						
Landless	11.66 (6.93)	—	1.58 (0.95)	—	128.72 (77.17)	6.75 (4.05)
Less than 2.5	14.82 (21.75)	0.43 (0.63)	12.45 (18.28)	2.71 (3.98)	4.37 (9.41)	14.00 (20.55)
2.5—5	26.94 (32.08)	3.25 (3.87)	2.08 (2.48)	12.01 (14.30)	2.31 (2.75)	8.05 (9.59)
5—10	33.38 (20.94)	0.14 (0.09)	1.95 (1.22)	37.86 (23.75)	16.03 (10.06)	12.71 (7.97)
10 & above	32.96 (18.34)	0.98 (0.54)	4.54 (2.53)	55.47 (23.86)	1.25 (0.70)	19.39 (10.79)
Total	119.66 (18.19)	4.80 (0.73)	22.60 (3.44)	108.05 (16.42)	152.68 (23 .20)	60.90 (6.26)
B.C.						
Landless	0.93 (0.50)	—	0.09 (0.05)	—	172.26 (92.29)	9.99 (5.34)
Less than 2.5	8.83 (16.26)	—	2.15 (3.96)	9.40 (17.30)	2.11 (3.89)	25.93 (47.75)
2.5—5	11.20 (27.34)	—	1.29 (4.69)	6.71 (16.38)	1.55 (3.78)	6.97 (17.01)

Table 11.8 (*Contd.*)

1	2	3	4	5	6	7
5—10	7.89	—	0.96	3.21	13.51	5.64
	(18.72)		(2.28)	(7.62)	(32.06)	(13.38)
10 & above	18.52	—	0.80	3.31	0.63	17.60
	(42.39)		(1.83)	(7.59)	(1.45)	(40.33)
Total	47.35	—	5.92	22.63	190.06	66.13
	(12.88)		(1.60)	(6.15)	(51.69)	(17.98)
S.C.						
Landless	0.15	6.19	2.19	—	24.58	1.84
	(0.49)	(0.62)	(6.16)		(80.30)	(6.01)
Less than 2.5	2.02	—	3.48	1.19	0.84	2.80
	(13.65)		(16.28)	(5.55)	(3.93)	(13.09)
2.5—5	5.83	—	—	—	4.50	2.55
	(36.26)				(27.99)	(15.86)
5—10	4.96	—	—	1.58	4.53	4.26
	(32.36)			(1 .30)	(29.55)	(27.79)
10 & above	1.26	—	—	—	—	2.00
	(38.65)					(61.35)
Total	15.12	0.19	5.67	2.77	34.45	13.45
	(17.12)	(0.21)	(6.54)	(3.20)	(39.75)	(15.52)

1	2	3	4	5	6	7
MUSLIM						
Landless	—	—	—	—	168.43 (95.20)	3.88 (2.19)
Less than 2.5	2.24 (12.49)	0.80 (4.46)	1.33 (7.41)	1.60 (8.92)	4.92 (27.42)	3.45 (19.23)
2.5—5	5.37 (26.82)	—	0.20 (1.00)	—	5.66 (28.27)	4.92 (24.58)
5—10	3.20 (31.59)	0,52 (5.13)	—	—	2.68 (26.46)	3.00 (29.61)
10 & above	—	—	—	—	—	—
Total	10.81 (4.80)	1.32 (0.59)	1.53 (0.68)	1.60 (0.71)	181.69 (80.74)	15.25 (6.78)
Grand Total	192.94 (14.43)	6.31 (0.47)	35.72 (2.68)	135.05 (10.10)	558.88 (41.79)	157.73 (11.64)

Table 11.8 (*Contd.*)

Size Category	REASONS				
	Purchase of machinery & equipment	House construction	Domestic Consumption	Miscellaneous	Total
1	8	9	10	11	12
H.C.H.					
Landless	1.90	—	0.54	15.74	166.79
	(1.14)		(0.32)	(9.44)	(100.00)
Less than 2.5	3.42	0.88	—	15.05	68.13
	(5.02)	(1.29)		(22.09)	(100.00)
2.5—5	3.23	2.00	12.89	11.21	83.97
	(3.85)	(2.38)	(15.35)	(13.35)	(100.00)
5—10	8.54	0.07	29.35	19.37	145.40
	(5.36)	(0.04)	(18.41)	(12.16)	(100.00)
10 & above	1.49	—	22.26	41.37	179.71
	(0.83)		(12.39)	(28.02)	(100.00)
Total	18.58	2.95	65.04	102.74	658.00
	(2.82)	(0.45)	(9.88)	(15.61)	(100.00)

	8	9	10	11	12
B.C.					
Landless	2.63 (9.34)	—	2.76 (1.48)	—	186.66 (100.00)
Less than 2.5	0.20 (0.37)	0.32 (0.54)	2.43 (4.48)	2.93 (5.40)	54.30 (100.00)
2.5—5	0.20 (0.44)	—	10.21 (24.92)	2.21 (5.39)	40.97 (100.00)
5—10	0.18 (0.43)	4.00 (9.40	0.02 (0.05)	6.73 (15.97)	42.14 (100.00)
10 & above	0.80 (1.83)	—	2.00 (3.58)	—	43.64 (100.00)
Total	2.01 (0.55)	4.32 (1.18)	17.42 (4.73)	11.87 (3.23)	367.71 (100.00)
S.C.					
Landless	—	—	0.52 (1.70)	1.14 (3.72)	30.61 (100.00)
Less than 2.5	—	—	7.15 (33.43)	3.01 (14.07)	21.39 (100.09)
2.5—5	—	—	1.04 (6.46)	2.16 (13.43)	16.08 (100.00)
5—10	—	—	—	—	15.33
10 & above	—	—	—	—	3.26 (100.00)
Total	—	—	8.71 (10.05)	6.31 (7.28)	86.67 (100.00)

	8	9	10	11	12
MUSLIM					
Landless	—	—	2.32	2.30	176.93
			(1.31)	(1.30)	(100.00)
Less than 2.5	—	—		3.60	17.94
				(20.07)	(100.00)
2.5—5	0.47	—	—	3.40	20.02
	(2.35)			(16.98)	(100.00)
5—10	0.26	—	—	0.47	10.13
	(2.57)			(4.64)	(100.00)
Total	0.73	—	2.32	9.77	225.02
	(0.33)	—	(1.03)	(4.34)	(100.00)
Grand Total	21.32	7.27	93.49	130.69	1337.40
	(1.59)	(0.54)	(6.99)	(9.77)	(100.00)

N.B.—Figures in parentheses are percentages.

Castes it accounted for 40 per cent of the alienated land. Among the high caste Hindus it accounted for 23 per cent of the land alienation. Understandably it was landless which accounted for the overwhelmingly large part of such land among all the castes.

Repayment of old debts accounted for 9 per cent of all land transfers among high caste Hindus while among the Backward and Scheduled Caste it accounted for 18 per cent and 16 per cent respectively of the land transfers. Among Muslims it accounted for only 7 per cent of the land transfers.

'Purchase of other land' accounted for 16 per cent of all land transfers among high caste Hindus but was quite low among Backward Castes (6 per cent), Scheduled Caste (3 per cent) and Muslims (1 per cent). Among the two higher categories of high caste Hindus it accounted for more than one fourth each of the land transferred but among the Backward Castes the two lowest landed categories accounted for one-sixth each of the land transferred due to this reason. Among the Scheduled Castes it was confined to two categories of less than 2.5 acres and 5—10 acres while among the Muslims it was confined to less than 2.5 acre category.

Purchase of machinery and implements accounted for less than 2 per cent of the land sold in the eastern region. Among the middle categories of high caste Hindus it accounted for nearly 5 per cent of the land sold whereas among the Backward castes as a whole it accounted for less than 1 per cent of the land sold.

Land was also sold to meet domestic consumption needs other than marriage, medicine and education. Such factors accounted for 7 per cent of the alienated land in eastern U.P. It accounted for nearly 10 per cent of alienated land among high caste Hindu, 5 per cent in case of Backward Castes, 10 per cent in case of Scheduled Castes and 1 per cent in case of Muslims. What is intriguing about it is the fact that land was sold generally by higher categories so far as high caste Hindus were concerned for meeting such needs and lessthan 2.5 acre category among them did not sell any land on this count. Among the Backward Castes although all the categories sold land on this count yet nearly one-fourth of the land was sold by 2.5—5 acres category on this count. Understandably one-third of the alienated land of Scheduled Castes in the category of less than 2.5 acres was sold on this count.

A caste and size-wise classification of reasons for land transfers in central U.P. is shown in Table 11.9. Among the high caste Hindus marriage accounted for 34 per cent of land alienation followed by Backward Castes (21 per cent) Muslims (18 per cent) and Schdeduled Caste (13 per cent). Among the high caste Hindus 57 per cent of the land sold in the size category of less than 2.5 acres was due to this factor followed by the highest category at 50 per cent. Among the Backward Caste 46 per cent of the land sold in the highest category was due to this factor as against 12 per cent among the Muslims of the same category. Among the Scheduled Caste 68 per cent of the land sold in the size categories of 5—10 acres was due to this reason.

Next in importance was the migration factor. Among the high caste Hindus 20 per cent of the land was sold on account of this factor. Among the Backward Castes it accounted for 35 per cent of the land followed by Scheduled Caste (22 per cent) and Muslims (12 per cent).

Repayment of old debts was responsible for 21 per cent of land alienation in the region and its incidence was most marked among Muslims where it accounted for 35 per cent of the land followed by Scheduled Castes (29 per cent), Backward Caste (25 per cent) and high caste Hindus (11 per cent).

Purchase of machinery and equipment accounted for less than 2 per cent of land alienation and was mainly confined to high caste Hindus. Among them the highest category resorted to it most as 14 per cent of their land alienation was due to it.

Education accounted for only 1 per cent of the alienated land and it was confined to high caste Hindus alone. No other caste had sold land to meet educational expenses. Significantly it was the highest category among them which accounted for 82 per cent of the total land sold for the purpose in this region. It shows that the richest among high caste Hindus are keen on imparting education to their wards even by selling land.

But unlike education, medicine accounted for 9 per cent of

TABLE 11.9

Reason-Wise Land Transfers in Central U.P. According to Size Category of Landholding and Caste

(Area in acres)

Size Category	Marriage	Education	Medicine	Purchase of other land	Left of the village	Repayment of old debts
1	2	3	4	5	6	7
H.C.H.						
Landless	—	—	2.05 (3.38)	—	43.73 (72.16)	2.22 (3.66)
Less than 2.5	9.88 (56.52)	1.26 (7.21)	2.20 (12.59)	—	0.91 (5.20)	3.23 (18.48)
2.5—5	29.82 (37.12)	—	6.86 (8.54)	9.00 (11.20)	6.35 (7.90)	16.80 (20.91)
5—10	34.66 (41.16)	—	18.61 (22.10)	7.26 (8.62)	6.13 (1.28)	9.72 (11.54)
10 & above	24.26 (50.12)	5.93 12.25	5.53 (11.43)	0.80 (1.65)	2.20 (4.55)	0.51 (1.06)
Total	98.62 (33.89)	7.19 (2.47)	35.25 (12.11)	17.06 (5.86)	59.32 (20.38)	32.48 (11.16)

1	2	3	4	5	6	7
B.C.						
Landless	0.75 (1.30)	—	—	—	44.77 (77.58)	6.87 (11.90)
Less than 2.5	14.93 (23.50)	—	6.29 (9.90)	2.60 (4.09)	9.29 (14.62)	28.72 (45.21)
2.5—5	18.72 (37.36)	—	3.68 (7.29)	6.94 (13.74)	3.35 (6.63)	11.97 (23.79)
5—10	6.00 (11.82)	—	2.32	2.32 (4.57)	23.19 (45.68)	11.40 (22.45)
10 & above	10.76 (45.83)	—	0.50 (2.13)	—	6.30 (26.82)	2.42 (10.31)
Total	51.16 (20.80)	—	10.47 (4.25)	11 86 (4.82)	86.90 (35.33)	61.38 (24.95)
S.C.						
Landless	—	—	—	—	—	1.40 (26.07)
Less than 2.5	2.50 (9.92)	—	6.48 (25.71)	—	6.41 (25.44)	8.04 (31.90)
2.5—5	0.39 (5.98)	—	0.93 (14.26)	0.32 (4.91)	2.51 (38.50)	1.89 (28.99)
5—10	2.57 (68.35)	—	—	—	—	0.54 (14.36)
10 & above	—	—	—	—	—	—
Total	5.46 (13.37)	—	7.41 (18.14)	0.32 (0.78)	8.92 (21.84)	11.87 (29.06)

1	2	3	4	5	6	7
MUSLIM						
Landless	—	—	—	—	9.85 (44.37)	7.35 33.11)
Less than 2,5	0.80 (3.16)	—	6.20 (24.51)	2,07 (1.18)	2.85 (11.26)	9.38 37.08)
2.5—5	4.77 (29.41)	—	0.80 (4.93)	1,73 (10.66)	—	6.20 (38.22)
5—10	12.39 (40.15)	—	1,25 (4.05)	0.74 (2.40)	1.25 (4.05)	11.14 (36.10)
10 & above	2.94 (11.74)	—	0.25 (1,00)	0.60 (2.40)	0.90 (3.59)	7.25 (28.05)
Total	20.90 (17.47)	—	8.50 (7.11)	5.14 (4.30)	14.85 (12.41)	41.35 (34.54)
SIKH						
Landless	—	—	—	—	—	—
Less than 2.5	—	—	—	—	—	—
2.5—5	—	—	—	—	—	—
5—10	—	—	—	—	—	—
10 & above	—	—	—	—	—	—
Total	—	—	—	—	—	—
Grand Total	176.14 (25.21)	7.19 (1.03)	61.63 (8.82)	34.38 (4.92)	169.99 (24.33)	147.05 (21.04)

Table 11.9 (*Contd.*)

	Purchase of Machinery & equipment	House construction	Domestic consnmption	Miscellaneous	Total
1	8	9	10	11	12
H.C.H.					
Landless	—	—	1.45 (2.40)	11.15 (18.40)	60.60 (100.00)
Less than 2.5	—	—	—	—	17.48 (100.00)
2.5—5	3.67 (4.57)	—	—	7.84 (9.76)	80.34 (100.00)
5—10	0.04 (0.05)	—	4.34 (5.15)	3.45 (4.10)	84.21 (100.00)
10 & above	6.99 (14.44)	—	—	2.18 (4.50)	48,40 (100.00)
Total	10.70 (3.68)	—	5.79 (1.99)	24.62 (8.46)	291.03 (100.00)

Table 11.9 (*Contd.*)

B.C.					
Landless	1.06 (1.84)	—	—	4.26 (7.38)	57.71 (100.00)
Less than 2.5	—	—	—	1.70 (2.68)	63.53 (100.00)
2.5—5	—	—	—	5.85 (11.58)	50.51 (100.00)
5—10	—	—	—	7.86 (15.48)	50.77 (100.00)
10 & above	—	—	—	3.50 (14.91)	23.48 (100.00)
Total	1.06 (0.43)	—	—	23.17 (9.42)	246.00 (100.00)
S.C.					
Landless	—	—	—	3.97 (73.93)	5.37 (100.00)
Less than 2.5	—	—	0 11 (0.44)	1.66 (6.59)	25.20 (100.00)
2.5—5	—	—	—	0.48 (7.36)	6.52 (100.00)
2.5—5	—	—	—	0.65 (17.29)	3.76 (100.00)
10 & above	—	—	—	—	—
Total	—	—	0.11 (0.26)	6.76 (16.55)	40.85 (.00.00)

1	8	9	10	11	12
MUSLIM					
Landless	—	—	0.98 (4.41)	4.02 (18.11)	22.20 (100.00)
Less than 2.5	0.90 (3.56)	—	3.10 (12.25)	—	25.30 (100.00)
2.5—5	—	—	—	2.72 (16.79)	16.22 (100.00)
5—10	—	—	—	4.09 (13.25)	30.86 (100.00)
10 & above	—	—	—	13.10 (52.32)	25.04 (100.00)
Total	0.90 (0.75)	—	4.08 (3.41)	23.93 (20.01)	119 62 (100.00)
SIKH					
Landless	—	—	—	—	—
Less than 2.5	—	—	—	—	—
2.5—5	—	—	—	—	—
5—10	—	—	-	1.26 (100.00)	1.26 (100.00)
10 & above	—	—	—	—	—
Total	—	—	—	1.26 (100.00)	1.26 (100 00)
Grand Total	12.66 (1.81)	—	9.98 (1.43)	79.74 (11.41)	698.76 (100.00)

N.B.—Figures in parentheses are percentages.

land alienation. Its incidence was highest among Scheduled Caste where it accounted for 18 per cent of their alienated land followed by high caste Hindus (12 per cent), Muslims (7 per cent) and Backward Caste (4 per cent).

Purchase of other land accounted for 5 per cent of the land sold in this egion. High caste Hindus accounted for half the land sold for this purpose. They also accounted for more than half (58 per cent) of the land sold to meet domestic consumption needs followed by Muslims (41 per cent). It was largely confined to poorer categories.

Land trānsfers in western U.P. according to size of land holding as well as caste is shown in Table 11.10. It will be seen that repayment of old debts occupied the first place and accounted for 35 per cent of the land alienation in this region. Among the Scheduled Caste and Muslims it was responsible for slightly more than half of the total land sold by them. The proportion was also quite high among high caste Hindus (29 per cent) and Backward Caste (39 per cent) as well.

'Left the village' was next in importance as nearly 22 per cent of the land alienation was on account of this factor. Sikhs appear to be particularly afflicted by it as nearly 90 per cent of the land alienation among them was because of this factor. Next came Backward Caste with 28 per cent of the total land alienated because of it. Among high caste Hindus the proportion was 18 per cent followed by 9 per cent among Scheduled Caste and 2 per cent among Muslims.

Marriage occupied the third place as nearly 12 per cent of the land alienation was due to it. Its incidence was highest at 16 per cent among high caste Hindus followed by Backward Castes (11 per cent), Muslims (7 per cent), Scheduled Caste (3 per cent) and Sikhs (1 per cent). Among the high caste Hindus the 5—10 acres category was particularly afflicted by it as 41 per cent of their land alienation was due to this factor.

'Purchase of other land' accounted for 4 per cent of the total alienated land in this region. It accounted for 9 per cent of the alienated land of Scheduled Castes followed by Backward Caste (6 per cent), Muslims (3 per cent), Sikhs and high caste Hindus (2 per cent) each. Purchase of agricultural and non-agricultural machinery and equipment accounted for

TABLE 11.10

Reason-wise Land Transfers in Western U.P. According to Size Category of Land-holding and Caste

(Area in acres)

Size Category	Marriage	Education	Medicine	Purchase of other land	Left the village	Repayment of old debts
1	2	3	4	5	6	7
H.C.H.						
Landless	1.00 (0.81)	—	—	—	60.70 (49.09)	9.13 (7.39)
Less than 2.5	7.90 (24.43)	—	3.45 (10.67)	—	1.56 (4.82)	12.43 (38.43)
2.5—5	9.52 (22.76)	—	0.75 (1.79)	3.60 (8.61)	1.25 (2.99)	18.61 (44.50)
5—10	32.29 (41.17)	1.25 (1.59)	2.36 (3.01)	4.45 (5.67)	4.12 (3.98)	25.58 (32.62)
10 & above	9.65 (10.23)	—	1.91 (2.02)	1.00 (1.06)	0.28 (0.30)	42.61 (45.18)
Total	60.36 (16.29)	1.25 (0.34)	8.47 (2.29)	9.05 (2.44)	66.91 (18.06)	108.36 (29.24)

1	2	3	4	5	6	7
B.C.						
Landless	—	—	0.78 (2.02)	—	28.52 (73.98)	5.93 (15.38)
Less than 2,5	0.60 (23.08)	—	0.54 (20.77)	0.05 (1.92)	—	42.31 (1.10)
2,5—5	3.83 (15.68)	0.63 (2.58)	2.73 (11.17)	2.54 (10.40)	1.09 (4.46)	12.29 (50.31)
5—10	7.30 (24.82)	—	5.08 (17.27)	3.82 (12.99)	—	8.63 (29.35)
10 & above	2.30 (6.94)	—	—	0.84 (2.53)	6.25 (18.84)	21.77 (65.63)
Total	14.03 (10.95)	0.63 (0.49)	9.13 (7.12)	7.25 (5.66)	35.86 (27.98)	49.72 (38.79)
S.C.						
Landless	—	—	1.85 (7.56)	—	5.54 (22.65)	4.99 (20 40)
Less than 2.5	—	—	1.73 (7.86)	1.75 (7.96)	1.07 (4.86)	14.33 (65.14)
2.5—5	0.30 (1.58)	—	0.75 (3.95)	—	—	16.50 (86.93)
5—10	—	—	0.06 (1.37)	3.75 (85.62)	—	0.57 (13.01)
10 & above	1.71 (34.40)	—	—	1.39 (27.97)	—	1.87 (37.63)
Total	2.01 (2.69)	—	4.39 (5.87)	6.89 (9.20)	6.61 (8.84)	38.26 (51.16)

Table 11.10 (*Contd.*)

1	2	3	4	5	6	7
MUSLIM						
Landless	0.47 (1.93)	—	—	—	0.63 (2.59)	18.99 (78.18)
Less than 2.5	0.84 (6.04)	—	0.40 (2.88)	—	1.58 (11.37)	9.57 (68.85)
2.5—5	2.81 (15.04)	0.63 (3.37)	1.42 (7.60)	2.87 (15.36)	—	6.29 (33.65)
5—10	1.10 (3 08)	—	0.93 (2.61)	—	—	12.71 (35.64)
10 & above	2.44 (14.94)	—	—	0.31 (1.90)	—	7.87 (48.19)
Total	7.66 (7.04)	0.63 (0.58)	2.75 (2.53)	3.18 (2.92)	2.21 (2.03)	55.43 (50.91)
SIKH						
Landless	—	—	—	—	44.49 (100.00)	—
Less than 2.5	—	—	—	—	1.88 (100.00)	—
2.5—5	—	—	—	—	—	—
5—10	0.63 (12.16)	—	0.32 (6.18)	1.10 (21.24)	1.00 (19.30)	2.13 (41.12)
10 & above	—	—	—	—	—	1.10 (100.00)
Total	0.63 (1.20)	—	0.32 (0.10)	1.10 (2.09)	47.37 (89.97)	3.23 (6.13)
Grand Total	84.69 (11.52)	2.51 (0.34)	25.06 (3.41)	27.47 (3.74)	158.96 (21.53)	255.00 (34.69)

Table 11.10 (*Contd.*)

	Purchase of machinery & equipment	House construction	Domestic consumption	Miscellaneous	Total
1	8	9	10	11	12
H.C.H.					
Landless	0.93 (0.75)	1.09 (0.88)	—	50.80 (41.08)	123.65 (100.00)
Less than 2.5	—	6.25 (19.33)	—	0.75 (2.32)	32.34 (100.00)
2.5—5	—	—	—	8.09 (19.35)	41.82 (100.00)
5—10	—	0.45 (0.57)	2.50 (3.19)	6.43 (8.20)	78.43 (100.00)
10 & above	2.31 (2.45)	0.37 (0.39)	3.87 (4.10)	32.32 (34.27)	94.32 (100.00)
Total	3.24 (0.87)	8.16 (2.20)	6.37 (1.72)	98.39 (26.55)	370.56 (100.00)

1	8	9	10	11	12
B.C.					
Landless	—	—	3.32 (8.62)	—	38.55 (100.00)
Less than 2.5	—	—	—	0.31 (11.92)	2.60 (100.00)
2.5—5	1.00 (4.09)	—	—	0.32 (1.31)	24.43 (100.00)
5—10	2.70 (9.18)	—	—	1.88 (6.39)	29.41 (100 00)
10 & above	1.42 (4.28)	—	0.06 (0.18)	0.53 (1.60)	33.17 (100.00)
Total	5.12 (4.00)	—	3.38 (2.64)	3.04 (2.37)	128.16 (100.00)
S.C.					
Landless	6.67 (22.27)	—	—	5.41 (22.12)	24.46 (100.00)
Less than 2.5	—	—	—	3.12 (14.18)	22.00 (100.00)
2.5—5	1.25 (6.59)	—	—	0.18 (0.95)	18.98 (100.00)
5—10	—	—	—	—	4.38 (100.00)
10 & above	—	—	—	—	4.97 (100.00)
Total	7.92 (10.59)	—	—	8.71 (11.65)	74.79 (100.00)

1	8	9	10	11	12
MUSLIM					
Landless	—	—	1.76 (7.25)	2.44 (10.05)	24.29 (100.00)
Less than 2.5	—	—	—	1.51 (10.86)	13.90 (100.00)
2.5—5	—	1.87 (10 00)	1.17 (6.26)	1.63 (8.72)	18.69 (100.00)
2—10	0.63 (1.77)	3.58 (10.04)	—	16.71 (46.86)	35.66 (100.00)
10 & above	2.71 (16.60)	1.42 (8.70)	0.58 (3.55)	1.00 (6.12)	16.33 (100.00)
Total	3.34 (3.07)	6.87 (6.31)	3.51 (3.22)	23.29 (21.39)	108.87 (100.00)
SIKH					
Landless	—	—	—	—	44.49 (100,00)
Less than 2.5	—	—	—	—	1.88 (100.00)
2.5—5	—	—	—	—	—
5—10	—	—	—	—	5.18 (100.00)
10 & above	—	—	—	—	1.10 (100.00)
Total	—	—	—	—	52.65 (100.00)
Grand Total	19.62 (2.67)	15.03 (2.05)	13,26 (1.80)	133.43 (18.15)	735.03 (100.00)

N.B.—Figures in parentheses are percentages.

nearly 3 per cent of the alienated land. It accounted for 11 per cent of land alienation among Scheduled Caste followed by Backward Castes (4 per cent), Muslims (3 per cent) and high caste Hindus (1 per cent). Land alienation for house construction was confined to high caste Hindus and Muslims alone. Among the former it accounted for 2 per cent of the alienated land and among the latter it accounted for 6 per cent of the same. Land alienation to meet household consumption needs accounted for nearly 3 per cent of the land alienated among Backward Castes and Muslims each followed by 2 per cent among high caste Hindus. Significantly Scheduled Castes did not sell any land on this count. Medical expenses accounted for 7 per cent of the land alienated among Backward Castes followed by Scheduled Caste (6 per cent), Muslims (3 per cent), and high caste Hindus (2 per cent). Education was not an important factor and it accounted for less than half per cent of the alienated land among high caste Hindus as well as Backward Castes. Among Muslims it accounted for slightly more than half per cent and was absent among Scheduled Castes.

Reasons for land alienation in Bundelkhand according to size category of owned holding and caste is shown in Table 11.11. Among the high caste Hindus marriage accounted for 36 per cent of the alienated land followed by Backward Caste and Muslims (20 per cent) each and Scheduled Caste (9 per cent).

Next to marriage was the factor of repayment of old debts which accounted for 29 per cent of the alienated land. Among the Scheduled Caste its incidence was highest at 62 per cent which possibly shows the hardships that poorer sections have to face in repayment of debts. Significantly the higher categories among the Scheduled Castes were free from this type of land alienation and the phenomenon was most pronounced in lessthan 25 acre category where 84 per cent of the alienated land was due to this factor. More than 40 per cent of the alienated land among Backward Caste and Muslims was also due to this factor. The same was 22 per cent among high caste Hindus.

Purchase of other land accounted for 14 per cent of the alienated land but this was a phenomenon which was more pronounced among high caste Hindus among whom the highest category had sold almost half of its alienated land with a view

TABLE 11.11

Reason-wise Land Transfers in Bundelekhand According to Size Category of Landholding and Caste

(Area in acres)

Size Category	Marriage	Education	Medicine	Purchase of other land	Left the village	Repayment of old debts
1	2	3	4	5	6	7
H.C.H						
Landless	—	—	—	—	4.00 (66.67)	2.00 (33.33)
Less than 2.5	—	—	1.90 (27.54)	—	—	4.70 (68.11)
2.5—5	11.31 (13.85)	—	3 43 (13.30)	0.51 (1.98)	—	8.14 (31.56)
5—10	13.59 (46.34)	—	8.14 (27.75)	2.60 (8.87)	—	4.00 (13.64)
10 & above	10.24 (34.70)	0.80 (2.71)	1.97 (6.68)	14.00 (47 44)	—	2.50 (8.47)
Total	35.14 (36.03)	0.80 (0.82)	15.44 (13.83)	17.11 (17.54)	4.00 (4.10)	21.34 (21.88)

Table 11.11 (*Contd.*)

1	2	3	4	5	6	7
B.C.						
Landless	1.00 (15.46)	—	0.72 (11.13)	—	2.75 (42.50)	2.00 (30.91)
Less than 2.5	1.94 (37.52)	—	— (33.66)	1.74 (33.66)	—	0.87 (16.83)
2.5—5	1.50 (20.98)	—	1.30 (32.17)	—	—	3.35 (46.85)
5—10	—	—	—	—	—	3.00 (100.00)
10 & above	—	—	—	—	—	—
Total	4.44 (20.37)	—	3.02 (13.86)	1.74 (7.99)	2.75 (12.62)	9.22 (42.31)
S.C.						
Landless	—	—	2.80 (57.73)	—	—	2.05 (42.27)
Less than 2.5	0.78 (15.85)	—	—	—	—	4.14 (84.15)
2.5—5	0.20 (25.00)	—	0.20 (25.00)	—	—	0.40 (50.00)
5—10	—	—	—	—	—	—
10 & above	—	—	—	—	—	—
Total	0.98 (9.27)	—	3.00 (28.38)	—	—	6.59 (62.35)

1	2	3	4	5	6	7
MUSLIM						
Landless	0.50 (20.00)	—	1.00 (40.00)	—	—	1.00 (40.00)
Less than 2.5	—	—	—	—	—	—
2.5—5	—	—	—	—	—	—
5—10	—	—	—	—	—	—
10 & above	—	—	—	—	—	—
Total	0.50 (20.00)	—	1.00 (40.00)	—	—	1.00 (40.00)
Grand Total	41.06 (31 02)	0.80 (0.60)	22.46 (16.97)	18.85 (14.24)	6.75 (5.10)	38.15 (28.82)

Table 11.11 (*Contd.*)

Size Category	Purchase of machinery & equipment	House construction	Domestic consumption	Miscellaneous	Total
1	8	9	10	11	12
H.C.H.					
Landless	—	—	—	—	6.00 (100.00)
Less than 2.5	—	—	—	0.30 (4.35)	6.90 (100.00)
2.5—5	—	—	—	2.40 (9.31)	25.79 (100.00)
5—10	—	—	0.50 (1.70)	0.50 (1.70)	29.33 (100.00)
10 & above	—	—	—	—	29.51 (100.00)
Total	—	—	0.50 (3.51)	3.20 (3.29)	97.53 (100.00)

Table 11.11 (*Contd.*)

1	8	9	10	11	12
B C.					
Landless	—	—	—	—	6.47 (100.00)
Less than 2.5	—	—	—	0.62 (11.99)	5.17 (100.00)
2,5—5	—	—	—	—	7.15 (100.00)
5—10	—	—	—	—	3.00 (100.00)
10 & above	—	—	—	—	—
Total	—	—	—	0.62 (2.85)	21.79 (100.00)
S.C.					
Landless	—	—	—	—	4.85 (100.00)
Less than 2.5	—	—	—	—	4.92 (100.00)
2,5—5	—	—	—	—	0.80
5—10	—	—	—	—	(100.00)
10 & above	—	—	—	—	—
Total	—	—	—	—	10.57 (100.00)

1	8	9	10	11	12
MUSLIM					
Landless	—	—	—	—	2.50 (100.00)
Less than 2.5	—	—	—	—	—
2.5—5	—	—	—	—	—
5—10	—	—	—	—	—
10 & above	—	—	—	—	—
Total	—	-	—	—	2.50 (100.00)
Grand Total	—	—	0.50 (0.38)	3.82 (2.86)	132.39 (100.00)

N.B.—Figures in parentheses are percentages.

to purchase other land. Among the Backward Castes accounted for 8 per cent of the alienated land. No other caste sold land on this count.

Interestingly no land was sold to purchase machinery and equipment in this region. This was so in case of house construction also. Domestic consumption as a factor for land alienation was almost absent save among high caste Hindus. But expenditure on medicine accounted for as high as 17 per cent of the total land alienated. in this region. Its incidence was high at 58 per cent among landless Scheduled Castes and 40 per cent among landless Muslims.

Reasons for land alienation in the state as a whole according to size category of owned holdings and caste is presented in Table 11.12. It will be seen that total migration or left the village as a factor for land alienation accounted for 31 per cent of the land that was alienated in the state during the reference period. It accountrd for 88 per cent of the land sold by Sikhs followed by Muslims (44 per cent), Backward Caste (41 per cent), Scheduled Caste (23 per cent) and high caste Hindus (20 per cent).

Repayment of old debts came next in importance. It accounted for 20 per cent of the land alienated in the state. This factor was responsible for 33 per cent of all the land sold by Scheduled Castes followed by Muslims (25 per cent) Backward Caste (24 per cent), high caste Hindus (16 per cent) and Sikhs (6 per cent).

Marriage as a factor for land alienation accounted for 22 per cent of the alienated land of high caste Hindus followed by Backward Caste (15 per cent) Scheduled Caste (11 per cent) and Muslims (9 per cent).

Purchase of other land as a reason for land sale accounted for 10 per cent of the alienated land among high caste Hindus followed by Backward Castes and Scheduled Caste (5 per cent each) and Muslims and Sikhs (2 per cent each).

Purchase of machinery and equipment accounted for 4 per cent of the land alienation among Scheduled Caste followed by high caste Hindus (2 per cent) and Backward Caste and

TABLE 11.12

Reason-wise Land Transfers in U.P. according to Size Category of Landholding and Castes

(Area in acres)

Size Category	Marriage	Education	Medicine	Purehase of other land	Left the village	Repayment of old debts
1	2	3	4	5	6	7
H.C.H.						
Landless	12.56	—	3.63	—	237.15	20.10
	(3.52)		(1.02)		(66.42)	(5.53)
Less than 2.5	32.60	1.69	20.00	2.71	6.84	34.36
	(25.62)	(1.33)	(15.72)	(2.13)	(5.37)	(27.00)
2.5—5	77.59	3.25	13.12	26.12	9.91	51.60
	(33.31)	(1.40)	(5.63)	(10.79)	(4.26)	(22.15)
5—10	133.92	1.39	31.06	53.17	25.28	52.01
	(32.11)	(0.39)	(8.76)	(14.71)	(7.13)	(14.66)
10 & above	77.11	7.71	13.95	73.66	3.73	65.01
	(21.91)	(2.19)	(3.96)	(20.25)	(1.06)	(18.47)
Total	313.78	14.04	81.76	155.66	282.91	223.08
	(22.04)	(0.99)	(5.74)	(10.90)	(19.87)	(15.67)

1	2	3	4	5	6	7
B.C.						
Landless	2.68 (0.93)	—	1.59 (0.55)	—	248.30 (85.80)	24.79 (8.57)
Less than 2.5	26.30 (20.94)	—	8.98 (7.15)	13.79 (10.98)	11.40 (9.08)	56.62 (45.08)
2,5—5	35.25 (28.64)	0.63 (0.51)	10.63 (8.64)	17.19 (13.16)	5.99 (4.87)	34.58 (28.10)
5—10	21.19 (16.91)	—	6.04 (4.82)	9.35 (7.47)	36.70 (29.28)	28.67 (22.88)
10 & above	31.56 (31.47)	—	1.30 (1.30)	4.15 (4.14)	13.18 (13.14)	41.79 (41.67)
Total	116.98 (15.32)	0.63 (0.08)	28.54 (3.74)	44.48 (5.14)	315,57 (41.32)	186.45 (24.41)
S.C.						
Landless	0.15 (0.23)	0.19 (0.29)	6.84 (10.48)	—	30.12 (46.13)	10.28 (15.74)
Less than 2.5	6.20 (8.43)	—	11.69 (15.90)	2.94 (4.00)	8.32 (11.32)	29.31 (39.87)
2.5—5	6.72 (15.86)	—	1.88 (4.44)	0.32 (0.76)	7.01 (16.54)	21.34 (50.35)
5—10	7.53 (32.08)	—	0.06 (0.26)	5.33 (22.71)	4.53 (19.30)	5.37 (22.88)
10 & above	2.97 (36.09)	—	—	1.39 (16.89)	—	3.87 (47.02)
Total	23.57 (11.07)	0.19 (0.09)	20.47 (9.62)	9.98 (4.69)	49.98 (23.48)	70.17 (32.96)

1	2	3	4	5	6	7
MUSLIM						
Landless	0.97 (0.43)	—	1.00 (0.44)	—	178.91 (79.19)	31.22 (13.82)
Less than 2.5	3.88 (6.79)	0.80 (1.40)	7.93 (13.88)	3.67 (6.42)	9.35 (16.36)	22.40 (39.20)
2.5—5	12.95 (23.58)	0.63 (1.15)	2.42 (4.41)	4.60 (8.36)	5.96 (10.30)	17.41 (31.70)
5—10	16.69 (21.77)	1.52 (0.68)	2.18 (2.84)	0.74 (6.97)	3.93 (5.13)	26.85 (35.03)
10 & above	5.38 (13.00)	—	0.25 (0.60)	0.91 (2.20)	0.90 (2.17)	15.12 (36.55)
Total	39.87 (8.74)	1.95 (0.43)	13.78 (3 02)	9.92 (1.71)	198.75 (43.58)	113.00 (24.78)
SIKH						
Landless	—	—	—	—	44.49 (100.00)	—
Less than 2.5	—	—	—	—	1.88 (100.00)	—
2.5—5	—	—	—	—	—	—
5—10	0.63 (9.78)	—	0.32 (4.97)	1.10 (17.08)	1.00 (15.53)	2.13 (33.18)
10 & above	—	—	—	—	—	— (100.00)
Total	0.63 (1.17)	—	0.32 (0.59)	1.10 (2.04)	47.37 (87.87)	3.23 (5.99)
Grand Total	494.83 (17.00)	16.81 (0.58)	144.87 (4.98)	221.14 (7.60)	894.58 (30.74)	595.93 (20.48)

Table 11.12 (*Contd.*)

Size Category	Purchase of machinery & equipment	House construction	Domestic consumption	Miscellaneous	Total
1	8	9	10	11	12
H.C.H.					
Landless	2.83 (0.79)	1.09 (0.30)	1.99 (0.56)	77.69 (21.76	357.04 (100.00)
Less than 2.5	3.42 ;2.69)	7.13 (5.60)	—	18.50) (14.54)	127.25 (100.00)
2.5—5	6.90 (2.96)	2.00 (0.86)	11.89 (5.53)	30.54 (13.11)	231.92 (100.00)
5—10	8.58 (2.42)	0.52 (0.15)	35.59 (10.34)	33.10 (9.33)	354.72 (100.00)
10 & above	10.79 (3.07)	0.37 (0.10)	23.74 (7.43)	75.87 (21.56)	351.94 (100.00)
Total	32.52 (2.28)	11.11 (0.78)	73.31 (6.04)	235.70 (16.55)	1422.87 (100.00)
B.C.					
Landless	1.69 (0.58)	—	6.08 (2.10)	4.26 (1.47)	289.39 (100.00)
Less than 2.5	0.20 (0.16)	0.32 (0.25)	2.43 (1.93)	5 56 (4.43)	125.60 (100.00)
2.5—5	1.20 (0.97)	—	9.21 (8.30)	8.38 (6.81)	123.06 (100.00)

Table 11.12 (*Contd.*)

1	8	9	10	11	12
5—10	2.88 (2.30)	4.00 (3.18)	0.02 (0.02)	16.47 (13.14)	125.32 (100.00)
10 & above	2.22 (2.21)	—	2.06 (2.05)	4.03 (4.02)	100.29 (100.00)
Total	8.19 (1.07)	4.32 (0.57)	19.80 (3.28)	38.70 (5.07)	763.66 (100.00)
S.C.					
Landless	6.67 (10.22)	—	0.52 (0.80)	10.52 (16.11)	65.29 (100.00)
Less than 2.5	—	—	7.26 (9.88)	7.79 (10.60)	73.51 (100.00)
2.5—5	1.25 (2.95)	—	1.04 (2.45)	2.82 (6.65)	42.38 (100.00)
5—10	—	—	—	0.65 (0.77)	23.47 (100.00)
10 & above	—	—	—	—	8.23 (100.00)
Total	7.92 (3.72)	—	8.82 (4.14)	21.78 (10.23)	212.88 (100.00)
MUSLIM					
Landless	—	—	5.06 (2.24)	8.76 (3.88)	225.92 (100.00)
Less than 2.5	0.90 (1.58)	—	3.10 (5.43)	5.11 (8.94)	57.14 (100.00)
2.5—5	0.47 (0.86)	1.87 (3.40)	1.17 (2.13)	7.75 (14.11)	54.93 (100.00)

1	8	9	10	11	12
5—10	0.89 (1.16)	3.58 (4.67)	—	21.27 (27.75)	76.65 (100.00)
10 & above	2.71 (6.55)	1.42 (3.45)	0.58 (1.40)	14.10 (34.08)	41.37 (100.00)
Total	4.97 (1.09)	6.87 (1.51)	9.91 (2.64)	56.99 (12.50)	456.10 (100.00)
SIKH					
Landless	—	—	—	—	44.49 (100.00)
Less than 2 5	—	—	—	—	1.88 (100.00)
2.5—5	—	—	—	—	—
5—10	—	—	—	1.26 (19.56)	6.44 (100.00)
10 & above	—	—	—	—	1.10 (100.00)
Total	—	—	—	1.26 (2.34)	53.91 (100.00)
Grand Total	53.60 (1.84)	22.30 (0.77)	111.84 (3.83)	354.43 (12.18)	2910.33 (100.00)

N.B.—Figures in parentheses are percentages.

Muslim (1 per cent each). Its share was less than 2 per cent of all land alienation in the State.

House construction was not an important factor for land alienation. It accounted for 0.8 per cent of the alienated land among high caste Hindus, 0.6 per cent among Backward Caste and 1.5 per cent among Muslims. For all the castes and size categories its share was less than 1 per cent.

Significantly domestic consumption accounted for 6 per cent of the alienated land among the high caste Hindus followed by Scheduled Caste (4 per cent), Backward Caste and Muslim (3 per cent each). This factor accounted for 4 per cent of land alienation in the State.

Education also was not an important factor and it accounted for 1 per cent of the alienated land among high caste Hindus, less than half per cent among Muslims and less than 0.1 per cent each among Backward Castes and Scheduled Castes. For the state as a whole its share was only half per cent of total land alienation.

Medicine accounted for 10 per cent of the land alienation among Scheduled Castes. This probably shows that the poorer sections have nothing else but to sell the land if some calamity like illness befalls them. It is worth noting that the incidence was much higher in lower categories even among the Scheduled Castes. Its incidence was 6 per cent among higher caste Hindus, 4 per cent among Backward Castes, 3 per cent among Muslims and less than 1 per cent among Sikh. In the State as a whole this factor accounted for 5 per cent of total land alienation.

Miscellaneous reasons which accounted for 12 per cent of total land alienation were mainly confined to high caste Hindus as they accounted for two-thirds of the total land alienated on account of such factors.

12

The Case of Landless

As the land sold by landless *i.e.* those who sold their entire landholding constituted a significant portion of the total land alienated in the state it was deemed proper to analyse the phenomenon in some detail. As already noted, such persons as had left the village for good could not be contacted, no first hand knowledge could be had as to what forced them to leave their native villages. Of course, the size of their landholding could be ascertained from those who had purchased their land. Thus the size category to which they belonged could be know but the purchasers in most of the cases could not throw any light regarding the reasons as to why the sellers left the village. This is why "left the village" has been shown as a separate reason for leaving the village although in reality there must be some cause behind it. Those who had sold their entire holding but continued to live in the village naturally told the reason for doing so which has been classified in the tables.

The data for eastern U.P. (Table 12.1) show that out of total land sold by landless persons, marginal farmers alone accounted for as high as 56 per cent of such land followed by

TABLE 12.1

Reason-wise Distribution of Land Sold by Landless According to Size Category of owned Holding in eastern U.P.

(Area in acres)

Size Category (acres)	REASON					
	Marriage	Education	Medicine	Left the village	Repayment of old debts	Purchase of machinary & equipment
1	2	3	4	5	6	7
Less than 2.5	4,28 (1.35)	—	1.67 (0.53)	284.14 (89.87)	9.09 (2.87)	2.53 (0.81)
2.5—5.0	3.26 (3.08)	0.19 (0.18)	2.19 (2.07)	89.20 (84.30)	5.10 (4.82)	—
5.0—10	5.10 (8.34)	—	—	42.81 (69.97)	8.27 (13.52)	—
10 & above	—	—	—	77.87 (100.00)	—	—
Total	12.64 (2.25)	0 19 (0.04)	3.86 (0.69)	493.99 (88.06)	22.46 (4.00)	2.53 (0.45)

Table 12.1 (*Contd.*)

Size Category (acres)	House construction	Domestic consumption	Misc.	Total	As%of total land sold
1	8	9	10	11	12
Less than 2.5	—	5.83 (1.84)	8.62 (2.73)	316.13 (100.00)	56.35
2.5—5.0	—	0.31 (0.29)	5.56 (5.26)	105.81 (100.00)	18.86
5.0—10.0	—	—	5.00 (8.17)	61.18 (100.00)	10.91
10 & above	—	—	—	77.87 (100.00)	13.88
Total	—	6.14 (1.09)	19.18 (3.42)	560.99 (100.00)	100.00

N.B.—Figures in parentheses are percentages.

small farmers (19 per cent). The share of semi-medium farmers was 11 per cent and that of medium and large farmers was 14 per cent. That three-fourths of the land was sold by marginal and small farmers indicates that the phenomenon is confined to the poorest section of peasantry. 'Left the village' or total migration was the biggest factor responsible for selling the entire landholding as it accounted for 88 per cent of the total land alienated from the landless. Repayment of old debts and marriage accounted for 4 per cent and 2 per cent respectively of the alienated land. It is also quite distressing to find that of the total land that was sold by those who had left the village, 58 per cent of the land belonged to marginal farmers having holdings of less than 2.5 acres.

A caste and size-wise analysis (Table 12.2) will show that in eastern U.P. high caste Hindus accounted for 30 per cent of the total land sold by landless. While 41 per cent of such land was accounted for by marginal farmers among them the large farmers also accounted for 31 per cent of such land.

The Backward Caste accounted for 33 per cent of the total land sold by landless and nearly two-thirds of such land was accounted for by marginal farmers among the sellers. The share of largest category was only 9 per cent.

Scheduled Caste accounted for 5 per cent of such land more than half of which was accounted for by marginal farmers among the sellers. Significantly Muslims accounted for 31 per cent of the total land sold by landless and here also the marginal farmers accounted for nearly two-thirds of the alienated land. Thus it was mostly the marginal farmers in all the caste groups which accounted for the bulk of the land sold by landless.

'Left the village' was the most important factor for all the caste groups for selling the entire holding. It accounted for 77 per cent the land sold by high caste Hindus, 92 per cent by Backward Caste, 80 per cent by Scheduled Caste and 95 per cent by Muslims.

Repayment of old debts was the next important reason. It accounted for 4 per cent of the land sold by high caste

TABLE 12.2

Reason-wise Distribution of Land Sold by Landless in Eastern U.P. according to Size Category and Caste

(Area in Acres)

Size Category	REASONS					
	Marriage	Education	Medicine	Left the village	Repayment of old debts	Purchase of machinery & equipment
1	2	3	4	5	6	7
H.C.H.						
Less than 2.5	3.20 (4.69)	—	1.58 (2.32)	55.28 (81.10)	0.48 (0.71)	1.90 (2.79)
2.5 to 5.0	3.26 (16.85)	—	—	10.53 (54.42)		
5.0 to 10.0	5.10 (18.01)	—	—	11.96 (42.21)	6.27 (22.14)	
10 & above	—	—	—	50.95 (100.00)		
Total	11.56 (6.93)	—	1.58 (0.95)	128.72 (77.17)	6.75 (4.05)	1.90 (1.14)

1	2	3	4	5	6	7
B.C						
Less than 2.5	0.93 (0.76)	—	0.09 (0.07)	112.70 (91.93)	5.49 (4.48)	0.63 (0.51)
2.5—5.0	—	—		34.52 (93.25)	2.50 (6.76)	—
5.0 to 10.0	—	—	—	8.28 (80.54)	2.00 (19.46)	—
10 & above		—	—	16.76 (100.00)		—
Total	0.93 (0.50)	—	0.09 (0.05)	172.26 (92.28)	9.99 (8.35)	0.63 (0.34)
S.C						
Less than 2.5	0.15 (0.93)	—		12.81 (76.32)	1.84 (11.39)	—
2.5 to 5.0	—	0.19 (2.11)	2.19 (24.31)	6.32 (70.14)		—
5.0 to 10.0	—	—	—	5.45 (100.00)	—	—
10 & above	—	—	—	—	—	—
Total	0.15 (0.48)	0.19 (0.62)	2.19 (7.16)	24.58 (80.30)	1.84 (6.02)	—

1	2	3	4	5	6	7
MUSLIM						
Less than 2.5	—	—	—	103.32 (94.60)	1.28 (1.17)	—
2.5 to 5.0	—	—	—	37.87 (93.57)	2.60 (6.43)	—
5.0 to 10.0	—	—	—	17.12 (100.00)	—	—
10 & above	—	—	—	10.16 (100.00)	—	—
Total	—	—	—	168.43 (95.20)	3.88 (2.19)	—
Grand Total	12.64 (2.25)	0.19 (0.04)	3.86 (0.69)	493.99 (88.06)	22.46 (4.00)	2.53 (0.45)

Table 12.2 (*Contd.*)

Size Category	House construction	Domestic consumption	Misc.	Total	As % of total land sold
1	8	9	10	11	12
H.C.H.					
Less than 2.5	—	0.54 (0.79)	5.18 (7.60)	68.16 (100.00)	—
2.5 to 5.0	—	—	5.56 (28.73)	19.35 (100.00)	—
5.0 to 10.0	—	—	5.00 (17.64)	28.33 (100.00)	—
10 & above	—	—	—	50.95 (100.00)	—
Total	—	0.54 (0.32)	15.74 (9.44)	166.79 (100.00)	29.73

1	8	9	10	11	12
B.C.					
Less than 2.5	—	2.76 (2.25)	—	122.60 (100.00)	—
2.5 to 5.0	—	—	—	37.02 (100.00)	—
5.0 to 10.0	—	—	—	10.28 (100.00)	—
10 to above	—	—	—	16.76 (100.00)	—
Total	—	2.76 (1.48)	—	185.66 (100.00)	33.27
S.C.					
Less than 2.5	—	0.21 (1.30)	1.14 (7.06)	16.15 (100.00)	—
2.5 to 5.0	—	0.31 (3.44)	—	9.01 (100.00)	—
5.0 to 10.0				5.45 (100.00)	—
10 to above	—		—	—	—
Total	—	0.52 (1.70)	1.14 (3.72)	30.61 (100.00)	[illegible]

Table 12.2 (*Contd.*)

1	8	9	10	11	12
H.C.H.					
Less than 2.5	—	2.32 (2.12)	2.30 (2.11)	109.22 (100.00)	—
2.5 to 5.0	—	—	—	40.43 (100.00)	—
5.0 to 10.0	—	—	—	17.12 (100.00)	—
10 & above	—	—	—	10.16 (100.00)	—
Total	—	2.32 (1.31)	2.30 (1.30)	176.93 (100.00)	31.54
Grand Total	—	6.14 (1.09)	19.18 (3.42)	560.99 (100.00)	100.00

N.B.—Figures in parentheses are percentages.

Hindus, 5 per cent in case of Backward Caste, 6 per cent in case of Scheduled Caste and 2 per cent in case of Muslims.

In central U.P. out of the total land alienated from landless one-third was accounted for by marginal farmers. (Table 12.3). Small farmers accounted for 43 per cent of such land and the share of semi-medium farmers was 23 per cent. There was no such case among medium and large farmers.

Of the total land that was alienated from marginal farmers in central U.P. 56 per cent was accounted for by the factor of 'left the village'. Another 14 per cent was accounted for by repayment of old debts. Significantly 2 per cent of the land was sold to acquire some machinery and equipment and domestic consumption accounted for 5 per cent of such land. Among small farmers 59 per cent of the land was alienated on account of the factor of 'left the village' while 18 per cent was accounted for by repayment of old debts. Among semi-medium farmers the entire land was sold on account of the factor of 'left the village'.

A caste and size-wise distribution of such land in central U.P. (Table 12 4) shows that high caste Hindus accounted for 41 per cent of the land sold followed by Backward Caste (40 per cent), Muslims (15 per cent) and Scheduled Caste (4 per cent). 'Left the village' was the most important reason for all the castes except the Scheduled Caste as there was no such case among them. It ranged from 44 per cent among Muslims to 78 per cent among Backward Castes. Among Backward Castes marginal and small farmers accounted for bulk of the land (84 per cent) sold on account this factor but significantly among high caste Hindus semi-medium farmers accounted for half of such land.

Repayment of old debts was the next important reason. It accounted for 4 per cent of the land alienated among high caste Hindus. 12 per cent in case of Backward Caste, 26 per cent in case of Scheduled Caste and 33 per cent in case of Muslims. This phenomenon was confined to marginal and small farmers alone.

Domestic consumption accounted for 2 per cent of the land alienated among high caste Hindus and 4 per cent among

TABLE 12.3

Reason-wise Distribution of Land Sold by Landless in central U.P. According to Size Category of owned Holdinge

(Area in acres)

Landholdings	REASONS					
	Marriage	Education	Medicine	Left the village	Repayment of old debts	Purchase of machinery & equipment
1	2	3	4	5	6	7
Less than 2.5	0.75 (1.55)	—	2.05 (4.22)	27.04 (55.66)	6.65 (13.69)	1.06 (2.18)
2.5 to 5.0	—	—	—	37.35 (58.97)	11.19 (17.67)	—
5.0 to 10.0	—	—	—	30.96 (100.00)	—	—
10.0 & above	—	—	—	—	—	—
Total	0.75 (0.51)		2.05 (1.40)	98.35)67.42)	17.84 (12.23)	1.06 (0.73)

Table 12.3 (*Contd.*)

Landholdings	House construction	Domestic consumption	Misc.	Total	As % of Total land sold
1	8	9	10	11	12
Less than 2.5	—	2.43 (5.00)	8.60 (17.70)	48 58 (100.00)	33.30
2.5 to 5.0	—	—	14.80 (23.36)	63.34 (100,00)	43.42
5.0 to 10.0	—	—	—	33.96 (100.00)	23.28
10.0 & above	—	—	—	—	—
Total	—	2.43 (1.67)	23.40 (16.04)	145.88 (100.00)	100.00

N.B.—Figures in parentheses are percentages.

TABLE 12.4

Reason-wise Distribution of land Sold By Landless in Central U.P. According to Caste and size Category of Holdings

(Area in acres)

Size Category	REASONS					
	Marriage	Education	Medicine	Left the village	Repayment of old debts	Purchase machinery of& equipment
1	2	3	4	5	6	7
H.C.H.						
Less than 2.5	—	—	2.05 (13.70)	6.89 (46.06)	2.22 (14.84)	—
2.5—5.0	—	—	—	15.40 (63.64)	—	—
5.0—10	—	—	—	21.40 (100.00)	—	—
10 & above	—	—	—	—	—	—
Total	—	—	2.05 (3.38)	43.73 (72.16)	2.22 (3.67)	—
B.C.						
Less than 2.5	0.75 (3.72)	—	—	15.67 (77.81)	1.40 (6.95)	1.06 (5.26)
2.5—5.0	—	—	—	21.95 (72.16)	5.47 (17.98)	—
5.0 - 10	—	—	—	7.15 (100.00)	—	—
10 & above	—	—	—	—	—	—
Total	0.75 (1.30)	—	—	44.77 (77.58)	6.87 (11.90)	1.06 (1.84)

Table 12.4 (*Contd.*)

1	2	3	4	5	6	7
S.C.						
Less than 2.5	—	—	—	—	1.40 (59.07)	—
2.5—5.0	—	—	—	—	—	—
5.0—10	—	—	—	—	—	—
10 & above	—	—	—	—	—	—
Total	—	—	—	—	1.40 (26.07)	—
MUSLIM						
Less than 2.5	—	—	—	4.48 (40.32)	1.63 (14.67)	—
2.5—5.0	—	—	—	—	5.72 (100.00)	—
5.0—10	—	—	—	5.37 (100.00)		—
10 & above	—	—	—	—	—	—
Total	—	—	—	9.85 (44.37)	7.35 (33.11)	—
Grand Total	0.75 (0.51)		2.05 (1.40)	98.35 (67.42)	17.84 (12.23)	1.06 (0.73)

Table 12.4 (*Contd.*)

Size Category	House construction	Domestic consumption	Misc.	Total	As % of total land sold
1	8	9	10	11	12
H.C.H.					
Less than 2.5	—	1.45 (9.69)	2.35 (15.71)	14.96 (100.00)	—
2.5—5.0	—	—	8.80 (36.36)	24.20 (100.00)	—
5.0—10.0	—	—		21.44 (100.00)	—
10 & above	—	—	—	—	—
Total		1.45 (2.39)	11.15 (18.40)	60.60 (100.00)	41.54
B.C.					
Less than 2.5	—	—	1.26 (6.26)	20.14 (100.00)	—
2.5—5.0	—	—	3.00 (9.86)	30.42 (100.00)	—
5.0—10	—	—	—	7.15 (100.00)	—
10 & above	—	—	—	—	—
Total			4.26 (7.38)	57.71 (100.00)	39.56

Table 12.4 (*Contd.*)

1	8	9	10	11	12
S.C.					
Less than 2.5	—	—	0.97 (40.93)	2.37 (100.00)	—
2.5—5.0	—	—	3.00 (100.00)	3.00 (100.00)	—
5.0—10	—	—	—	—	—
10 & above					
Total	—	—	3.97 (73.93)	5.37 (100.00)	3.68
MUSILM					
Less than 2.5	—	0.98 (8.82)	4.02 (36.19)	11.11 (100.00)	—
2.5—5.0	—	—	—	5.72 (100.00)	—
5.0—10	—	—	—	5.37 (100.00)	—
10 & above	—	—	—	—	—
Total		0.98 (4.41)	4.02 (18.11)	22.20 (100.00)	15.22
Grand Total	—	2.43 (1.67)	23.40 (16.04)	145.88 (100.00)	100.00

N.B.—Figures in parentheses are percentages.

Muslims but significantly was absent among Scheduled Caste and Backward Caste.

In western U.P. out of the total land that was sold by landless 47 percent was accounted for by marginal farmers and 23 per cent by small farmers. (Table 12.5). The share of semi-medium farmers and large farmers was 20 per cent and 10 per cent respectively. In this region also it was the poorer farmer who accounted for bulk of the alienated land.

'Left the village' as a reason for selling the entire holding accounted for 65 per cent of the land in the case of marginal farmers, 42 per cent in the case of small farmers, 47 per cent in case of semi-medium farmers and 49 per cent in the case of medium and large farmers. For all the categories taken together it accounted for 55 per cent of the alienated land. Marginal farmers alone accounted for 57 per cent of the total land that was alienated on account of this factor.

Repayment of old debts as a reason for selling the entire holding accounted for 15 per cent of the alienated land in this region and accounted for 13,30, and 12 per cent respectively of the alienated land of marginal, small and semi-medium farmers.

A caste and size category-wise analysis shows (Table 12.6) that in western U.P. high caste Hindus accounted for the bulk of the land (48 per cent) sold by landless followed surprisingly by Sikhs (17 per cent), Backward Caste (15 per cent) and Scheduled Caste and Muslims (10 per cent) each.

Among high caste Hindus, 49 per cent of the alienated land was accounted for by those who completely left the village. It varied from 36 per cent among small farmers to 65 per cent among marginal farmers. There was no such case among medium and large farmers. Repayment of old debts accounted for 7 per cent of the land sold by landless among high caste Hindus which was confined to lower categories.

Among Backward Caste out of the total land sold by landless 74 per cent was accounted for by those who left the village. It ranged for 58 per cent among small farmers to cent per cent among semi-medium farmers ; there being no such case among medium and larger farmers. Repayment of old

TABLE 12.5

Reason-wise Distribution of Land Sold by Landless in western U.P. according to Size Category of owned Holdings

(Area in acres)

Size Category	Marriage	Education	Medicine	Left the village	Repayment of old debts	Purchase of machinery & equipment
1	2	3	4	5	6	7
Less than 2.5	1.47 (1.22)		2.63 (2.18)	79.14 65.55)	15.22 (22.61)	4.85 (4.02)
2.5—5.0	—	—	—	24.69 (41.89)	17.51 (29.71)	2.75 (4.67)
5.0—10.0	—	—	—	23.70 (46.68)	6.31 (12.43)	—
10 & above	—	—	—	12.35 (49.40)	—	—
Total	1.47 (0.58)	—	2.63 (1.03)	139.88 (54.75)	39.04 (15.29)	7.60 (2.98)

Table 12.5 (*Contd.*)

Size Category	House construction	Domestic consumption	Misc.	Total	As % of total land sold
1	8	9	10	11	12
Lsss than 2.5	1.09 (0.90)	5.08 (4.20)	11.25 (9.32)	120.73 (100.00)	47.26
2.5—5.0	—	—	13.99 (23.73)	58.94 (100.00)	23.07
5.0—10.0	—	—	20.76 (40.89)	50.77 (100.00)	19.88
10 & above	—	—	12.65 (50.60)	25.00 (100.00)	9.79
Total	1.09 (0.43)	5.08 (1.99)	58.65 (22.95)	255.44 (100.00)	100.00 —

N.B.—Figures in parentheses are percentages.

TABLE 12.6

Reason-wise Distribution of Land Sold by Landless in western U.P. According to Caste and Size Category of owned Holdings

(Area in Acres)

Size Category	REASONS Marriage	Education	Madicine	Left the village	Repayment of old debts	Purchase of machinery & equipment
1	2	3	4	5	6	7
H.C.H.						
Less than	1.00 (1.93)	—	—	33.80 (65.13)	6.52 (12.56)	0.93 (1.79)
2.5—5.0	—	—	—	9.33 (35.98)	2.61 (10.07)	—
5.0—10.0	—	—	—	17.57 (52.97)	—	—
10 & above	—	—	—	—	—	—
Total	1.00 (0.81)	—	—	60.70 (49.09)	9.13 (7.39)	0.93 (0.75)

1	2	3	4	5	6	7
B.C.						
Less than 2.5	—	—	0.78 (3.40)	16.32 (73.28)	2.03 (8.85)	—
2.5—5.0	—	—	—	5.57 (58.82)	3.90 (41.18)	—
5—10	—	—	—	6.13 (100.00)	—	—
10 & above	—	—	—	—	—	—
Total	—	—	0.78 (2.03)	28.52 (73.98)	5.93 (15.38)	—
S.C.						
Less than	—	—	1.85 (18.06)	2.73 (26.66)	1.49 (14.55)	3.92 (38.28)
2.5—5.0	—	—	—	2.81 (31.01)	3.50 (38.63)	2.75 30.36)
5—10						
10& above						
Total	—	—	1.85 (7.56)	5.54 (22.65)	4.99 (20.40)	6.67 (22.27)

Table 12.6 (*Contd.*)

1	2	3	4	5	6	5
MUSLIM						
Less than 2.5	0.47 (4.49)	—	—	0.63 (6.01)	5.18 (49.43)	—
2.5—5.0	—	—	—	—	7.50 (100.08)	—
5.0—10	—	—	—	—	6.31 (100.00)	—
10 & above	—	—	—	—	—	—
Total	0.47 (1.93)	—	—	0.63 (2.59)	18.99 (78.18)	—
SIKH						
Less than 2.5	—	—	—	25.16 (100.00)	—	—
2.5—5.0	—	—	—	6.98 (100.00)		—
5—10	—	—	—	—	—	—
10 & above	—	—	—	12.35 (100.00)	—	—
Total	—	—	—	44.49 (100.00)	—	—
Grand Total	1.47 (0.58)	—	2.63 (1.03)	139.88 (54.76)	39.04 (15.28)	7.60 (2.98)

N.B.—Figures in parenthese are percentages.

Table 12.6 (*Contd*)

Size Category	House construction	Domestic consumption	Misc.	Total	As % to total land sold
1	8	9	10	11	12
H.C.H.					
Less than 2.5	1.09 (2.10)		8.56 (16.49)	51.90 (100.00)	—
2.5—5.0	—	—	13.99 (53.95)	25.93 (100.00)	—
5.0—10	—	—	15.60 (47.03)	33.17 (100.00)	—
10 & above	—	—	12.65 (100.00)	12.65 (100.00)	—
Total	1.09 (0.88)	—	50.80 (41.08)	123.65 (100.00)	48.41

Table 12.6 (*Contd.*)

1	8	9	10	11	12
B.C.					
Less than 2.5	—	3.32 (14.47)	—	22.95 (100.00)	—
2.5—5.0	—	—	—	9.47 (100.00)	—
50—10	—	—	—	6.13 (100.00)	—
10 & above	—	—	—	—	—
Total	—	3.32 (8.61)	—	38.55 (100.00)	15.09
S.C.					
Less than 2.5	—	—	0.25 (2.45)	10.24 (100.00)	—
2.5—5.0	—	—	—	9.06 (100.00)	—
5.0—10	—	—	5.16 (100.00)	5.16 (100.00)	—
10 & above	—	—	—	—	—
Total	—	—	5.41 (22.12)	24.46 (100.00)	9.58

1	8	9	10	11	12
MUSLIM					
Less than	—	1.76 (16.79)	2.44 (23.28)	10.48 (100.00)	—
2.5—5.0	—	—	—	7.50 (100.00)	—
5.0—10	—	—	—	6.31 (100.00)	—
10 & above	—	—	—	—	—
Total	—	1.76 (7.25)	2.44 (10.05)	24.29 (100.00)	9.51
SIKH					
Less than 2.5	—	—	—	25.16 (100.00)	—
25—5.0	—	—	—	6.98 (100.00)	—
5.0—10	—	—	—	—	—
10 & above	—	—	—	12.35 (100.00)	—
Total	—	—	—	44.49 (100.00)	17.47
Grand Total	1.09 (0.43)	5.08 (1.99)	58.65 (22.95)	255.44 (100.00)	100.00

N.B.—Figures in parentheses are percentages.

debts accounted for 15 per cent of the land which was confined to marginal and small farmers.

Among Scheduled Caste the factor of 'left the village' accounted for 23 per cent of the land and was confined to marginal and small farmers. Repayment of old debts accounted for 20 per cent of the land sold by landless among Scheduled Caste. But interestingly 22 per cent of the land was sold to purchase some productive asset.

Among Muslims only 3 per cent of the land was accounted for by those who completely left the village and the same was confined to marginal farmers alone. But significantly repayment of old debts accounted for as high as 79 per cent of such land. Among Sikhs the entire land sold by landless was accounted for by those who left the village.

In Bundelkhand (Table 12.7) out of the total land sold by landless, marginal farmers accounted for 59 per cent of the land. The remaining 41 per cent of the land was sold by small farmers. It is significant to find that repayment of old debts was the biggest cause for land alienation among marginal farmers accounting for 60 per cent of their alienated land. Medicine and marriage accounted for 15 per cent and 13 per cent respectively of their alienated land. 'left the village' as a factor was responsible for only 13 per cent of their alienated land unlike in other regions but among the small farmers two-thirds of their alienated land was accounted for by this factor while medicine accounted for 34 per cent of their alienated land.

A caste-wise analysis (Table 12.8) shows that Backward Caste accounted for 33 per cent of the land sold by landless followed by high caste Hindus (30 per cent), Scheduled Caste (24 per cent) and Muslims (13 per cent). Among the high caste Hindus two-thirds of the alienated land was due to the factor of 'left the village' and remaining one-third to repayment of old debts. Among Backward Caste 'Left the Village' was again the biggest factor accounting for 42 per cent of the alienated land followed by, repayment of old debts (31 per cent) and marriage (15 per cent). Among the Scheduled Caste distressingly 58 per cent of the alienated land was on account of medicine and the remaining 42 per cent on account of

TABLE 12.7

Reason-wise Distribution of Land Sold by Landless in Bundelkhand according to Size Category of owned Holdings

Size Category	REASONS Marriage	Education	Medicine	Left the village	Repayment of old debts	Purchase of machinery & equipment
1	2	3	4	5	6	7
Less than 2.5	1.50 (12.80)	—	1.72 (14.68)	1.45 (12.37)	70.5 (60.15	—
2.5—5.0		—	2.80 (34.57)	5.30 (65.43)	—	—
5—10	—	—	—	—	—	—
10 & above	—	—	—	—	—	—
Total	1.50 (7.57)	—	4.52 (22.80)	6.75 (34.06)	7.05 (35.57)	—

Table 12.7 (*Contd.*)

Size Category	House con-struction	Domestic consumpation	Misc.	Total	As % to total land sold
1	8	9	10	11	12
Less than 2.5	—	—	—	11.72 (100 00)	59.13
2.5—5.0	—	—	—	8.10 (100.00)	40.87
5—10	—	—	—	—	—
10 & above	—	—	—	—	—
Total	—	—	—	19.82 (100.00)	100.00

N.B.—Figures in parentheses are percentages.

TABLE 12.8

Reason-wise Distribution of Land Sold by Landless in Bundelkhand according to Size Category and Caste

(Area in acres)

Size Category	REASONS Marriage	Education	Medicine	Left the village	Repayment of old debts	Purchase of machinery & equipment
1	2	3	4		6	7
H.C.H.						
Less than 2.5	—	—	—	1.45 (42.03)	2.00 (57.97)	—
2.5—5.0	—	—	—	2.55 (100.00)	—	—
5—10	—	—	—	—	—	—
10 — above	—	—	—	—	—	—
Total	—	—	—	4.00 (66.66)	2.00 (33.34)	—
B.C.						
Less than 2.5	1.00 (26.88)	—	0.72 19.36)	—	2.00 (53.76)	—
2.5—5	—	—	—	2.75 (100.00)	—	—

1	2	3	4	5	6	7
5—10	—	—	—	—	—	—
10 & above	—	—	—	—	—	—
Total	1.00 (15.46)	—	0.72 (11.13)	2.75 (42.50)	2.00 (30.91)	—
S.C,						
Less than 2.5	—	—	—	—	2.05 (100.00)	—
2.5—5	—	—	2.80 (100.00)	—	—	—
5—10	—	—	—	—	—	—
10 & above	—	—				—
Total	—	—	2.80 (57.63)	—	2.05 (42.27)	—
MUSLIM						
Less than 2.5	0.50 (20.00)	—	1.00 (40.00)	—	1.00 (40.00)	—
2.5—50	—	—	—	—	—	—
5.0—10	—	—	—	—	—	—
10 & above	—	—	—	—	—	—
Total	0.50 (20.00)	—	1.00 (40.00)	—	1.00 (40.00)	—
Grand Total	1.50 (7.57)	—	4.52 (22.80)	6.75 (34.06)	7.05 (35.57)	—

Size Category	House construction	Domestic consumption	Misc,	Totai	As % to total land sold
1	8	9	10	11	12
H.C.H.					
Less than 2.5	—	—	—	3.45 (100.00)	—
2.5—5.0	—	—	—	2.55 (100.00)	—
5—10	—	—	—	—	—
10 — above	—	—	—	—	—
Total	—	—	—	6.00 (100.00)	30.27
B.C.					
Less than 2.5	—	—	—	3.72 (100.00)	—
2.5—5	—	—	—	2.75 (100.00)	—
5—10	—	—	—	—	—
10 — above	—	—	—	—	—
Total	—	—	—	6.47 (100.00)	32.64

1	8	6	10	11	12
S.C.					
Less than 2.5	—	—	—	2.05 (100.00)	—
2.5—5	—	—	—	2.80 (100.00)	—
5—10	—	—	—	—	—
10 abore	—	—	—	—	—
Total	—	—	—	4.85 (100.00)	24.48
MUSLIM					
Less than 2.5	—	—	—	2.50 (100.00)	—
2.5—5.0	—	—	—	—	—
5.0—10	—	—	—	—	—
10 above	—	—	—	—	—
Total	—	—	—	2.50 (100.00)	12.61
Grand Total	—	—	—	19.82 (100.00)	100 00

N.B.—Figures in parentheses are percentages.

repayment of old debts. Among Muslims repayment of old debts and medicine accounted for 40 per cent each of the alienated land and marriage accounted for the remaining 20 per cent.

Taking the state as a whole it will be seen (Table 12.9) that of the total land sold by landless 51 per cent of the land was accounted for by marginal farmers. The share of small farmers was 24 per cent followed by medium farmers (15 per cent) and medium and large farmers (10 per cent). Of the total land sold by marginal farmers 79 per cent of the land was accounted for by those who had left the village for good. Nearly 8 per cent of their alienated land was on account of repayment of old debts. Other reasons were not significant.

Of the total land sold by small farmers two-thirds was accounted for by those who left the village for good and another 14 per cent was accounted for by the factor of repayment of old debts. Similar was the case of semi-medium farmers in whose case 69 per cent of the alienated land was accounted for by those who had left the village and another 10 per cent was accounted for by the factor of repayment of old debts. In case of medium and large farmers 88 per cent of their alienated land was accounted for by those who had left the village.

A caste-wise analysis (Table 12.10) shows that high caste Hindus accounted for 36 per cent of the alienated land of the landless followed by Backward Caste (29 per cent), Muslim (23 per cent), Scheduled Caste (7 per cent) and Sikhs (5 per cent). Among the high caste Hindus two-thirds of the alienated land was on account of the factor of total migration. Although the marginal farmers accounted for a larger chunk of such land yet it is significant to note that higher categories among them also accounted for a significant share. Repayment of old debts accounted for 6 per cent of their alienated land, marginal farmers accounting for more than half of such land. Among Backward Castes 86 per cent of the alienated land was on account of the factor of total migration ; the marginal farmers constituting the largest chunk of the same. Among the Scheduled Castes less than half of the alienated land was accounted for by those who had left the village and half of its was accounted for by marginal farmers. Significantly 10 per

TABLE 12.9

Reason-wise Distribution of Land Sold by Landless in U.P. acccording to Size Category of owned Holdings

(Area in acres)

Size Category	REASONS					
	Marriage	Education	Medicine	Left the village	Repayment of old debts	Purchase of machinery & equipment
1	2	3	4	5	6	7
Less than 2.5	8.00 (1.61)	—	8.07 (1.62)	391.74 (78.80)	38.01 (7.65)	8.44 (1.70)
2.5—5.0	3.26 (1.38)	0.19 (0.08)	4.99 (2.12)	156.54 (66.28)	33.80 (14.31)	2.75 (1.16)
5—10	5.10 (3.50)	—	—	100.47 (68.86)	14.58 (9.99)	—
10 & above	—	—	—	90.22 (87.70)	—	—
Total	16.36 (1.67)	0.19 (0.02)	13.06 (1.33)	738.97 (75.24)	86.39 (8.80)	11.19 (1.14)

Table 12.9 (*Contd.*)

	House construction	Domestic consumption	Misc.	Total	As % to total land sold
1	8	9	10	11	12
Less than 2.5	1.09 (0.22)	13.34 (2.68)	28.47 (5.72)	497.16 (100.00)	50.62
2.5—5.0	—	0.31 (0.13)	34.35 (14.54)	236.19 (100.00)	24.05
5—10	—	—	25.76 (17.65)	145.91 (100.00)	14.86
10 & above	—	—	12.65 (12.30)	102.87 (100.00)	10.47
Total	1.09 (0.11)	13.65 (1.39)	101.23 (10.30)	982.13 (100.00)	100.00

N.B.—Figures in parentheses are percentages.

TABLE 12.10

Reason-Wise Distribution of Land sold in U.P. by Landless according to Caste and Size Category of owned Holdings

(Area in acres)

Size Category	REASONS Marriage	Education	Medicine	Left the village	Repayment of old debts	Purchase of machinery & equipment
1	2	3	4	5	6	7
H.C.H.						
Less than 2.5	4.20 (3.03)	—	3.64 (2.63)	97.42 (70.36)	11.22 (8.10)	2.83 (2.04)
2.5—5.0	3.26 (4.53)	—	—	37.81 (52.49)	2.61 (3.62)	—
5.0—10.0	5.10 (6.15)	—	—	50.97 (61.45)	6.27 (7.56)	—
10 & above		—	—	50.95 (80.11)	—	—
Total	12.56 (3.52)	—	3.63 (1.02)	237.15 (66.41)	20.10 (5.63)	2.83 (0.79)

Table 12.10 (*Contd.*)

1	2	3	4	5	6	7
B.C.						
Less than 2.5	2.68 (1.58)		1.59 (0.94)	145.19 (85.70)	10.92 (6.45)	1.69 (0.99)
2.5—5	—	—	—	64.79 (81.33)	11.87 (14.90)	—
5—10	—	—	—	21.56 (91.51)	2.00 (8.49)	—
10 & above	—	—	—	16.76 (100.00)		—
Total	2.68 (0.93)	—	1.59 (0.55)	248.30 (85.80)	24.79 (8.57)	1.69 (0.58)
S.C.						
Less than 2.5	0.15 (0.49)	—	1.85 (6.00)	15.54 (50.44)	6.78 (22.00)	3.92 (12.73)
2.5—5		0.19 (0.80)	4.99 (20.90)	9.13 (38.25)	3.50 (14.66)	2.75 (11.52)
5—10	—	—	—	5.45 (51.36)	—	—
10 & above						
Total	0.15 (0.23)	0.19 (0.29)	6.84 (10.48)	30.12 (46.13)	10.28 (15.75)	6.67 (10.22)

1	2	3	4	5	6	7
MUSLIM						
Less than 2.5	0.97 (0.73)	—	1.00 (0.73)	108.43 (81.34)	9.09 (6.82)	—
2.5—5	—	—	—	37.83 (70.51)	15.82 (29.49)	—
5—10	—	—	—	22.49 (78.09)	6.31 (21.91)	—
10 & above	—	—	—	10.16 (100.00)	—	—
Total	0.97 (0.43)		1.00 (0.44)	178.91 (79.18)	31.22 (13.82)	—
SIKH						
Less than 2.5	—	—	—	25.16 (100.00)	—	—
2.5—5	—	—	—	6.98 (100.00)	—	—
5—10	—	—	—	—	—	—
10 & above	—	—	—	12.35 (100.00)	—	—
Total	—	—	—	44.49 (100.00)	—	—
Grand Total	16.36 (1.67)	0.19 (0.02)	13.06 (1.33)	738.97 (75.24)	86.39 (8.80)	11.19 (1.14)

Size Category	House construction	Domestic consumption	Misc.	Total	As % to total sold
1	8	9	10	11	12
H.C.H.					
Less than 2.5	1.09 (0.79)	1.99 (1.43)	16.09 (11.62)	138.47 (100.00)	—
2.5—5.0	—	—	28.35 (39.36)	72.03 (100.00)	—
5 0—10.0	—	—	20.60 (24.84)	82.94 (100.00)	—
10 & above	—	—	12.65 (19.80)	63.60 (100.00)	—
Total	1.09 (0.31)	1.99 (0.56)	77.69 (21.76)	357.04 (100.00)	36.35
B.C.					
Less than 2.5	—	6.08 (3.60)	1.26 (0.74)	169.41 (100.00)	—
2.5—5	—	—	3.00 (3.77)	79.66 (100.00)	—
5.0—10.0	—	—	—	23.56 (100.00)	—
10 & above	—	—	—	16.76 (100.00)	—
Total	—	6.08 (2.10)	4.26 (1.47)	289.39 (100.00)	29.47

1	8	9	10	11	12
S.C.					
Less than 2.5	—	0.21 (0.68)	2.36 (7.66)	30.81 (100.00)	—
2.5—5	—	0.31 (1.30)	3.00 (12.57)	23.87 (100.00)	—
5—10	—	—	5.16 (48.64)	10.61 (100.00)	—
10 & above	—	—	—	—	—
Total	—	0.52 (0.80)	10.52 (16.10)	65.29 (100.00)	6.65
MUSLIM					
Less than 2.5	—	5.06 (3.80)	8.76 (6.57)	133.31 (100.00)	—
2.3—5	—	—	—	53.65 (100.00)	—
5—10	—	—	—	28.80 (100.00)	—
10 & above	—	—	—	10.16 (100.00)	—
Total	—	5.06 (2.34)	8.76 (3.88)	225.92 (100.00)	23.00

Table 12.10 (*Contd.*)

1	8	9	10	11	12
SIKH					
Less than 2.5	—	—	—	25.16 (100.00)	—
2.5—5	—	—	—	6.98 (100.00)	—
5—10	—	—	—	—	—
10 & above	—	—	—	12.35 (100.00)	—
Total	—	—	—	44.49 (100.00)	4.53
Grand Total	1.09 (0.11)	13.65 (1.39)	101.23 (10.30)	982.13 (100.00)	100.00

N.B.—Figures in parentheses are percentages.

cent of their alienated land was on account of the factor of purchase of some machinery and equipment while repayment of old debts accounted for 16 per cent of the alienated land which was confined to marginal and small farmers. Among Muslims 79 per cent of the alienated land was on account of the factor of total migration, marginal farmers constituting 60 per cent such land while repayment of old debts accounted for 14 per cent of such land. Among Sikhs the entire land sold by landless was because of the factor of total migration. Marginal farmers among them accounted for 56 per cent of such land.

13

Source of Finance for Land Purchase

The purchasers of land were asked the source of finance for land purchased. In many cases there was not one single source. In such cases the respondents were asked to mention all the sources of income. In those cases where the respondents were unable to give the exact source and just mentioned that money was arranged from various sources a separate category was made andhas been shown in the Table 13.1 under the caption 'Mixed Source'. Table 13.1 shows the source of finance for land purchase.

It will be seen that in eastern U.P. savings from agriculture accounted for 39 per cent of the cases of land purchases. Non-agricultural income accounted for 14 per cent of the cases of land purchases. Roughly 9 per cent of the cases of land purchase was financed by sale of land. Significantly remittances from outside accounted for 29 per cent of the cases of land purchase. Mixed sources accounted for roughly 10 per cent of such cases.

That agricultural savings could finance slightly more than one-third of the cases of land purchase is not surrpising

TABLE 13.1

Source of Finance for Land Purchase in Different Regions of U.P.

(No.)

Source	Eastern	Central	Western	Bundel-khand	Hill Region	U.P.
1	2	3	4	5	6	7
1 Savings for agriculture	505 (38.85)	388 (61.61)	205 (52.97)	89 (61.81)	—	1187 (48.04)
2 Non agricultural Income	182 (14.00)	103 (16.25)	89 (23.00)	12 (8.33)	—	386 (15.62)
3 Sale of land	114 (8.77)	18 (2.82)	14 (2.58)	3 (2.08)	—	145 (5.87)
4 Remittances	373 (28.69)	120 (18.87)	71 (18.35)	36 (25.00)	2 (50.00)	602 (24.36)
5 Mixed Source	126 (9.69)	7 (1.10)	12 (3.10)	4 (2.78)	2 (50.00)	151 (6.11)
All Sources	1300 (100.00)	636 (100.00)	387 (100.00)	144 (100.00)	4 (100.00)	2471* (100.00)

N.B.—Figures in parentheses are percentages

*The number of cases of land purchase and the number of sources differ as land was purchased from more than one source in many cases.

for eastern U.P. as per household agricultural income are low mainly on account of small size of average holding and lower productivity. As the economy is not sufficiently diversified non-agricultural incomes could finance only 14 per cent of the cases of land purchases. As already mentioned remittance income financed nearly 29 per cent of such cases which was only 10 percentage points less than what was financed by agricultural savings. It shows that those who get jobs elsewhere are generally in a better economic position. Not only do they continue to maintain their links with their native villages but a significant portion of the land purchase in this region is financed by such remittances.

In central U.P. 61 per cent of the cases of land purchases was financed with money earned from agriculture. Non-agricultural income accounted for 16 per cent of such cases. Sale of land accounted for about 3 per cent of such cases while remittances accounted for about 19 per cent of such cases. Mixed sources accounted for 1 per cent of such cases. The picture in central U.P. was slightly different from eastern region. In the former agricultural income played a larger role in financing land purchases as compared to the latter while the role of remittances was of a lower order.

In western U.P. 53 per cent of the cases of land purchases was financed from savings from agriculture while non-agriculture income financed 23 per cent of such cases. Sale of land accounted for less than 3 per cent of such cases. Remittances accounted for 18 per cent of such cases while the share of mixed sources was only 3 per cent.

In Bundelkhand 62 per cent of the cases of land purchases was financed from agricultural savings and non-agricultural savings accounted for 8 per cent of such cases. Significantly remittances accounted for 25 per cent of such purchases. The share of sale of land and mixed sources was 2 per cent and 3 per cent respectively. In Hill region remittances and mixed income accounted for land purchases equally.

For the State as a whole 48 per cent of land purchase cases was financed from agricultural incomes while non-agricultural income accounted for 16 per eent of such cases. Remittances accounted for 24 per cent of such cases. The share of sale of land and mixed sources was 6 per cent each. Broadly it can be said that in the State only half of the cases of land purchases could be financed from savings from agriculture while another one-fourth of such cases was accounted for by remittance income. Non-agricultural income financed nearly one-sixth of such cases.

14

Some Policy Implications

One striking fact that has emerged from this empirical study is that land is passing from the hands of the lower categories of farmers to the higher categories. The bulk of the land is being sold by marginal and small farmers while semi-medium, medium and large farmers purchase nearly two-thirds of the land. Medium and large farmers accounted for 40 per cent of the net gain in land transactions. What is even more distressing is the fact that one-fifth of the land alienation was on account of repayment of old debts mainly incurred to meet consumption needs. Those who had left the village after selling their entire holding were generally marginal and small farmers who could not make both ends meet and preferred to move out to the informal sector of the urban areas.

The growth of shanty dwellings and slums in urban areas, more so in metropolitan cities bears testimony to the fact that rural poor are migrating to cities for sheer survival as they are becoming increasingly redundant in the village economy and are being pushed out.

If we have a look at the working of the economy it appears that marginalisation of the poor is inherent in the structure. On account of highly skewed distribution of land in rural areas the gains of development have accrued to the relatively larger landed groups. A significant part of the public resources goes to these sections via subsidy on inputs but the surplus that is generated with them is not made available for further investments as their incomes are nearly exempt from taxation.[1] The non-communitarian land ownership structure precludes their surplus from being utilised in a productive manner in the rural areas for raising the agricultural productivity through development and better management of land and water resources. Consequently the surplus after some initial utilisation in the agricultural/rural sector is, by and large, either wasted in wasteful consumption or is drained to the urban areas through the banking network.[2] In the absence of sustained and high level of investment in rural areas the rural poor find little opportunities for gainful employment.

Public investment in the agricultural/rural sector has played a crucial role in the rejuvenation of the rural economy but this investment has never been commensurate with the needs. Plan outlay on agriculture including cooperation and forestry is only 6 per cent of the total plan outlay during the Seventh Plan and has declined in percentage terms. It accounted for 10 per cent during the First Plan period. Likewise percentage distribution of plan outlay on irrigation and flood control has declined from 22 per cent during the First Plan to 9 per cent during the Seventh plan. Outlay on rural development which includes poverty alleviation programmes like IRDP, RLEGP etc. form only 5 per cent of the plan outlay. The meagre outaly on such programmes has failed to produce the desired effect[3] and the rural poor remain unintegrated with the developmental process. Gross capital formation in agriculture as a proportion of gross capital formation in the economy constituted 16.2 per cent in 1980-81 but it declined to 12.6 per cent in 1986-87. Growth rate in agricultural production has consequently declined and is no higher than the population growth rate. This has resulted in near stagnation in the per capita rural incomes in real terms and given the skewed nature of land ownership and vast landlessness, has resulted in decline in the incomes of the bottom most rural population. Employment in the agricultural sector which grew at a rate of 2.1 per cent during 1961-71 declined to 1.1 per cent during 1972-73 to 1983[4] despite growth in production. Decline in the employment elasticity in the agricultural sector cannot but have deleterious effect on the income of agricultural labourers in the absence of rapid diversification of the economy. The rising population of agricultural labourers in the population[5] and their increasing casualisation, growth of chronic unemployment among the rural areas and the high unemployment rate among agricultural labourers[7] the increase in marginal holdings[8] etc. point out to the increasing polarisation in the rural sector. This is also borne out by our study as poor households are selling their land to the richer households.

Given the skewed structure and the working of market forces there is little likelihood of reversal of the trends unless there is a drastic structural change or the Government effectively intervenes in the land market. Ceiling laws have been enacted in the country but they have not been effectively implemented. If ceiling limits are further lowered, it will be in the right direction but it will be of little use if the same is not rigorously implemented. But all the same the ceiling limit in U.P. should be further lowered as average sized holdings in the state is 1 hectare only and 70 per cent of the holdings are below 1 hectare accounting for only 25 per cent of the area. A further lowering of the ceilings will further deter the large landholders from purchasing more land and may indirectly increase the access of the smaller farmers to the land market.

But given the power equation it may be difficult to lower the ceilings. An alternative policy can be to ban the purchase of land by those who have say, more than 10 acres of land in the first instance. If such persons are eliminated from the land market it will also help in checking the price of land which has skyrocketted as large surplus owners can pay any price for it. The policy of the Government is to prevent concentration and disparity in the ownership of assets and wealth and to usher in a just and equitable social order. If market forces are working in an opposite direction the only option open is a drastic intervention on the part of the state.

It is equally imperative that conditions should be created

whereby the poor may not be forced to sell land to meet consumption needs. If poor households sell land after being absorbed in the urban sector there can be no objection to it but if it is to meet consumption needs or to repay old debts it is a serious matter. This is intimately connected with the wider question of credit policy and credit flows in the economy. While credit should be made available for meeting production needs the question remains as to what should be done to meet the consumption needs of the poorest section of the population. These consumption needs can also be divided into two categories. One which is connected with meeting the food needs, medical or educational requirements and the other, which is connected with social obligations like marriage, *Shradha etc.* While no one can advocate credit to meet such social obligations yet the credit needs to meet other unforeseen contingencies stands on a separate footing. Loans extended to meet foodgrains requirement or to meet medical expenses should be considered as productive loans for they are directly connected with the survival of such persons. If such loans can be made available in a liberal manner, the debt bondage of rural poor[9] can be eliminated.

There is no denying that it will be very difficult for credit institutions to realise the loans because the loanees happen to be so poor even when the loans may carry very nominal rate of interest or no interest at all. The existence of large number of bonded labours in the country bears it out. Consequently unless the credit institutions are subsidised in a big way while extending such loans they will hardly opt for it.[10] If the Union Government can set apart just 0.5 per cent of its revenue to assist banks in extending such loans to weaker sections a sum of Rs. 400 crores can be made available for it instead of Rs. 11 lakhs by way of risk finance as at present.

If a provision of interest-free loans for weaker sections to meet their subsistence requirements as also production needs is also introduced and the banks are reimbursed by way of interest subsidy it will hardly involve an amount of Rs. 300 crores.[11]

It may not be out of place to mention that the Central Government gives a subsidy of nearly Rs 9,000 crores annually to various sections of society who definitely are not the poorest and in many cases form the upper echelons. Take for example the export subsidy of about Rs. 2000 crores which is enjoyed by prosperous exporters. Even the food subsidy of more than Rs. 2000 crores essentially goes to large surplus farmers as they account for the bulk of the procurement. Fertilizer subsidy of nearly Rs. 4000 crores also mainly goes to upper segments of the farming community for they are its bulk users. The interest subsidy of Rs. 400 crores is also enjoyed by big organisations like Coal India Ltd., Steel Authority and National Textile Corporation etc. The point is that subsidies in large measures are being given but the question is whether they can be diverted to the poorest sections.

The bias is also reflected in so far as the credit policy of the banking and credit institutions is concerned. In the agricultural sector the credit is on the hypothecation of land and consequently the larger the area owned the larger is the access to institutional credit. The landless and marginal farmers are naturally out of its orbit.

If the policy is to help the rural poor, they too should have access to institutional credit. This is all the more imperative if the poor want to purchase land. There is no such existing provision. The rural affluent can get credit for purchase of tractors and other agricultural equipments but why the poor should not get credit if they want to purchase land. Land is also a productive asset and if the richer sections are eligible for credit to purchase certain assets, the poor too should not be denied credit to purchase land. In such cases. the land itself can be hypothecated as is the case when some agricultural machinery or equipment is purchased through institutional credit agencies. The banks and other credit institutions will have no difficulty in realising such loans. And if such credit is made interest free or given at a very nominal rate of interest it will prove of immense help to the poor to acquire land.[12] The rural bank branches which have a low credit deposit ratio can do well to cater to the needs of the poorest section which will not only raise the ratio[13] but will come to the rescue of the hitherto completely neglected section of the rural population.

Interest-free loans should likewise be extended to the rural poor to repay their old debts. Land alienation to repay outstanding debts is a significant factor and if such loans are available they need not sell their land.

Marriage has been found to be a big factor in land alienation even as regards marginal and small farmers.. In a tradition bound society embedded in feudal values and mores the process of transformation and modernisation will not be smooth more so, if the ruling classes have a vested interest in the old order. No society can modernise itself if the bulk of the population remains illiterate. Even after four decades and half of independence nearly two-thirds of the population is illiterate and at present there are more illiterate persons than were at the time of independence. The intelligentsia is no better where dowry rates have risen fast and the phenomenon of bride burning has surfaced. Some drastic steps are needed to curb dowry and marriage expenses. One measure can be to make registration of marriage compulsory. It will constitute a sharp break from traditional forms of marriage which involve lot of expenditure. Once registration is made compulsory which will be without any cost it is expected that more and more people will resort to it and old practice will die down. But again it requires a determined leadership to act on and implement it.

It can be asserted that unless the Government intervenes in the land market drastically in favour of the poor the process of land alienation on the part of poorer households cannot be arrested in a market economy characterised by gross inequalities.

NOTES AND REFERENCES

1. Agricultural taxation accounts for only 3 per cent of the revenue receipts.
2. The credit deposit ratio of rural branches of banks is hardly 50 per cent. Thus half of rural deposits is not utilised in rural areas and is transferred to urban areas.
3. In a concurrent evaluation of IRDP in 1985-86, it was found that 20 per cent of the assets were not intact and 24 per cent of the assets that survived failed to generate any income. Vide, Annual Report Ministry of Agriculture, 1987-88.

4. R. Thamarajakshi : Agricultural growth, Rural Development and Employment Generation". *Economic & Political Weekly*, March 25, 1989 p. A-6
5. Agricultural labourers as a percentage of total workers in the country increased from 16.7 per cent in 1961 to 22.7 per cent in 1981,
6. Male Casual Wage Labour as a percentage of rural wage labour increased from 64.6 per cent in 1972-73 to 72.8 per cent in 1982-83.
7. The unemployment rate among agricultural labours was 15.8 per cent according to N.S.S.
8. The number of marginal holdings in the country increased from 36 million in 1970-71 to 51 per cent in 1980-81, *Vide* Agricultual Census 1980-81 Ministry of Agriculture.
9. In a survey by Gandhi Peace Foundation and National Labour Institute it was estimated that there were 22 lakh bonded labourers in nine States of the Indian Union in 1978. Such persons or in many cases their forefathers had taken small loans and being unable to repay the loan or interest were undergoing lifelong bondage with their employers.
10. The Reserve Bank of India has initiated a Risk Finance Assistance scheme since 1977-78 throughout the country to assist the banks and cooperative banks in extending consumption loans to weaker sections in rural areas. But the assistance is so meagre that hardly the credit institutions will act upon it. There was a provision of Rs. 11 lakhs only for this purpose in the Central Budget of 1987-88 vide, Report on Currency and Finance, 1987-88 Vol. I. p. 229.
11. On the assumption that credit institutions will advance roughly Rs. 3000 crores annually as consumption loans for the above mentioned purposes to the poorest in rural India the interest subsidy will come to Rs. 300 crores. It will form only 3 per cent of the total subsidy given by Union Government.
12. In U.P. according to this study roughly 1 lakh acres of land is sold every year. Small and marginal farmers purchase one-third of the land from their own resources. In order that they may be in a position to purchase the remaining land also an annual credit of roughly Rs. 200 crores will be required to purchase it at a rate of Rs. 30,000 per acre,
13. One of the reasons advanced by the banking sector for low credit deposit ratio has been that there are not enough bankable projects. If the bank funds could be made available to purchase land by the poorer sections it will open a new avenue for deployment of funds leading to a higher ratio as compared to 45 per cent at present. If the percentage could go up by 5 points an additional amount of Rs. 500 crores can be made available for loaning in U.P. The total deposits of scheduled commercial banks in U.P. is of the order of Rs. 15000 crores.